READING BIBLICAL GREEK ENDORSEMENTS

An interesting and innovative approach to biblical Greek, providing a nice balance of theory, memorization, and practical exercises. This is one of the first introductory Greek grammars to introduce more nuanced theories of verbal aspect and the middle voice for the beginning student.

—*Mark L. Strauss, professor of New Testament, Bethel Seminary San Diego*

Con Campbell and Richard Gibson are to be congratulated for writing an introduction to biblical Greek that is informed by the latest studies in biblical linguistics and yet is accessible and user-friendly for instructors and students alike. This is not a fast-food-style crash course on Greek, nor a Greek grammar for budding scholars of classical antiquity. Rather, it is a book designed to teach you how to competently read the Greek text of the New Testament. Campbell and Gibson's *Reading Biblical Greek* is sure to become the standard introduction to Greek grammar in seminaries and colleges across the world.

—*Michael F. Bird, lecturer in theology, Ridley College, Melbourne, Australia*

Open this book to any page, and you will feel that a master teacher (i.e., Campbell or Gibson) is gently leading you to abundant pastures of reading the Greek New Testament. Students will love this book. Well done!

—*Robert L. Plummer, professor of New Testament interpretation, The Southern Baptist Theological Seminary*

Con Campbell and Richard Gibson's introductory Greek grammar and companion workbook reading Mark 1–4 will benefit beginning students greatly. As experienced and creative teachers they present key topics in bite-sized pieces with clear explanations and examples and good exercises to help students solidify their learning. The book's innovative three-column layout is visually helpful in distinguishing learning grammar, examples, and vocabulary. They draw well on recent studies of the Greek verb to make this book up-to-date. The focus on Mark 1–4 for examples and translation will encourage students as they see that they can read the New Testament in Greek for themselves. Bravo!

—*Steve Walton, professorial research fellow in New Testament, St Mary's University, Twickenham, UK*

RICHARD J. GIBSON
— AND —
CONSTANTINE R.
CAMPBELL

READING
BIBLICAL
GREEK

A GRAMMAR
FOR STUDENTS

ZONDERVAN®

ZONDERVAN

Reading Biblical Greek
Copyright © 2017 by Richard J. Gibson and Constantine R. Campbell

This title is also available as a Zondervan ebook.

Requests for information should be addressed to:

Zondervan, 3900 Sparks Dr. SE, Grand Rapids, Michigan 49546

ISBN 978-0-310-52799-2

Summary of *Greek Accents in Eight Lessons* (Sydney: Macquarie University) by John A. L. Lee, ©2005. Used with permission.

All Scripture quotations, unless otherwise indicated, are the authors' own translations.

Cover design: Brand Navigation
Cover art: Shutterstock.com; 123RF.com
Interior design: Matthew Van Zomeren

Printed in China

17 18 19 20 21 22 23 24 /CTC/ 20 19 18 17 16 15 14 13 12 11 10 9 8 7 6 5 4 3 2 1

Dedication

To Kay Avery
student and colleague
par excellence
and
to Kim
'my stunning,
mystery companion'

PREFACE

This book is the product of countless hours and incalculable pain, but not mine. I wish it could come with the disclaimer: "No students suffered in the making of this book." The reality is that its distinctive approach has been shaped by lessons learned over decades from students struggling with the inherent challenge of language acquisition, the limitations of inherited learning methods, and the ineptitude of their teachers. So this book is dedicated to all those students.

The effort put in over decades to redesign, reorganize, and refine has been motivated by these students in attempts to reduce the hours and the pain required to start translating the New Testament. The goals have been clarity, convenience, and currency. The quest for clarity is reflected in visual layout, the three-column structure to each lesson. Convenience accounts for the apparent minimalism of the material. User-friendly explanations to students first encountering an idea readily become clutter for the student revising essential information. In terms of currency, the material also seeks to reflect the latest developments in verbal aspect, middle lexical forms, and other issues without burdening the beginner with detailed discussions better suited to intermediate-level study.

The overarching goal is to equip students to read the text of Mark's Gospel as soon as is practicable. The approach is informed by the dictum, "If you can translate one chapter of the New Testament, you can translate any chapter." Experience has taught me the enormous value of enabling students to translate early, for motivation. This is why students enroll in the course, so they can read the text for themselves.

There is a selfish dimension to this process as well. There is no greater thrill for the teacher than when the alchemy of education turns our base-metal explanation into the precious gold of understanding a verse in Mark's Gospel; when the tedious calculus of tense, voice, and mood yields a moment of insight and doxology; when the parsing turns to praise.

Among the students who have inspired and helped me, special mention goes to the class of '94, where it all began. Rod and Karen Morris deserve special mention for the double grace of pointing out their teacher's limitations and then offering ideas for how to initiate a fresher, better approach. Special thanks goes to Laura Blyth, who kept asking, "What do you mean?" in the editing process. Thanks must go to the colleagues at Moore College who have encouraged, critiqued, and contributed, notably Perry Wiles, Bill Salier, and Kay Avery.

This book would simply not have seen publication without the sponsorship and hard work of my ever-precocious coauthor. It was a privilege to teach Con. Since then I have known the joy of teaching with him and now cooperating to produce this volume. I have been happy to be exceeded by him and struggled to keep up with him. Having fallen behind, it has been kind of him to wait for me to make this volume possible.

Finally, it would be remiss of me to omit those who demonstrated the value of engaging with the Greek text in exegesis and exposition, my revered teachers Peter O'Brien, Donald Robinson, David Peterson, and Bill Dumbrell.

My hope is that this material will usher people into the joy of encountering the text of the New Testament with surprising ease, whether they are eager or apprehensive, novice or nervous, bilingual or barbarian. Teachers can't do the learning for their students. Nor can the best methods remove the need for methodical, disciplined, and regular learning. Yet the sometimes painful hours offer the prospect of being "like the owner of a house who brings out of his storeroom new treasures as well as old" (Matt 13:52).

Richard J. Gibson

TABLE OF CONTENTS

A NOTE TO TEACHERS

This Greek grammar is designed to optimize the learning experience. It revolves around three core elements: grammar, vocabulary, and reading & translation.

A. Grammar	B. Vocabulary	C. Reading and Translation

A. Grammar

The first core element is grammar. The pedagogical philosophy embraced here is called minimalism. Students are introduced to essential information—no more and no less. Clarity too is of utmost importance.

This is not a reference grammar. It is strictly for first year Greek students, aimed at optimizing their grasp of the fundamentals of the Greek language. While minimalist in approach, the grammar is informed by the latest and best of Greek and linguistic scholarship. It enables students to move seamlessly into further study.

The grammar consists of **micro-lessons**, which break up information in small, digestible chunks. Each micro-lesson addresses a **single** point. This arrangement makes for easy comprehension and review. Lessons are structured in three columns (like this page). Each column serves a particular function, which is explained in Lesson 1.

The instructor may choose to teach more than one micro-lesson in a single session. We do not prescribe how much content should be covered in a single period of teaching. The teacher should discern how to pace the material, based on the degree of difficulty of the content, the abilities of the students, and the time available for learning.

The order of material is deliberate. New learning comes in incremental steps, in a recursive fashion, so that each new piece builds on prior learning, which is also reinforced. Material is also arranged to most quickly enable reading the Greek of Mark 1–4.

B. Vocabulary

Vocabulary is an essential complement to grammar. In this text, vocabulary is introduced at strategic points. Rather than lists arranged purely by frequency, the vocabulary is arranged first by what the student has been learning in grammar, and then by frequency.

The vocabulary lists are collated together at the back of the book, rather than interspersed with each chapter. This enables convenient study of vocabulary, since all lists can be consulted in the same place.

The first 13 vocabulary lists are keyed to Mark's Gospel (Mark 1–4 is used for reading and translation in this grammar). The number in the middle column of lists 1–13 represents the first verse in which the word can be found in Mark (1:3 = Mark 1:3; 2:10 = Mark 2:10). For example:

οὐρανός   1:10   heaven

The position of words found in later chapters is indicated by standard referencing (e.g., 15:1).

Πιλᾶτος   15:1   Pilate

As students begin to acquire vocabulary, it is recommended that they take note of new words as they appear in the Greek text of Mark 1–4. This helps students to integrate their vocabulary learning with "real" Greek text.

C. Reading and Translation

The goal of this grammar is to enable students to read and translate the Greek of the New Testament. Learning grammatical information and vocabulary is simply a means to this end. Thus, the content is structured to enable reading as soon as possible.

The grammar is tied to a specific Greek text. The student will have read and translated the whole of Mark 1–4 by the end of the course. Rather than reading a variety of Greek texts in a piecemeal fashion, our approach values reading through a substantial block of the Greek New Testament. This will enhance student satisfaction, and enables students to encounter real Greek usage "in the wild" as it were.

The companion book, *Reading Biblical Greek Workbook: A Reading & Translation Guide to Mark 1–4,* is a vital part of the grammar. It breaks up the text of Mark 1–4 into manageable chunks, and provides vocabulary and grammatical assistance as required. This information is coordinated with the grammar, so that students are given assistance only for what they are not yet expected to know. The volume of such information decreases as the student progresses through grammatical and vocabulary learning. Translation work, using *Reading Biblical Greek Workbook*, is incorporated into the exercises beginning in Lesson 42.

Students are also instructed to "mark up the text" in such a way that helps them to recognize parts of speech and clause structures. This will greatly help the student to understand how Greek conveys meaning.

In class settings, it is recommended that *Reading Biblical Greek Workbook* be used in small groups of 3 or 4 students each, for at least one hour per week. The instructor should "hover over" the small groups to answer questions and help to solve problems. It is also recommended that students complete at least one chunk on their own at home each week. (A sample course schedule is available at www.zondervanacademic.com.)

1. Our Approach to Learning

You will find that most pages in this grammar are divided into three columns. Each column has a specific function, as indicated below.

A. Introducing a New Topic	B. Material to Be Memorized	C. Examples and Exercises
The first column introduces new material and provides explanation of the significance of this part of the language.	The middle column usually presents material that needs to be remembered, such as noun and verb paradigms, and rules of grammar.	The final column provides examples to illustrate principles taught in the lesson, and exercises to reinforce their application. (This column includes space for students to complete the exercises. If more room is needed, blank pages are found at the back of the book.)
1. Engage When you first encounter a new topic, you are expected to engage thoughtfully with this material, clarifying anything that is unclear and understanding what is the most important information.	**2. Rehearse** The first time through, rehearse the paradigms, ensuring that you sound them out correctly, and become familiar with the patterns of the rhythms.	**3. Observe** Initially, you should observe carefully how the examples demonstrate the new material. These exercises are designed to consolidate your understanding.
4. Learn After studying the lesson, you will be expected to learn this material. You won't be expected to remember every detail, but should have a confident grasp of the key information.	**5. Memorize** After studying the lesson, you need to practice and memorize paradigms and relevant vocab lists (back of this grammar) so that you can reproduce them. You will also be expected to commit some rules of grammar to memory.	**6. Complete & Check** You will be expected to complete the exercises and check your answers against those in the back of the grammar. This consolidation will build your confidence and highlight points you should review.

2. History of Koine Greek

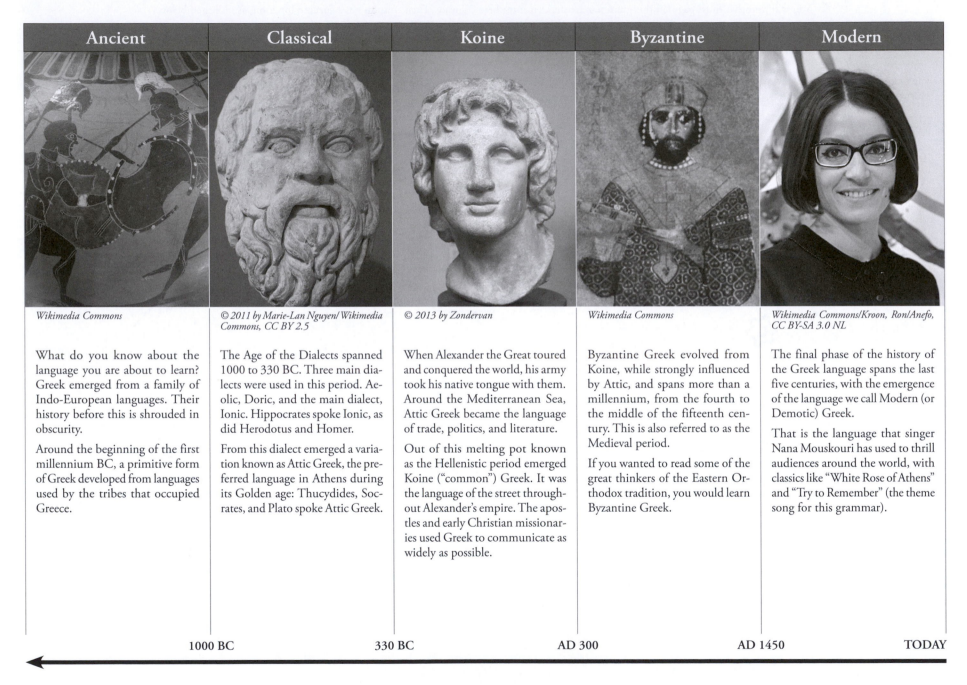

Ancient	Classical	Koine	Byzantine	Modern
Wikimedia Commons	*© 2011 by Marie-Lan Nguyen/ Wikimedia Commons, CC BY 2.5*	*© 2013 by Zondervan*	*Wikimedia Commons*	*Wikimedia Commons/Kroon, Ron/Anefo, CC BY-SA 3.0 NL*

Ancient

What do you know about the language you are about to learn? Greek emerged from a family of Indo-European languages. Their history before this is shrouded in obscurity.

Around the beginning of the first millennium BC, a primitive form of Greek developed from languages used by the tribes that occupied Greece.

Classical

The Age of the Dialects spanned 1000 to 330 BC. Three main dialects were used in this period. Aeolic, Doric, and the main dialect, Ionic. Hippocrates spoke Ionic, as did Herodotus and Homer.

From this dialect emerged a variation known as Attic Greek, the preferred language in Athens during its Golden age: Thucydides, Socrates, and Plato spoke Attic Greek.

Koine

When Alexander the Great toured and conquered the world, his army took his native tongue with them. Around the Mediterranean Sea, Attic Greek became the language of trade, politics, and literature.

Out of this melting pot known as the Hellenistic period emerged Koine ("common") Greek. It was the language of the street throughout Alexander's empire. The apostles and early Christian missionaries used Greek to communicate as widely as possible.

Byzantine

Byzantine Greek evolved from Koine, while strongly influenced by Attic, and spans more than a millennium, from the fourth to the middle of the fifteenth century. This is also referred to as the Medieval period.

If you wanted to read some of the great thinkers of the Eastern Orthodox tradition, you would learn Byzantine Greek.

Modern

The final phase of the history of the Greek language spans the last five centuries, with the emergence of the language we call Modern (or Demotic) Greek.

That is the language that singer Nana Mouskouri has used to thrill audiences around the world, with classics like "White Rose of Athens" and "Try to Remember" (the theme song for this grammar).

| 1000 BC | 330 BC | AD 300 | AD 1450 | TODAY |

3. Signs and Symbols

Signs and Symbols	Approach to Learning	Exercises
Any language system relies on a set of symbols that are arranged to express meaning. So the first step in learning New Testament Greek is to become familiar with those symbols and their significance. For Koine Greek, this includes (1) the letters of the alphabet, (2) punctuation marks, (3) breathings, and (4) accents. These are the topics of the next few lessons (Lessons 4–8).	Greek uses a very different set of symbols from English. Before we meet the Greek alphabet, it is important to be aware of our approach to learning it.	1. Other than the twenty-six letters of the alphabet, what symbols does English use to communicate meaning?

Pronunciation: Two Approaches

There are no recordings of first century Greek-speakers. While there would have been some diversity of pronunciation across the Roman empire, evidence from papyri and ostraca (pieces of clay pots) indicates the likely pronunciation, by revealing phonetically-based spelling mistakes.* There are two main conventions for assigning values to the Greek letters.

1. Modern

Growing in popularity among scholars is the use of modern Greek pronunciation (or variations of it). There is strong evidence that modern Greek is closer to the way Greek was spoken in the first century than traditionally taught alternatives. Modern pronunciation also has the advantage of being the way Greek people speak today.

A disadvantage with Modern Greek pronunciation is that the same sound is given to more than one letter or letter combination. For example, six different symbols are given the same sound. So for someone new to the language, this can be bewildering! And yet this is the difficulty when learning most languages.

2. Erasmian

The traditional approach is based on a system developed in the 16th century by the Dutch scholar, Erasmus. It has been demonstrated that Erasmus was probably right for *Attic* Greek, but not Koine. However, most students still learn Greek with this system, and it has the advantage that every letter and letter combination has a distinctive sound.

In keeping with recent trends, this grammar presents both systems of pronunciation. Where needed, the Erasmian and Modern alternatives will be indicated. The student or instructor should choose one system or another.

At this stage, you need to master the letters of the Greek alphabet in 3 ways:

1. Recognize the shape of each letter.
2. Give a distinctive sound to each letter.
3. Be able to write each letter.

The most efficient way to learn is to practice these three steps at the same time. For each letter:

a. Observe the form
b. Rehearse the sound
c. Draw the shape

You will need to be able to write the letters in order to complete the exercises.

Remember, there is no substitute for repetition.

2. Find an adult who has learned another language in the last decade. What features of the language have they found most difficult?

---

* For more information about this evidence, and Greek pronunciation in general, see ch. 9 in Constantine R. Campbell, *Advances in the Study of Greek: New Insights for Reading the New Testament* (Grand Rapids: Zondervan, 2015).

4. Alphabet

Alphabet

The Greek alphabet developed from the Phoenician alphabet; it emerged in a distinctive form at about 900 BC.

Letters: Names, Symbols, Sounds

There are twenty-four letters in the Greek alphabet. The table opposite gives their name and Greek forms, lower case and upper case, and their transliteration. The value or sound of each letter is also given, according to the Erasmian pronunciation system. The final column provides the value given by modern pronunciation, where it differs from this approach.

Take time to observe some key features, using Exercises 1–3.

Memorize

It is now your job to learn and rehearse the letters of the alphabet (Exercises 4–6). Write each letter correctly and associate it with its correct sound. You should aim to memorize the twenty-four lower case letters in order. You could start by learning four letters at a time.

Letters of the Greek Alphabet

Name	Lower	Upper	Trans.	Erasmian	Modern
alpha	α	A	*a*	father	**a**way
bēta	β	B	*b*	**b**at	**v**at
gamma	γ	Γ	*g*	**g**et	**g**et, **y**et
delta	δ	Δ	*d*	**d**ig	**th**is
epsilon	ε	E	*e*	m**e**t	
zēta	ζ	Z	*z*	**z**oo or bi**ds**	
ēta	η	H	*ē*	**ai**r	sp**i**t, p**e**tite
thēta	θ	Θ	*th*	**th**in	
iōta	ι	I	*i*	h**i**t *or* **y**et	sp**i**t, p**e**tite
kappa	κ	K	*k*	**k**id	
lambda	λ	Λ	*l*	**l**eg	
mu	μ	M	*m*	**m**at	
nu	ν	N	*n*	**n**ut	
xi	ξ	Ξ	*x*	fo**x**	
omicron	ο	O	*o*	n**o**t	
pi	π	Π	*p*	**p**it	
rho	ρ	P	*r*	**r**ug	
sigma	σ, ς	Σ	*s*	**s**it	
tau	τ	T	*t*	**t**ip	
upsilon	υ	Y	*u*	b**oo**k	sp**i**t, p**e**tite
phi	φ	Φ	*ph*	**ph**oto *or* **f**oot	
chi	χ	X	*ch*	lo**ch**	lo**ch**, **h**uge
psi	ψ	Ψ	*ps*	li**ps**	
ōmega	ω	Ω	*ō*	t**o**ne	n**o**t

Exercises

1. Which letter of the Greek alphabet:

   takes two forms?

   makes two sounds?

2. In terms of form, which letters of the Greek alphabet are:

   most like their English equivalent?

   most different from their English equivalent?

   similar to another English letter?

3. Which letters do you initially find most difficult to:

   write?

   pronounce?

4. On some paper, write out a full line of each lower case Greek letter.

5. Practice making each of the sounds.

6. Learn the lower case letters and sounds in order. Try to sing the alphabet to the tune of *Twinkle, Twinkle, Little Star*.

5. Vowels and Consonants

Vowels and Consonants

Like English, the Greek language distinguishes between vowels and consonants. This distinction is important and will impact the way some words are formed. In the Greek alphabet there are seven vowels and seventeen consonants.

1. Vowels

The English language uses five vowels: a, e, i, o, u. Greek has seven: *alpha* (α), *epsilon* (ε), *ēta* (η), *iōta* (ι), *omicron* (o), *upsilon* (υ) and *ōmega* (ω).

2. Consonants

Of the seventeen consonants, ten are worth noting now. This is because the way they combine with certain letters will impact the way words are spelled and sounded.

a. Rho

The consonant *rho* (ρ) is a special letter: it leads a double life. While it is a consonant, *rho* sometimes behaves like a vowel. The relevance of this will become clear later.

b. Mutes

Nine consonants are collectively known as "mutes." They are divided into groups of three, depending on where in the mouth the sound is formed.

Velars: roof of the mouth and tongue.
Labials: lips.
Dentals: teeth and tongue.

Greek Vowels and Consonants

Vowels

English (5)	Greek (7)
a	α
e	ε η (Erasmian)
i	ι η (Modern)
o	o ω
u	υ

Note: the consonant ρ can behave like a vowel

Mute Consonants

Mutes (9)

Velars:	γ	κ	χ
Labials:	β	π	φ
Dentals:	δ	τ	θ

Exercises

1. Underline the vowels and circle the mute consonants in the following text from Mark 1:9–10. If you are unsure about upper case letters, consult the previous lesson:

[9] Καὶ ἐγένετο ἐν ἐκείναις ταῖς ἡμέραις ἦλθεν Ἰησοῦς ἀπὸ Ναζαρετ τῆς Γαλιλαίας καὶ ἐβαπτίσθη εἰς τὸν Ἰορδάνην ὑπὸ Ἰωάννου.

[10] καὶ εὐθὺς ἀναβαίνων ἐκ τοῦ ὕδατος εἶδεν σχιζομένους τοὺς οὐρανοὺς καὶ τὸ πνευμα ὡς περιστερὰν καταβαινον εἰς αὐτόν·

2. Attempt to read this text aloud, pronouncing each sound carefully.

6. LETTER COMBINATIONS

Letter Combinations	Diphthongs	Exercises

Letter Combinations

Some letters combine with other letters to form a new, distinct sound, rather than each letter retaining its own value.

1. VOWELS COMBINED: DIPHTHONGS

When two vowels combine, the new unit of sound is called a diphthong. The Greek language uses eight different vowel combinations in this way.

2. WHEN VOWELS ARE NOT COMBINED

a. DIAERESIS

Occasionally, a combination, which would usually be pronounced as a diphthong, will sound out as two separate letters. When this is the case Greek signifies it by two dots above the second vowel. This is called a *diaeresis*.

For example, the Greek word for *and* (καί) is pronounced as one sound or syllable. The name for the high priest at Jesus's trial is pronounced Κα-ϊ-α-φας. The *diaeresis* signals two separate sounds for α-ι, rather than one diphthong.

b. ENGLISH-ONLY VOWEL COMBINATIONS

To English speakers, some combinations look like diphthongs. These include εα, εε, or οο. Nevertheless, these are never combined in Greek to form one sound. Each letter is given its own value. E.g., δω-ρε-α (not *doe-ree*).

3. CONSONANT COMBINATIONS: GAMMA NASAL

Consonants are always given their own sound value, except for γ. When a *gamma* comes immediately before another velar consonant, γ, κ, χ, or ξ, the first *gamma* is pronounced *n* like the letter *nu* (ν). E.g., ἄγ-γε-λος is *an-ge-los* not *ag-ge-los*.

When *gamma* behaves like this, it is called a *gamma nasal*.

Diphthongs

GREEK	ERASMIAN		MODERN	
αι	ai	**ai**sle	e	m**e**t
αυ	ou	**ou**th**ou**se	av	cad**av**er
ει	ei	v**ei**l	i	sp**i**t, pet**i**te
ευ, ηυ	eu	**eu**logy	ev	**ev**angel
οι	oi	**oi**l	i	sp**i**t, pet**i**te
ου	ou	r**ou**te	ou	r**ou**te
υι	whi	q**ui**t, **whi**sker	i	sp**i**t, pet**i**te

Exercises

1. Practice sounding out the following words. Circle the diphthongs.

θησαυρον

πνευματος

προορισας

ποιησατε

Καφαρναουμ

δικαιος

Καϊαφα

βασιλεια

γενεαν

Βοος

παισιν

χειρας

μετανοιας

σταυρου

νηστευσας

δωρεαν

βουλευσεται

7. Other Sounds and Symbols

Other Sounds and Symbols	Sounds and Symbols	Exercises

Other Sounds and Symbols

There are still some symbols to recognize before reading the text of the New Testament. The earliest manuscripts of the New Testament do not contain these marks; they were added later for greater clarity. These include:

1. Breathings

Breathings are placed over the beginning of words that begin with a vowel or *rho*. You will find them placed over the first letter, or the second when a word begins with a diphthong. The are two types:

a. Smooth breathings make no difference to the sound of the word.

b. Rough breathings are pronounced like the English *h*, by breathing over the initial sound.

2. Punctuation Marks

Punctuation marks function much as they do in English, to signal the end of a sentence, or an idea, or to ask a question. Of the four main marks, two are the same symbol as English (full-stop, comma) and two differ (semi-colon, question mark).

3. *Iōta* Subscript

Sometimes the *iōta* in a diphthong will appear as a small letter under the other vowel rather than alongside it. This can occur only under long vowels, α, η and ω. This *iōta* subscript is never pronounced. However, an *iōta* subscript does affect the meaning of the word and must be noted.

4. Apostrophe

An apostrophe looks just like a smooth breathing mark, but will appear at the end of a word rather than the beginning. It signals the fact that a vowel has dropped out for ease of pronunciation. Compare English usage of the apostrophe in words like *isn't* and *didn't*. When a vowel is dropped out, it is called "elision"; the vowel is "elided."

Sounds and Symbols

1. Breathings

a. Smooth
Not pronounced
ἑν, αὐτου, Ἰωαννης

b. Rough
Pronounced like English *h*
ὁδον, οὑτος, Ἱεροσολυμιται, ῥαββι

2. Punctuation

Full-stop (period): closes a sentence
καὶ εὐθυς ἐκαλεσεν αὐτους.

Comma: separates and connects ideas
ἐβαπτισα ὑμας ὑδατι, αὐτος δε βαπτισει

Semi-colon: introduces direct speech, separates and connects ideas
Και ἐκηρυσσεν λεγων· ἐρχεται

Question mark: signals a question
ἠλθες ἀπολεσαι ἡμας;

3. *Iōta* Subscript

Ἡσαϊα τω προφητῃ, ᾐτησατο

4. Apostrophe

ὑπο + αὐτου = ὑπ᾽ αὐτου
μετα + αὐτου = μετ᾽ αὐτου

Exercises

1. Match these Greek words on the right (from Mark 1) with the features on the left:

gamma nasal	ἱερει
smooth breathing	λεγων·
rough breathing	τουτο;
iōta subscript	προσενεγκε
diaeresis	κατ᾽ ἐξουσιαν
semi-colon	πλοιῳ
question mark	πρωϊ
apostrophe	αὐτον

2. Practice reading aloud Mark 1:1–15, pronouncing each sound carefully.

3. Learn Vocab #1 well enough to match Greek and English words.

8. ACCENTS

Accents	Accents: Types and Usage	Exercises

Accents

Accents originally indicated intonation. But by the time of the New Testament, it is more likely that accents were used to identify which part of a word to emphasize or stress. Though accents were *pronounced* for hundreds of years before Jesus, they were introduced only into *written* Greek in the 3rd century AD.

Most Greek words have an accent. On rare occasions, a word will have two. You are not expected to learn the rules for accents. However, all New Testament text and vocabulary used in this grammar are fully accented so that you become familiar with text as it appears in the Greek New Testament.

1. THREE TYPES

There are three different accents: acute (ά), grave (ὰ) and circumflex (ᾶ). Some Greek fonts will display the circumflex in a slightly different form. Accents may also be placed over the same letter as breathings or a *diaeresis*.

2. TWO USES

a. PRONUNCIATION

As you learn vocabulary, try to place the stress on the accented syllable.

b. DISTINGUISHING WORDS

Accents will also help you distinguish between two words when they would otherwise be spelled the same.

Learning the rules of accents requires great effort even for the advanced student. You are not expected to know the rules nor remember where accents occur in words. You are expected only to place accents on a few words that are distinguished only by their accent.

However, students who wish to learn the rules of accentuation should consult the summary provided in an appendix at the back of this grammar. The best time to learn the rules is from the beginning of your vocabulary learning.

Accents: Types and Usage

3 TYPES

acute	ά, ᾰ
grave	ὰ, ᾱ̀
circumflex	ᾶ, αῖ

2 USES

1. PRONUNCIATION

When learning vocabulary, place the stress on the accented syllable

E.g., ἐκκλησία   *ek-klair-si-a (E)*
                   ek-kli-si-a (M)

2. DISTINGUISHING WORDS

Some words are distinguished only by an accent mark, e.g.,

masculine article (*the*)	ὁ
neuter relative pronoun (*which*)	ὃ

🔒

Vocab #1

Exercises

1. Count the number of each type of accent found in the first two verses of Mark's Gospel.

Ἀρχὴ τοῦ εὐαγγελίου Ἰησοῦ Χριστοῦ υἱοῦ

θεοῦ. Καθὼς γέγραπται ἐν τῷ Ἠσαΐᾳ τῷ

προφήτῃ· ἰδοὺ ἀποστέλλω τὸν ἄγγελόν

μου πρὸ προσώπου σου, ὃς κατασκευάσει

τὴν ὁδόν σου·

2. How many words lack an accent?

3. How many have two accents?

9. Earliest Manuscripts

Earliest Manuscripts	Today's New Testament

Having learned the alphabet and the other signs and symbols used in Greek, we turn now to consider the text of the Greek New Testament. The original texts of the Gospels and Epistles of the New Testament, known as autographs, are no longer available. The earliest surviving manuscripts (abbreviated to mss) are dated to approximately AD 125.

Early manuscripts were written in upper case letters. There was rarely a gap between words and very little punctuation. Words were broken up at the end of a line if they did not fit, but syllables were kept intact. There were no breathings or accents. Chapter and verse numbers were not introduced until centuries later. So this is how a page of an early manuscript appears; this is 2 Corinthians 10:11–11:2.

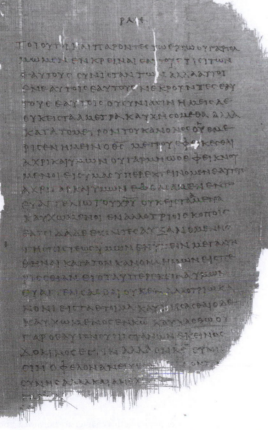

Image digitally reproduced with the permission of the Papyrology Collection, Graduate Library, University of Michigan, P.Mich.inv. 6238

Today, the same text in the United Bible Society's Greek New Testament (UBS[5]) and the Nestle-Aland Greek New Testament (NA28) is written in lower case letters. Occasionally upper case letters indicate a proper name, direct speech, or a new paragraph. Note the inclusion of headings, verse numbers, punctuation, accents, and footnote references. It is important to be clear that these were added later.

> καὶ ἐν σαββάτῳ περιτέμνετε ἄνθρωπον. **23** εἰ περιτομὴν λαμβάνει ἄνθρωπος ἐν σαββάτῳ ἵνα μὴ λυθῇ ὁ νόμος Μωϋσέως, ἐμοὶ χολᾶτε ὅτι ὅλον ἄνθρωπον ὑγιῆ ἐποίησα ἐν σαββάτῳ; **24** μὴ κρίνετε κατ᾽ ὄψιν, ἀλλὰ τὴν δικαίαν κρίσιν κρίνετε.

Division Over Who Jesus Is

> **25** Ἔλεγον οὖν τινες ἐκ τῶν Ἱεροσολυμιτῶν, Οὐχ οὗτός ἐστιν ὃν ζητοῦσιν ἀποκτεῖναι; **26** καὶ ἴδε παρρησίᾳ λαλεῖ καὶ οὐδὲν αὐτῷ λέγουσιν. μήποτε ἀληθῶς ἔγνωσαν οἱ ἄρχοντες ὅτι οὗτός ἐστιν ὁ Χριστός; **27** ἀλλὰ τοῦτον οἴδαμεν πόθεν ἐστίν· ὁ δὲ Χριστὸς ὅταν ἔρχηται οὐδεὶς γινώσκει πόθεν ἐστίν.

How do modern translators know where to divide words and sentences? This is not as disconcerting as it may seem. The text below is the NRSV of the same portion (John 7:38–45) in upper case letters, with punctuation and spaces removed. Words are broken at the end of the line but syllables are kept intact. Try reading and working out where words and sentences begin and end.

ASTHESCRIPTUREHASSAIDOUTOFTHEBELIEVERSHEARTSHALL
FLOWRIVERSOFLIVINGWATERNOWHESAIDTHISABOUTTHESPI
RITWHICHBELIEVERSINHIMWERETORECEIVEFORASYETTHEREWAS
NOSPIRITBECAUSEJESUSWASNOTYETGLORIFIEDWHENTHEYHEARD
THESEWORDSSOMEINTHECROWDSAIDTHISISREALLYTHEPRO
PHETOTHERSSAIDTHISISTHEMESSIAHBUTSOMEASKEDSURE
LYTHEMESSIAHDOESNOTCOMEFROMGALILEEDOESHEHASNOT
THESCRIPTURESAIDTHATTHEMESSIAHISDESCENDEDFROMDA
VIDANDCOMESFROMBETHLEHEMTHE

Understanding Meaning

Meaning Is a Product of Choices

In preparation for reading Greek, we need to do some thinking about how language conveys *meaning*. We convey meaning by the choices we make. We understand meaning by appreciating the choices made by someone else. The meaning of any text is generated by choices made along two different axes—vocabulary and syntax.

A. Vocabulary

In any given position in a sentence, its author could choose a range of alternatives. E.g.:

> The old man just said, "You missed the boat."

In the slot occupied by the adjective *old,* a number of other adjectives could have been chosen. Synonyms like *aged, elderly, senior,* or *venerable* would each create a subtly different effect. The author could name another feature of the man with adjectives such as *tall, angry,* or *third.*

Similarly, in the noun slot occupied by *man,* synonyms such as *male, gentleman, bloke,* or *fellow* could have been chosen, or more specific terms like *deckhand, captain,* or *sailor.* Also, *ferry, yacht, ship,* or *ocean liner* could be substituted for *boat.*

To discern the significance of choices made by the original authors of the New Testament, you need to appreciate the choices they made in the context of the alternatives available to them. To this end you will learn a substantial amount of vocabulary.

However, for most people it will not be realistic, nor desirable, to memorize the entire vocabulary of the New Testament. You will learn to consult reference tools like a lexicon (dictionary) and a concordance to bridge the gap.

B. Syntax

At the same time, an author makes choices about how words relate to each other in a sentence. The same words used above could be rearranged to create a very different relationship between them, and a very different meaning:

> You said, "The old boat just missed the man."

> OR

> You, the just man, missed the said old boat.

> BUT NOT:

> Boat just man missed old said the the you.

This combination breaks too many rules to be a meaningful sentence.

In the first two sentences *just* and *missed* take exactly the same form. However, they are used in quite different ways, simply by altering their position in the sentence. *Just* could mean *by a small distance* in the first sentence, but in the second it means *righteous.* In the same way, *missed* could mean *failed to collide,* but in the second means *failed to catch.*

The way words are related to each other in a sentence is governed by certain conventions, called syntax. To understand New Testament Greek, we will also need to be aware of the conventions that first-century authors used to indicate the relationships between words.

Exercises

Try to work out the meaning intended by the author of the following. Where do they:

a) choose the wrong word?

b) combine words in the wrong way?

- *Two signs from a Majorcan shop entrance:* English well speaking. Here speeching America.

- *Hotel brochure, French Alps:* The hotel also has a heated of course swimming pool. Thus, even by thunder weather, dare to give in and in case of congestion, the barmaid owning proper diplomas will help.

- *A sign posted in Germany's Black Forest:* It is strictly forbidden on our black forest camping site that people of different sex, for instance, men and women, live together in one tent unless married with each other or that purpose.

- *From a Russian airline safety brochure:* Airlines staff can ask you for something concerning smoking and we beg you to follow its advices and recommendations. If you possess strong will and are able to decline smoking during the flight, non-smoking passengers and the crew will appreciate your generosity and respect for them.

- *From a Tokyo car rental brochure:* When passenger of foot heave in sight, tootle the horn. Trumpet him melodiously at first, but if he still obstacles your passage then tootle him vigorously.

- *On the menu of a Polish restaurant:* Salad a firm's own make; limpid red beet soup with cheesy dumplings in the form of a finger; roasted duck let loose; beef rashers beaten up in the country people's fashion.*

* The examples in this chapter are borrowed from users.tinyonline.co.uk/gswithenbank/mangeng.

11. Parts of Speech

Parts of Speech

To communicate meaning, every language consists of a set of "building blocks," called "parts of speech." Each part of speech, or building block, contributes something to the whole. Just in case you are not confident about English grammar, here is a quick review.

Verbs

Verbs portray processes, actions, or states. Because of the wide range of activities in life, verbs need to be complex and subtle. At times, English uses more than one word to describe a single verbal process.

Adverbs

Adverbs qualify or add more information about a verb. In English, they are usually formed by adding −ly to an adjective. E.g., badly, thoughtfully, well.

Nouns

Nouns name a person such as *Jesus*, a thing like the *treasury* or a state of being, like *anger*.

Pronouns

Pronouns are noun substitutes. They refer back to a person or thing without naming them again.

Articles

English uses two articles, to indicate whether a thing named by the noun is definite (*the*) or indefinite (*a* or *an*). They precede their noun but may be separated by some words. E.g., *the* house, *the* very large, green house.

Adjectives

Adjectives qualify or give more information about a noun. Sometimes an adjective can be used on its own as a noun substitute.

Prepositions

Prepositions show how something is positioned in relation to something else in terms of space, time, or logic. They immediately precede the noun to which something else is related. For example, he hid "*behind* the house," "the hour *before* lunch," "ask *about* the test."

Conjunctions

Conjunctions join clauses, phrases and words together. Words like *and, but, for,* or *because* are commonly-used conjunctions.

Participles

Participles are verbal forms that cannot stand as the main verb. They usually qualify the main verb in some way. In English, participles are often indicated by adding -*ing* to the end of a verb.

Particles

"Particle" is the name reserved for a part of speech that doesn't fit into the other categories. While *truly* is an adverb in English, the underlying Greek word, ἀμήν, is regarded as a particle.

Examples

Then he called his disciples and said to them, "Truly I tell you, this poor widow has put in more than all those who are contributing to the treasury."

Mark 12:43 (NRSV)

Verbs: called, said, tell, has put

Adverbs: more

Nouns: disciples, widow, treasury

Pronouns: he, his, them, I, you

Article: the

Adjectives: this, poor

Prepositions: to, in, to

Conjunctions: Then, and

Participles: contributing

12. RELATING WORDS IN CLAUSES

Relating Words in Clauses

In order to read Greek well, it is essential to appreciate the differences between Greek and English. One of the most significant differences between English and Greek is the way they show the relationship between nouns and the verb in a clause. We will misunderstand the New Testament at many points if we simply assume the same rules as English.

ENGLISH: WORD ORDER

In English, the order of words is the main way to indicate the relationship between nouns and a verb. In the English examples opposite, note how the form *Peter* remains unchanged, but the word's location, relative to the verb, changes.

The subject of a verb performs the action or experiences the state indicated by the verb. As subject of the verb *answered*, Peter immediately precedes it. To indicate possession, we add the word *of* or *'s* in English. The indirect object is affected by the process, but not directly. To show the indirect object, we add *to* or *for* in front of the relevant noun. The (direct) object indicates the person or thing directly affected by the process. As object of the verb *saw*, Peter follows the verb in English.

Standard English word order is:

> Subject + verb + object + indirect object
> E.g., John spoke the message to Herod.

Greek is much less reliant on the order in which words are arranged to convey meaning. It does make use of word order, but it often differs from English. The Greek of the same sentence may read:

> Verb + conjunction + subject + indirect object + object
> E.g., ἔλεγεν γὰρ ὁ Ἰωάννης τῷ Ἡρῴδη ὅτι

GREEK: NOUN INFLECTION

To show the relationship between nouns and their verb, Greek makes much more use of inflection. This is where the end of the noun changes according to the noun's function in a clause or sentence. Now look at the Greek for the examples opposite. Note the way that the noun Πέτρος changes its form to indicate its function. Also, compare the position of verb and noun.

In Greek, nearly every noun is inflected. Encoded in each ending is a range of information about the noun. The endings usually carry the case, that is, its relationship to the verb; number, that is whether it is singular or plural, and gender, which is a grammatical category, rather than a biological one.

English is not a highly inflected language, but some nouns, and especially pronouns (e.g., third person pronoun) do inflect to indicate their relationship to the verb.

ADJUSTING YOUR FOCUS

One of the greatest challenges in learning Greek is retraining our eyes to focus on form, rather than word order, to determine a noun's function in its context. Because this takes time, we will spend an extended period becoming familiar with nouns and noun-related parts of speech, before turning to verbs.

Examples

Subject of the verb

Peter answered him
ὁ Πέτρος λέγει αὐτῷ
(Mark 11:21)

Possession or content

When Jesus entered *Peter's* house
Καὶ ἐλθὼν ὁ Ἰησοῦς εἰς τὴν οἰκίαν Πέτρου
(Matt 8:14)

Indirect object

But turning, he said to *Peter*
ὁ δὲ στραφεὶς εἶπεν τῷ Πέτρῳ·
(Matt 16:23)

Object of the verb

When she saw *Peter*
ἰδοῦσα τὸν Πέτρον
(Mark 14:67)

Direct Address

Jesus said, "*Peter*, I tell you…"
ὁ δὲ εἶπεν· λέγω σοι, Πέτρε,
(Luke 22:34)

ENGLISH PRONOUN INFLECTION
3rd Person Singular Personal Pronoun

	Masculine	**Feminine**	**Neuter**
Subject	he	she	it
Possessive	his	her	its
Indirect object	to him	to her	to it
Direct object	him	her	it

13. Nouns

Nouns

The first part of speech we will focus on is the noun. Remember from Lesson 11 that nouns name a person such as *Jesus*, a thing like the *treasury*, or a state of being, like *anger*.

Each Greek noun carries information about its meaning and its function in its context. Because Greek is heavily dependent on inflection, Greek nouns carry more information than English nouns. To translate from Greek into English, we need to decode that information and then convey this meaning and function in appropriate English expressions.

To decode a Greek noun's form, it is convenient to break it into two parts: the stem and the ending. Each carries information about the word that needs to be decoded. Some textbooks draw attention to the "connecting vowel" in the ending, but we will simply refer to two parts. For the noun λόγος:

stem	ending
λόγ	ος

Noun Stem

The root meaning of a noun is carried by the front part, or stem. Depending on the context, λόγ- can have a range of English "meanings." These include *word, assertion, computation, Word* with a capital "W," etc.

Vocabulary lists often give one English equivalent, or "gloss," for each Greek word. However, this may be misleading. There is rarely one-to-one correspondence between words in two languages. Words overlap in meaning, so a number of glosses may be needed to reflect a word's possible meanings, or "semantic range."

Noun Endings

The ending, or inflection, of the noun carries three pieces of information: case, number, and gender.

1. Case

Case usually defines a noun's relationship to its verb (use with prepositions is an exception). There are 5 cases:

Nominative indicates the subject of the verb. In English, this person or thing will be placed before the verb.

Genitive is the case of possession, translated by *of* ... or *'s*. The case may also be used to indicate the content of something.

Dative shows the indirect object of the verb—involved in the action of the verb, but not directly. English translation usually uses *to* ... or *for* ....

Accusative indicates the direct object of the verb. This will be placed after the verb in English.

Vocative is the case of direct address. English usually places this within quotation marks.

2. Number

Singular or Plural

This indicates one item (*word*), or more than one (*words*).

3. Gender

Masculine, Feminine, or Neuter

This should not to be confused with "natural" or biological gender. Some words are the gender we expect, but many are not. For instance, Israel is masculine in Greek, rock is feminine, while Sanhedrin is neuter. λόγος is regarded as masculine, grammatically.

Examples

Greek Case Endings

Nominative (Subject)
ὁ *λόγος* σὰρξ ἐγένετο
The *Word* became flesh
(John 1:14)

Genitive (Possession or Content)
οἱ ... ὑπηρέται γενόμενοι τοῦ *λόγου*
Those who were servants *of* the *word*
(Luke 1:2)

Dative (Indirect Object)
συνείχετο τῷ *λόγῳ* ὁ Παῦλος
Paul devoted himself *to* the *word*
(Acts 18:5)

Accusative (Direct object)
ἐλάλει αὐτοῖς τὸν *λόγον*
He preached the *word* to them
(Mark 2:2)

Vocative (Direct Address)
οὐδὲ καταισχυνῶ σε, φιλόσοφε *λόγε*
"I will not shame you, philosophic *reason*!"
(4 Maccabees 5:35)

N.B. The vocative is used rarely, and is usually obvious in its context. This grammar will focus on the other four cases.

14. The Article

The Article	Paradigm for the Article	Exercises

The Article

Before we go further with nouns, the second part of speech we will focus on is the article. Greek does not have an indefinite article like English (*a* or *an*). So when we refer to the Greek article we mean a small word, which functions like *the* in English, placed before a noun to show that it is definite.

Articles are closely related to nouns. This is because each article modifies the noun that follows it. So, any article will have the same case, number, and gender as its noun.

Form

As a result, the Greek article needs to have a range of forms flexible enough to agree with a noun of any combination of case (x 4), number (x 2), and gender (x 3). This means there are 24 forms of the Greek article to express the potential combinations.

Note that some forms are repeated. In translation, any ambiguity is normally clarified by the context.

"Paradigm"

This structured layout is generally referred to as a *paradigm*. All nouns, pronouns and adjectives will be learned according to this structure. So this is the "paradigm for the Greek article."

Once a paradigm is learned, you will be able to decode the function of any word that follows that pattern. If a word matches the third word in a given list it will be the dative singular; if it matches the last of the eight it will be the accusative plural.

Paradigm for the Article

	Masculine	Feminine	Neuter
Sg Nom	ὁ	ἡ	τό
Gen	τοῦ	τῆς	τοῦ
Dat	τῷ	τῇ	τῷ
Acc	τόν	τήν	τό
Pl Nom	οἱ	αἱ	τά
Gen	τῶν	τῶν	τῶν
Dat	τοῖς	ταῖς	τοῖς
Acc	τούς	τάς	τά

Memorizing paradigms

You are expected to memorize nouns and noun-related words according to their paradigm. Thorough memorization is basic to translating the Greek New Testament. Memorize this paradigm, column by vertical column.

Exercises

1. Find each definite article in Mark 1:1–5. Identify case, number, and gender from the table.

Verse	Form	Case	Number	Gender
1	τοῦ	gen	sg	masc/neut
2				
2				
2				
2				
3				
3				
3				
4				
4				
5				
5				
5				
5				

2. Begin to learn the full declension of the article, that is, its various forms in a paradigm. Memorize the masculine article.

15. Masculine Nouns

Masculine Nouns

Now back to nouns. Every noun in the Greek language is assigned a gender: masculine, feminine, or neuter. A noun's gender is not evident from its form alone. To learn the gender of a noun we will rely on vocabulary lists, which introduce new nouns in groups according to their gender.

The noun λόγος (*word, assertion*) is masculine. Its paradigm is representative of a large number of other masculine nouns. Masculine nouns like λόγος that occur in Mark 1 and 2 are listed in Vocab #2. There are also some irregular feminine nouns that follow this same pattern.

The paradigm for λόγος, like the article, is organized into two groups of four, according to case and number. Once the endings for λόγος are memorized, the endings for many other masculine nouns will also be known. For instance, Mark 2:2 uses the form λόγον. By referring to the paradigm, λόγον occurs fourth on the list, and is therefore accusative. Since it occurs in the top group of four, the noun is singular. The vocabulary list tells us that any form of λόγος is always masculine. So, λόγον is the accusative, singular, masculine of λόγος.

Mark 10:24 contains λόγοις, which matches the third word in the lower group. So λόγοις is dative, plural, and masculine.

The word κύριος (*Lord,* see Vocab #2) follows the same pattern as λόγος. The ending of κυρίου in Mark 1:3 matches the second line in the top group of the paradigm for λόγος. So κυρίου is the genitive, singular form of κύριος. Vocab #2 indicates it is also a masculine noun.

The Name, Jesus

The word for Jesus's name (Vocab #1) is irregular but is a variation on λόγος. Note that the genitive and dative take the same form. The plural is not used in the New Testament.

Masculine Nouns Like λόγος, ου, ὁ

Sg	Nom	λόγος	a word
	Gen	λόγου	of a word
	Dat	λόγῳ	to/for a word
	Acc	λόγον	a word
Pl	Nom	λόγοι	words
	Gen	λόγων	of words
	Dat	λόγοις	to/for words
	Acc	λόγους	words

Jesus in Greek

Sg	Nom	Ἰησοῦς	Jesus
	Gen	Ἰησοῦ	of Jesus, Jesus's
	Dat	Ἰησοῦ	to/for Jesus
	Acc	Ἰησοῦν	Jesus

Vocab #2

Exercises

1. Find each word from Vocab #2 in the verse given with it. Compare each with λόγος and work out its case, number, and gender.

2. Learn the declension for λόγος.

16. Marking Nouns

Marking Nouns	Symbols for Marking Nouns	Examples
Preparing the Text for Reading We are moving toward reading from Mark's Gospel. "Marking the text" is a useful step in preparing the Greek text for reading and translation. It is a discipline worth practicing and persevering with. We will adopt a number of conventions for showing the relationship of the noun to its verb and for showing how to render them into English. These symbols are placed above the final two letters of a noun. These instructions are also found in *Reading Biblical Greek Workbook*. **Nominative:** an arrow pointing right above the nominative reminds us that in English this noun will be the subject of the verb. So regardless of the Greek word order, the verb should be placed to the right of the subject in your English translation. **Genitive:** the Greek genitive is nearly always translated by *of* in English, for a large range of relationships (e.g., "bucket *of* balls," "bucket *of* plastic," "bucket *of* Bob"). So *of* is placed above the final letters of the genitive. **Dative:** the dative case often expresses the indirect object, rendered by *to* or *for* in English. So the numbers *2/4* are placed above a dative noun to represent these possibilities. **Accusative:** since the accusative indicates the direct object, an arrow pointing to the left serves as a reminder that in English the verb will precede the accusative noun.	**Nominative** → λόγος **Genitive** *of* λόγου **Dative** 2/4 λόγῳ **Accusative** ← λόγον	**Nominative** → πεπλήρωται ὁ καιρὸς The *time* is fulfilled (Mark 1:15) **Genitive** *of* ἑτοιμάσατε τὴν ὁδὸν κυρίου Prepare the way *of the Lord* (Mark 1:3) **Dative** 2/4 Εἶπεν κύριος τῷ κυρίῳ The Lord said *to the Lord* (Mark 12:36) **Accusative** ← ἀποστέλλω τὸν ἄγγελόν I am sending *the messenger* (Mark 1:2)

17. The Way Words Mean

The Way Words Mean	Exercises

Meaning Is More Than the Meaning of Words

Reading Greek involves more than substituting Greek words with equivalent meanings in English. There is much more to *meaning* than simply adding individual words together. Think back (Lesson 10) to the sentence,

> *The old man just said, "You missed the boat."*

It is possible to paraphrase this sentence:

> *The geriatric male recently explained, "You're late for the ferry."*

However, since the meaning of a sentence is more than simply the sum of the words, this could be a complete misunderstanding. The sentence could consist of two idiomatic expressions. *The old man* is a common colloquial expression for *my father*. *You missed the boat* could be slang for *you wasted the opportunity*.

In that case:

> *My dad just said, "You blew your chance,"*

would be a much more accurate rendering of the intended meaning.

Deciding which paraphrase is more accurate is difficult when reading a sentence by itself. To clarify the meaning of *man* we would need to take account of the paragraph around the sentence, perhaps the whole text.

While we speak of "the meaning of a word," meaning depends on the relationship between words within language units, that is: phrases, sentences, paragraphs, and whole documents, or "discourses."

To understand the meaning of New Testament texts we need to take account of all the language units that contribute to meaning. The wider context enables us to limit the possible meanings of words.

For practical purposes, we will begin with individual words, but we need to remember that our aim is ultimately to be competent at reading whole texts. The exercise in the next column illustrates the relationship between a whole text and individual sentences within it.

Reading English involves complex and sophisticated skills. So, the skills you already have will be foundational to reading Greek. Rather than learning to do something completely new, we will be building on your skills as a reader of English.

Exercises

1. How good are you at recognizing the genre of a document from just a sentence or two? Match the following genres with the quotes below.

2. Which clues give the genre away?

   a. Constitutional code   d. Science textbook
   b. Sports journalism   e. Letter/Epistle
   c. Apocalyptic/Prophecy   f. Fantasy

   i. *Hewitt has suffered another injury setback, citing an ailment in his left foot for his late withdrawal from the French Open.*

   ii. *His heart pounded. The doorknob turned again. All he could do was wait, hoping the music box would soon stop before the shadows had a chance to find him.*

   iii. *Photosynthesis is a process that converts carbon dioxide into organic compounds, especially sugars, using the energy from sunlight.*

   iv. *Immediately after they shall be assembled in consequence of the first election, they shall be divided as equally as may be into three classes.*

   v. *James, a servant of God and of the Lord Jesus Christ, To the twelve tribes scattered among the nations: Greetings.*

   vi. *Then I saw a Lamb, looking as if it had been slain, standing at the center of the throne, encircled by the four living creatures and the elders.*

18. Feminine Nouns

Feminine Nouns

Back again to nouns. We have already learned one paradigm of masculine nouns (Lesson 15). Nouns that are *feminine* in gender have distinctive feminine endings. Nouns in the group of feminine nouns introduced in this lesson have the same plural endings. However, there are three variations within the singular endings.

The feminine noun paradigm in the middle column contains these three types. Variations in the noun endings are determined by the final letter of the noun stem.

1. Like γραφή

These have a stem ending in a consonant. In the singular forms these nouns have exactly the same endings as the feminine article, with *ēta* (η) as the dominant vowel (Lesson 14). This type includes words like παραβολή (*parable*), ἀγάπη (*love*), and γῆ (*earth*). The only exceptions to this rule are feminine nouns that end with the consonants *rho, sigma*, or *xi* (ρ, σ, or ξ.)

2. Like ὥρα

These have a stem that ends with a vowel or *rho* (ρ; a situation in which *rho* behaves just like a vowel). Greek prefers the distinctive α sound in the singular when the stem ends with a vowel or *rho*. This type includes καρδία (*heart*), γενέα (*generation*), θύρα (*door*).

3. Like δόξα

When the stem ends in *sigma* or *xi*, the singular forms include a mixture of *alpha* and *ēta* endings. Their singular nominative and accusative contain *alpha* (α), while the genitive and dative, *ēta* (η). Only three nouns in this category occur often enough to rate inclusion in the vocab lists: γλῶσσα (*tongue*), δόξα (*brightness*), θάλασσα (*sea, lake*).

Feminine Nouns Like
γραφή, ῆς, ἡ; ὥρα, ας, ἡ; δόξα, ης, ἡ

Sg	**Nom**	γραφή	ὥρα	δόξα
	Gen	γραφῆς	ὥρας	δόξης
	Dat	γραφῇ	ὥρᾳ	δόξῃ
	Acc	γραφήν	ὥραν	δόξαν
Pl	**Nom**	γραφαί	ὧραι	δόξαι
	Gen	γραφῶν	ὡρῶν	δοξῶν
	Dat	γραφαῖς	ὥραις	δόξαις
	Acc	γραφάς	ὥρας	δόξας

Vocab #3

Exercises

1. Find each of the feminine nouns in Vocab #3, which occur in Mark 1 (the relevant verse is given). Identify the case, number, and gender of each one.

2. Write out the full declension of βασιλεία, φωνή, and θάλασσα.

3. Learn the declension of the feminine definite article.

4. Learn the declension of γραφή and familiarize yourself with the variations in the other two feminine nouns.

19. ANALYZING NOUNS

Analyzing Nouns

Reading Greek nouns involves deciphering the information carried in their endings. To do that, we need to recognize the family of noun they belong to.

1. LEXICON ENTRIES

A Greek dictionary is referred to as a *lexicon*. Nouns are listed in a lexicon according to a consistent pattern. This lexicon entry for ποταμός (Mark 1:5) is typical:

ποταμός, οῦ, ὁ — *river, stream*

Along with English glosses, three pieces of information are given. It is listed under its nominative singular form (ποταμός), its genitive singular ending (οῦ) and its article (ὁ). The masculine article makes it clear that ποταμός is a masculine word.

This entry tells us even more than just these three pieces of information. It tells us that ποταμός follows the same pattern as λόγος (Lesson 15), since it is listed in the same way, as λόγος, ου, ὁ. From this we can infer all the paradigm endings for ποταμός by recalling the paradigm for λόγος. So, since ποταμῷ matches λόγῳ (upper group, third line), it is dative, singular, and masculine.

2. NOUN FAMILY-GROUPS (DECLENSIONS)

Each Greek noun belongs to one of three families. These families are known as declensions, another name for a noun paradigm.

Each Greek noun belongs to either the 1st, 2nd, or 3rd declension, according to similarities in the way they form, or "decline." Vocab lists are ordered by these declensions. Three nouns represent the variations in 1st declension feminine nouns. These have the same plural endings (αι, ων, αις, ας)

λόγος, ου, ὁ represents masculine 2nd declension nouns. Neuter second declension nouns follow ἔργον, ου, τό (*work*). The genitive and dative endings (sing. and plur.) for these nouns are the same. We will encounter 3rd declension nouns later.

3. "PARSING" A NOUN

"Parsing" is the technical term for analyzing the form of a Greek word for its meaning. To parse a noun, identify the case, number, and gender of the form in the text, along with an English gloss. This follows a four step process:

1. Determine the noun stem and its English meaning (see vocab lists or a lexicon).

2. Identify the noun declension it follows. This gives you the noun's gender.

3. Locate the noun's endings on the declension of the representative noun to decode case and number.

4. Parse the noun fully by providing the case, number, gender, the Greek nominative singular, and English gloss.

Examples

NOUNS FROM VOCAB #1

1ST DECLENSION

	Feminine			Masculine	
γραφή	ὥρα	δόξα		προφήτης	Ἀνδρέας
	Γαλιλαία			Ἰορδάνης	Ἡσαΐας
	Ἰουδαία			Ἰωάννης	(σατανᾶς)

2ND DECLENSION

Masculine	Neuter
λόγος	ἔργον
Ζεβεδαῖος	
θεός	
Ἰάκωβος	
Ἰησοῦς	
Ἰουδαῖος	
Πέτρος	
Πιλᾶτος	
Χριστός	

3RD DECLENSION

Masc/Fem	Neuter		Masc	Fem
ἀνήρ	σῶμα	γένος	βασιλεύς	πόλις
Σίμων				

INDECLINABLE
(N.B. often from Hebrew)

Ἀβραάμ, ὁ

Δαυίδ, ὁ

Ναζαρά or Ναζαρέτ, ἡ

20. NEUTER NOUNS

We've learned 2nd declension masculine and 1st declension feminine nouns. *Neuter* nouns, like ἔργον, ου, τό (*work*) complete the 2nd declension.

Bear in mind that gender in Greek is a grammatical category. For example, the words for *Holy Spirit*, *Jerusalem* and *Sanhedrin* are grammatically neuter. Avoid reading too much into the gender of a word.

At this stage, there are two features to note about these neuter nouns:

1. LEXICON ENTRY

These nouns are grouped with masculine nouns like λόγος in the second declension because they share genitive and dative endings in the singular and plural. So ἔργον will be listed in a lexicon under ἔργον, ου, τό.

2. SAME NOMINATIVE & ACCUSATIVE

A distinctive feature of neuter nouns is that they have the same nominative and accusative form in the singular; and also the same form in the nominative and accusative plural. This is true in the singular and in the plural. This makes for some ambiguity when reading the New Testament. But this is most often resolved by the context.

Usually when marking the text, you will be unfamiliar with the context. So in marking neuter nouns that could be nominative or accusative, use an arrow pointing both ways to mark these possibilities:

E.g.,   ἔργα↔

NEUTER NOUNS LIKE ἔργον, ου, τό

Sg	Nom	ἔργον
	Gen	ἔργου
	Dat	ἔργῳ
	Acc	ἔργον
Pl	Nom	ἔργα
	Gen	ἔργων
	Dat	ἔργοις
	Acc	ἔργα

Vocab #4

Exercises

Using vocab lists if necessary:

1. Write out the full declension of εὐαγγέλιον and πρόσωπον.

2. Work out the lexicon entry under which you would find the following nouns from Mark 1:

ἁμαρτίας	ἁμαρτία, ας, ἡ
οὐρανούς	
θάλασσαν	
ἀνθρώπων	
ἐρήμῳ	
ἐξουσίαν	
δαιμόνια	
τόποις	

3. Parse the following nouns:

	Case	No	Gender	Greek	Eng
πλοίῳ	Dat	Sg	Neut	πλοῖον	boat
συναγωγάς					
προσώπου					
ἡμέραις					
φωνή					
υἱοῦ					
διδαχήν					
οἰκίαν					

21. 1st Declension Masculine Nouns

1st Declension Masculine Nouns	Exercises

1st Declension Masculine Nouns

We've learned 1st declension *feminine* nouns (Lesson 18). Two paradigms complete nouns in the 1st declension. Words like προφήτης, and a variation, Ἀνδρέας, represent 1st declension *masculine* nouns.

Nouns Like προφήτης, ου, ὁ

Vocab #5 contains only two nouns whose stems end in a consonant and that follow this pattern; nevertheless, they are significant words in the NT: *prophet* and *disciple*. Two names from Vocab #1 also follow this pattern: Ἰορδάνης and Ἰωάννης. Note the distinctive features of these nouns:

1. They have the same plural endings as 1st declension feminine nouns: γραφή, ὥρα, and δόξα. Their singular dative and accusative forms also echo these feminine nouns.

2. However, they have the same genitive singular ending as masculine nouns like λόγος and are masculine in gender. So they are listed in the lexicon under: προφήτης, ου, ὁ

Nouns Like Ἀνδρέας, ου, ὁ

1st declension noun stems ending in a vowel or *rho*, like Ἀνδρέας, ου, ὁ, represent a variation on προφήτης.

One other name in Vocab #1 follows this pattern: Ἡσαΐας. For some reason σατανᾶς also does so, despite its stem ending in a consonant. Since these are all proper nouns and have no plural forms in the New Testament, only the singular forms are given.

1st Declension Masculine Nouns Like προφήτης, ου, ὁ; Ἀνδρέας, ου, ὁ

Sg	**Nom**	προφήτης	Ἀνδρέας
	Gen	προφήτου	Ἀνδρέου
	Dat	προφήτῃ	Ἀνδρέᾳ
	Acc	προφήτην	Ἀνδρέαν
Pl	**Nom**	προφῆται	
	Gen	προφητῶν	
	Dat	προφήταις	
	Acc	προφήτας	

Vocab #5

Exercises

1. Parse the following first declension masculine nouns from Mark 1:

Ἡσαΐᾳ

προφήτῃ

Ἰωάννης

Ἰορδάνῃ

Ἰορδάνην

Ἰωάννου

Ἰωάννην

Ἀνδρέαν

Ἀνδρέου

22. Memorizing Vocabulary and Paradigms

Memorizing Vocabulary and Paradigms		Examples
Principles	**Methods**	

Principles

This grammar includes nearly 130 items of Greek vocabulary and numerous paradigms. Committing these to memory can be daunting. Try to develop good habits at the outset.

1. **Be regular:** A small amount of regular time is more effective for long-term memory than cramming in one sitting. It's best to set aside 15 minutes nearly every day.

2. **Be organized:** To make the most of these opportunities you need to be organized. The earlier you set up your patterns of learning the better.

3. **Be active:** It is easy to waste time going over and over long lists. Some words will come easily. Some will prove to be slippery. Identify these early and give them more attention.

4. **Be varied:** There is no avoiding repetition, so variety is important. Make the most of computer tools. Make sure you can sound out words and paradigms and write them out on paper. Practice with a friend if possible.

5. **Be precise:** Pronounce words correctly from the beginning. You must sound out rough breathings. Place stress on the accented syllable of the word. Also, as you learn each new word, learn the paradigm that the word follows. Rather than memorizing υἱός, ου, ὁ in full, simply recall that υἱός is like λόγος.

For further practical advice, see Constantine R. Campbell, *Keep Your Greek: Strategies for Busy People* (Grand Rapids: Zondervan, 2010).

Methods

Computer Tools

There are numerous, excellent electronic tools available for computers, phones, and tablets. These are constantly developed and improved. The most useful tools can be customized to correspond to the vocab lists and paradigms for this grammar.

Traditional Methods

These illustrate principles of effective learning.

a. **Flash cards:** Small cards with Greek on one side and English on the back are a time-honoured method. These can be purchased but be aware that they are not synced to this grammar. You may also make your own by following the samples opposite.

b. **Recordings:** Students can make their own recordings of Greek vocab and paradigms. Make your own sound files and listen to them as you walk, shop, or travel.

c. **Lists:** Lists and tables on walls, beside beds, on bathroom doors, etc. have also proven very effective. This grammar provides handy tables with all the verb and noun paradigms to be memorized.

d. **Coffee:** Students have also benefited from meeting with a friend to practice Greek together. This gentle accountability helps regularity and precision, and tends to be more enjoyable.

Examples

Sample Flash Cards

Noun λόγος, ου, ὁ υἱός	son
Verb λύω βάλλω	I throw, expel, put
Adj ἀγαθός, ή, όν ὀλίγος	little, few
Prep ὑπό + gen + acc	by under

A Reminder

No one can memorize Greek vocab and paradigms for you. Take responsibility for your own learning. The sooner you get organized and develop effective patterns, the less painful learning Greek will be. More importantly, you will be better prepared to start reading the Greek New Testament!

23. PERSONAL PRONOUNS: 3RD PERSON

Personal Pronouns 3rd Person

Pronouns belong to the world of nouns and behave like them. They are *noun substitutes*—a convenient way of referring to someone or something without naming them again. There is a wide variety of pronouns:

personal *I, you, he, she, it*   **demonstrative** *this, that*

relative *who, which*   **interrogative** *who?, which?*

indefinite *someone, anyone*   **reflexive** *myself, yourself*

reciprocal *one another*

Personal pronouns represent over two-thirds of pronoun use, so they warrant attention first, beginning with the 3rd person personal pronoun: Greek words for *he, she, it* in the singular and *them* in the plural. With this little bit of learning, the student will be able to recognize over 5,500 words in the Greek New Testament.

USAGE

The third person pronoun is used extensively. The pronoun substitutes for a noun or name already mentioned, known as the pronoun's "antecedent." The pronoun saves referring to a character or item by its full name. Usually the person or thing referred to is clear from the context; e.g., though Jesus's name is not used between Mark 3:7 and 5:6, he is unmistakably the focus of the action in 4:38:

But he (αὐτός) was in the stern, asleep on the cushion; and they woke him (αὐτόν) up and said to him (αὐτῷ), "Teacher . . ."

FORM

The form for each gender has close affinities to the article. The pronoun is listed in a lexicon under its three nominative singular endings, αὐτός, ή, ό (like adjectives).

TRANSLATION

Note the way the equivalent English pronouns decline. The pronoun usually agrees with grammatical number and gender, but may reflect natural gender or the plurality in a collective noun. So, the word for child, παιδίον, is neuter. If this refers to a boy, an author may choose *he* rather than *it* when referring back to this noun. Your translation should reflect appropriate English usage.

		Masculine	Feminine	Neuter
Sg	**Nom**	αὐτός	αὐτή	αὐτό
	Gen	αὐτοῦ	αὐτῆς	αὐτοῦ
	Dat	αὐτῷ	αὐτῇ	αὐτῷ
	Acc	αὐτόν	αὐτήν	αὐτό
Pl	**Nom**	αὐτοί	αὐταί	αὐτά
	Gen	αὐτῶν	αὐτῶν	αὐτῶν
	Dat	αὐτοῖς	αὐταῖς	αὐτοῖς
	Acc	αὐτούς	αὐτάς	αὐτά

ENGLISH EQUIVALENTS

Sg	**Nom**	he	she	it
	Gen	his	her	its
	Dat	to him	to her	to it
	Acc	him	her	it
Pl	**Nom**	they	they	they
	Gen	their	their	their
	Dat	to them	to them	to them
	Acc	them	them	them

Exercises

1. Count how many times the 3rd person pronoun occurs in Mark 1:1–20. Identify the number, gender, and case in each instance. Compare your findings with an English translation of these pronouns.

2. Parse and translate the following uses of αὐτός in Mark:

   καὶ παρεκάλει αὐτὸν πολλὰ (5:10)

   ἦλθεν καὶ προσέπεσεν αὐτῷ καὶ εἶπεν αὐτῷ πᾶσαν τὴν ἀλήθειαν (5:33)

   καὶ εἶπεν αὐτοῖς· ἄφετε τὰ παιδία ἔρχεσθαι πρός με, μὴ κωλύετε αὐτά (10:14)

   ὁ δὲ λέγει αὐταῖς· μὴ ἐκθαμβεῖσθε· . . . ἴδε ὁ τόπος ὅπου ἔθηκαν αὐτόν. (16:6)

   εἶχεν γὰρ αὐτὰς τρόμος καὶ ἔκστασις (16:8)

24. OTHER USES OF CASE: TIME

Other Uses of Case: Time

An important element in learning about nouns is to understand the role of *cases*. The case system is one of the significant differences between Greek and English. Greek makes extensive use of cases. We have already seen the most fundamental use: showing the relationship between nouns and verbs in sentences.

Cases figure in Greek in other ways too:
- in time phrases
- with prepositions
- after certain verbs where the accusative would be expected for the object
- other special uses (e.g., accusative of respect, genitive absolute, instrument of a passive verb).

There is a sense in which the three "oblique" cases (genitive, dative, accusative) contribute to these constructions. The following are generalizations, so they do not always apply.

The genitive is often used for the type or "genus" to which something belongs, hence possession. Related to this is the idea of separation. It is used to express motion away from something.

The dative is used to place or locate a person or event at a point in space or time. *In, on,* and *at* are usually expressed with the help of the dative because of this "locative" function.

The accusative is referred to as the case of "extension." It is used to express distance travelled, or length.

Time Expressions

The easiest way to appreciate the contribution that case can make is to see the way that time is expressed.

GENITIVE CASE

time during which or within which

νηστεύω δὶς **τοῦ σαββάτου** (Luke 18:12)

I fast twice **a week**

προσμένει ταῖς δεήσεσιν καὶ ταῖς προσευχαῖς **νυκτὸς** καὶ **ἡμέρας** (1 Tim 5:5)

continues in supplications and prayers **night** and **day**

DATIVE CASE

time at which or when

προσεύχεσθε δὲ ἵνα μὴ γένηται ἡ φυγὴ ὑμῶν χειμῶνος μηδὲ **σαββάτῳ** (Matt 24:20)

Pray your flight may not be in winter or **on the sabbath**

καὶ **τῇ τρίτῃ ἡμέρᾳ** ἐγερθήσεται (Matt 17:23)

and **on the third day** he will be raised

ACCUSATIVE CASE

time how long or duration

νηστεύσας **ἡμέρας τεσσεράκοντα** καὶ **νύκτας τεσσεράκοντα** (Matt 4:2)

fasting **forty days** and **forty nights**

ἐγὼ μεθ᾽ ὑμῶν εἰμι **πάσας τὰς ἡμέρας** ἕως τῆς συντελείας τοῦ αἰῶνος (Matt 28:20)

I am with you **always**, to the end of the age

Exercises

1. Each of the following verses uses ἡμέρα (*day*) in a time phrase. Identify the kind of time phrase being used (i.e., *time during, time when,* or *time how long*). Give the case that you expect the Greek to have used for ἡμέρα.

Keep awake therefore, for you do not know on what day your Lord is coming. (Matt 24:42)

We worked night and day, so that we might not burden any of you. (1 Thess 2:9)

We greeted the believers and stayed with them for one day. (Acts 21:7)

Its gates will never be shut by day—and there will be no night there. (Rev 21:25)

For three days he was without sight, and neither ate nor drank. (Acts 9:9)

25. Prepositions

Prepositions

They may be small, but prepositions are extremely important and frequently used words in Greek. Prepositions are words used to place parts of a sentence in a relationship. They indicate relationships in terms of space (in, on, under, over, before), motion (toward, away from, out of), time (after, during, before), or logic (for).

The Object of a Preposition

Prepositions are followed by their noun or pronoun. This is referred to as the *object* of the preposition. (This needs to be distinguished from the *object* of the verb.) The object immediately follows its preposition.

Case

The meaning of any preposition is the product of the preposition and the case of the noun that follows. The objects of some prepositions take only one case; some take two, others three. The impact on meaning of the different cases varies. For instance, ἐπί means *on* with all three cases, but carries a slightly different nuance with each. While μετά can carry two quite different meanings, either *with* or *after*, depending on the case of its object.

Marking the Text

Bracketing prepositional phrases is a vital step in the process of marking the text. Prepositions expose the fact that nouns may take a case for a very different reason from showing a noun's relationship to the verb, in the way they combine with the preposition. So, prepositional phrases are bracketed to avoid confusion. In fact, it makes sense to bracket nouns in their prepositional phrases before marking other nouns.

Mark prepositional phrases with a round bracket (), opening them before the preposition and closing them after any articles, adjectives, nouns, and pronouns in the same case that follow the preposition (see "Marking the Greek Text" in *Reading Biblical Greek Workbook*).

E.g., Mark 1:2

Καθὼς γέγραπται (ἐν τῷ Ἠσαΐᾳ τῷ προφήτῃ·)

Prepositions of Space

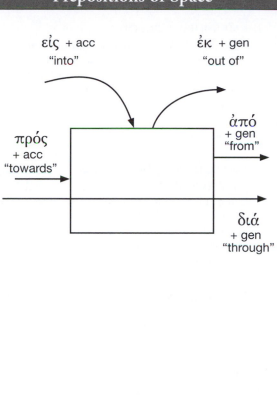

εἰς + acc "into"   ἐκ + gen "out of"

ἀπό + gen "from"

πρός + acc "towards"

διά + gen "through"

Vocab #6

Exercises

1. Translate these prepositional phrases from Mark 1 (refer to vocab lists if necessary):

   ἐν τῷ Ἠσαΐᾳ τῷ προφήτῃ

   ἐν τῇ ἐρήμῳ

   πρὸς αὐτόν

   ἐν τῷ Ἰορδάνῃ ποταμῷ

   ἐν ἐκείναις (*those* dat.) ταῖς

   ἡμέραις

   ἐκ τοῦ ὕδατος (gen. of *water*)

   εἰς αὐτόν

   ἐκ τῶν οὐρανῶν

   εἰς τὴν ἔρημον

   ἐκ τῆς συναγωγῆς

   πρὸς τὴν θύραν

   ἀπʼ αὐτοῦ

   πρὸς αὐτόν

2. Learn the prepositions and their cases from the vocab list according to the pattern:
   εἰς + accusative = *into, in*

3. Learn to reproduce the diagram to the left.

26. An Introduction to Verbs

An Introduction to Verbs

Verbs portray processes, actions, or states. Verbs require more learning than nouns because of their relative complexity, caused by a number of factors:

1. Centrality

In Greek, verbs are the engine room of clauses and sentences. While a clause may contain many nouns, it will contain only one verb. This makes verbs very significant and places greater burden on their form.

E.g., Mark 1:16a contains one finite verb
but seven nouns:

Passing along the Sea of Galilee, Jesus saw Simon and his brother Andrew casting a net into the sea.

2. Flexibility

In describing a process, action, or state, verbs need to be very flexible. They express what *happens*, *is thought*, *said*, or *done by* or *to* the participants in a sentence. They present a process, action, or state from a certain viewpoint or perspective (see Lesson 31 for more on this). To convey and distinguish these subtleties, verbs inflect much more than other parts of speech.

3. Amount of Information

In Greek, verbs often carry more information than their English equivalents. A process in English may be described by a group of words, known as "auxiliary verbs," e.g., *am teaching*, *will teach*, *have been teaching*. In Greek, a single verbal form nearly always carries all such information by itself.

4. Embedded Subject

Also, English verbs do not contain the subject of the verb; a separate noun or pronoun is required. E.g., *I am teaching*, *she taught*, *they will be teaching*. In Greek, the verb conveys the first, second, or third person subject of the verb in its form:

E.g., ἐδιδάσκετε   *you* (2nd pers. pl) *were teaching*.

5. Inflection at Both Ends

The ways in which verbs inflect or change reflects these factors. Like nouns, verbs are inflected through the addition of endings. Unlike nouns, Greek verbs may also be inflected at the beginning of the verb stem. Or they may be turned into "compound" verbs by the addition of a preposition at the front of the verb stem.

Agreement Between Noun and Verb

Verbs agree with their subjects in person (1st, 2nd, 3rd) and number (singular or plural). This is how a verb is tied or attached to a particular noun in a clause as its subject.

In English we say, *I teach* and *Laura teaches*, not *I teaches* and *Laura teach*. Similarly, Greek uses endings to indicate the person and number of a verb and as a rule these must agree with the subject. There are exceptions. For example, neuter plural nouns take a singular verb. E.g., Mark 4:36:

ἄλλα πλοῖα (pl) ἦν (sg) μετ᾽ αὐτοῦ

(lit. but boats was with him)

Some singular "collective" nouns occur with plural verbs. E.g., Mark 4:1:

ὁ ὄχλος (sg) πρὸς τὴν θάλασσαν ἐπὶ τῆς γῆς ἦσαν (pl)

Exercises

1. Read this famous text with verbs removed. What is lost as a result?

   We … not … nor … We … on to the end. We … in France and on the seas and oceans; we … with growing confidence and growing strength in the air. We … our island whatever the cost … ; we … on beaches, landing grounds, in fields, in streets and on the hills. We … never…

   Winston Churchill

2. Account for the forms of the verb *swim* below. When would you use them and how do they nuance the process being described?

   swim

   swims

   swam

   swum

   swimmed

   swimming

3. Circle the verb and noun that agree:

   The dog chews OR The dog chew

   The boy and his dog runs OR The boy and his dog run

   The flock flies OR The flock fly

27. CHARACTERISTICS OF THE VERB

Characteristics of the Verb | Examples

The complexity of verbs is reflected in the characteristics that one needs to master. Like nouns, verbs carry a range of information that must be decoded in order to read and translate. Due to their greater complexity, verbs carry greater amounts of information. This lesson provides an overview of the five key characteristics:

1. TENSE-FORM

There are six key tense-forms in Greek:

1. present
2. imperfect
3. aorist
4. future
5. perfect
6. pluperfect

Each tense-form expresses *verbal aspect*. The significance of aspect has been the subject of much discussion and debate; more about this in Lesson 31.

2. VOICE

In English, active and passive voices distinguish between a process done *by* the subject and one done *to* the subject. In the sentences, *John baptized Jesus* and *John was baptized by Jesus* the meaning is inverted by changing the verb from an active to a passive voice. Greek also has a middle voice, which indicates *subject-affectedness*. This voice is also a topic of some debate among grammarians.

3. MOOD

Mood refers to the mode or manner of the process, action, or state described. There are three key moods—Indicative, Imperative, and Subjunctive. The Optative mood also exists, but is rare in the NT as it was dying out in the Koine period.

4. PERSON

Three categories of person—1st (*I, we*), 2nd (*you*), and 3rd (*he, she, it, they*)—correspond to the one performing the action of the verb: *I make, you make, she makes*, etc.

5. NUMBER

Verbs are either singular or plural. This is what distinguishes *I* from *we*, and *you* (singular) from *you* (plural) etc. English has lost the useful distinction between 2nd person singular and plural that the *King James Version* used (*thou, thee* versus *you, ye*). Greek has different endings that clearly distinguish number, and this needs to be remembered in reading and translation.

PARSING VERBS

Like nouns, verbs are parsed in order to list all the information conveyed by a Greek verbal form. Again, the relative complexity of the verb will mean a longer list is needed than is offered for nouns. Note the increased amount of information needed to parse the two verbs from Mark 1 (*to the right*).

These examples highlight the sophisticated skills needed for recognizing the information encoded in verbs. This might seem overwhelming at this stage. But remember that this is an overview of material that will be introduced gradually over an extended period.

Examples

γέγραπται

Tense-form:	Perfect
Voice:	Middle/Passive
Mood:	Indicative
Person:	3rd
Number:	Singular
Lexical Form:	γράφω
English:	I write
Translation:	It is written

ἑτοιμάσατε

Tense-form:	Aorist
Voice:	Active
Mood:	Imperative
Person:	2nd
Number:	Plural
Lexical Form:	ἑτοιμάζω
English:	I prepare
Translation:	Prepare!

28. Verbs Ending in ω, Like λύω

Verbs Ending in ω, Like λύω

It's time to begin learning verb forms. The verb λύω (*I loose, untie, destroy*) is representative of a large group of regular verbs. It has the advantage of the stem remaining constant throughout all moods, tenses and voices. It is also a short word. So λύω will serve as the basic verb pattern throughout the grammar.

Verb Conjugations

A verb paradigm is known as a "conjugation." While nouns decline, verbs "conjugate." There are six lines within a verb conjugation, to account for three persons in the singular and three in the plural.

The conjugation for λύω (*see right*) is present in tense-form, active in voice, and indicative in mood. The conjugation shows the different forms for person and number.

λύω may be translated *I am loosing* or *I loose*. It is best to begin translating by the former to stress continuous action. The present tense-form is made up of two parts: the stem λυ- and the personal endings ω, εις, ει, etc. The ending often contains a connecting vowel to make pronunciation easier. In practice it will be simpler to think of this vowel as part of the personal ending.

Using the conjugation for λύω it is possible to work out the person and number of forms of other verbs from Vocab #7. They are all present, indicative and active. E.g., Mark 1:30:

λέγουσιν is a form of λέγω, meaning, *I say*

The 3rd person plural translates, *they are saying*.

Present Active Indicative of λύω

Sg	1st	λύω	I loose
	2nd	λύεις	you loose
	3rd	λύει	he/she/it looses
Pl	1st	λύομεν	we loose
	2nd	λύετε	you loose
	3rd	λύουσιν	they loose

Vocab #7

Exercises

Using the table to the left, and vocab lists:

1. Form the present active indicative:

   2nd person plural of ἔχω

   3rd person singular of πιστεύω

   1st person plural of θεραπεύω

   2nd person singular of φέρω

2. Parse (Tense, Voice, Mood, Pers, Num, Gk, Eng):

   ἄγετε

   βάλλουσιν

   ἐσθίω

3. Translate

   πιστεύομεν

   γράφει

   ἐγείρεις

4. Begin to learn Vocab #7.

5. Find each of the verbs from Vocab #7 in Mark 1. How has the stem been built on/altered in each case?

29. CONTRACT VERBS ENDING IN εω

Contract Verbs Ending in εω (ποιέω)

A key variation on the λύω verb paradigm is seen with contract verbs. Contract verbs have a vowel at the end of the verb stem. They take the same personal endings as λύω but this vowel combines with the personal endings in a number of ways.

CONTRACTION

This combination of short vowels to form diphthongs is known as contraction. Some simple rules govern the formation of the present and imperfect forms of these verbs (see right).

ποιέω (I do, make) is representative of verbs that have an *epsilon* (ε) at the end of the verb stem, known as εω verbs (i.e., its stem is ποιέ). Greek also has αω and οω contract verbs (see Lessons 76, 77).

While these verbs are entered in a lexicon under their non-contracted form (e.g., ποιέω), they occur only in the New Testament in their contracted form (e.g., ποιῶ). The non-contracted lexical form (e.g., ποιέω) provides the key to the contracted forms of these verbs. Also note the circumflex accent (ῶ) that accompanies contraction.

RULES OF CONTRACTION

Note the differences from λύω. Rather than learning a new paradigm for ποιέω, you should learn the *Rules of Contraction* and apply them to the conjugation you have already learned.

εω CONTRACT VERBS LIKE ποιέω

Sg	**1st**	ποιῶ	I do
	2nd	ποιεῖς	you do
	3rd	ποιεῖ	he/she/it does
Pl	**1st**	ποιοῦμεν	we do
	2nd	ποιεῖτε	you do
	3rd	ποιοῦσιν	they do

RULES OF CONTRACTION (εω VERBS)

1. *Epsilon* drops out with the addition of:
   long vowels (ω, η)
   diphthongs (ει, ου)

2. *Epsilon* forms diphthongs with the addition of short vowels:

$$\varepsilon + o = ou$$
$$\varepsilon + \varepsilon = \varepsilon\iota$$

Vocab #8

Exercises

1. Form the present active indicative:

   1st person plural of ἀκολουθέω

   2nd person plural of ποιέω

   3rd person plural of κρατέω

2. Parse (Tense, Voice, Mood, Pers, Num, Gk, Eng):

   διακονῶ

   φωνεῖτε

   ὑπάγεις

   λαλοῦμεν

3. Translate:

   ἰδοὺ (*look*) ἀποστέλλω τὸν ἄγγελόν μου (*my*) πρὸ προσώπου σου (*your*) (Mark 1:2)

   ἦλθεν (*he came*) Ἰησοῦς ἀπὸ Ναζαρὲτ τῆς Γαλιλαίας (Mark 1:9)

30. Analyzing Verbs

Analyzing Verbs

We continue to unpack the complexity of verbs. Like nouns, verbs are grouped into families. Verbs are grouped together according to their endings. There are five basic types (*see far right*), although these types do not cover all the variations found in *compound verbs*, *liquid stem* verbs, and verbs with a *middle lexical form*.

1. Lexical Entries

Verbs are listed in a Greek lexicon according to these variations in endings. The lexicon lists a single word, the present active indicative first person singular of the verb (e.g. λύω, ποιέω, τίθημι), the same form found the vocabulary lists. Some older textbooks and lexicons list verbs by their infinitive form (i.e., λύειν).

Unlike nouns, verbs may be inflected at the beginning of their stem. This means the way a verb in the New Testament begins is not always the same as the way its lexicon entry begins. This makes understanding the way verbs form (called *morphology*) vital.

2. Parsing Verbs

Decoding verbs requires a sophisticated ability to recognise the different parts of each verb. The presence or absence of an augment, the verb stem, and the personal endings, all combine to specify the five characteristics of the verb. Through a process of elimination, using verb tables and vocab lists, the verb can be parsed in full, ready for translation.

3. Table of the Verb

This grammar provides a full verb table of the regular verb (λύω; see p. 123). Eventually, to read and translate the New Testament competently, you should master the *Full Table of the Regular Verb*.

4. Marking Verbs

As with nouns, we will mark verbs in preparation of the text for reading and translation. Double underline any indicative, imperative, or subjunctive verb forms. This marks them as the "finite" or main verb in a clause. A finite verb is one that has person and number.

Single underlining is used for marking other verbal forms such as participles and infinitives. These are not finite verbs nor the main verb in a clause. The single line indicates that they are normally dependent on or subordinate to the main verb.

One Verb Per Clause

For Mark 1:1 – 2, vertical lines show where each clause begins and ends. Note that each clause has only one verb. Mark 1:1 is a verb-less clause:

¹ Ἀρχὴ τοῦ εὐαγγελίου Ἰησοῦ Χριστοῦ υἱοῦ θεοῦ. |
² Καθὼς γέγραπται ἐν τῷ Ἡσαΐᾳ τῷ προφήτῃ·| ἰδοὺ ἀποστέλλω τὸν ἄγγελόν μου πρὸ προσώπου σου, | ὃς κατασκευάσει τὴν ὁδόν σου·

Stay Calm

An overview like this can be intimidating, but it is useful in providing the "big picture" of the variety of verbs. Each type will be introduced gradually.

Examples

Representative Verbs

Five Basic Types

1. ω
λύω

Contract Verbs

2. εω	3. αω	4. οω
ποιέω	γεννάω	φανερόω

5. μι verbs

ε	α	ο
τίθημι	ἵστημι	δίδωμι

Decoding ἐβαπτίζοντο (Mark 1:5)

ἐβαπτίζοντο consists of three parts:

ἐ βαπτίζ οντο

An ἐ augment is found in imperfect and aorist tense-forms in the indicative mood.

βαπτιζ, the stem, means *baptize*. This is the "present" stem, on which the present and imperfect tense-forms are based (aorist and future are based on βαπτιδ). The personal ending οντο is found only in the passive voice of the imperfect tense-form. It indicates 3rd person plural.

ἐβαπτίζοντο is therefore the imperfect passive indicative 3rd person plural of the verb βαπτίζω. The NRSV translates *(they) were baptized*.

31. Verbal Aspect

Verbal Aspect	Examples

Verbal Aspect

A vital element for understanding verbs is known as "verbal aspect." This is a way of describing the essential contribution of any tense-form to its meaning. A speaker or author can choose to use, say, the present, the aorist, or the imperfect to present the action or state in a particular way.

Verbal aspect can be a confusing topic and it's a matter of debate amongst scholars. It is difficult to find two textbooks that define the significance of verbal aspect in the same way. Even shared terminology is used in different ways. Three factors have shaped the history of the discussion:

1. Time (Tense)

In English, the verb and the time of the action are closely related, as our terminology implies (*present, past, future*). Older grammars, from the 19th and early 20th century, tended to describe the Greek tense-forms in a similar way (especially in the indicative mood). Thus, the present was said to be used for events occurring in the *present*, while the aorist described *past events*.

However, unlike English, Greek tense-forms are not concerned primarily with time, although they are often translated in terms of time in the indicative mood. So, using the term *tense*, even for convenience, is misleading when it comes to Greek. In this grammar, we refer to *tense-form* to reflect the fact that we are referring to a verbal *form*, rather than a fixed time-frame.

2. Types of Action (*Aktionsart*)

Most traditional grammars published in the middle of the 20th century describe the core idea of tense-forms in terms of the *type of action* being described (they tended to use the German word *Aktionsart*.) According to this approach, the present and imperfect tense-forms were used for *linear* or continuous processes (e.g., *I am walking* or *I was walking*). The aorist tense-form was chosen for *punctiliar* events, that is, something occurring at a point in time (e.g., *I hit*). The perfect tense-form reflected a current state resulting from a past action (e.g., *I have learned*).

More recently, the limitations of this approach have been recognized when it comes to explaining how Greek verbs actually work. Often, information about the type of action owes more to the context than the verb's tense-form.

Examples

1. Time

G. Curtius, *A Smaller Grammar of the Greek Language* (15th ed.; London: John Murray, 1885), 152, 154, 157.

PRESENT: "denotes, as in English and Latin, an action going on or in progress *at the present time.*"

AORIST: expresses "a Momentary action, and therefore denotes the actual beginning of an action in the past, similar to the Historical Perfect of the Latins."

PERFECT: "is the *Present* of a completed action, *i.e.* by the Perfect the Greeks denoted an action completed *for* and *with reference to the Present.*"

2. Type of Action

"The original function ... was not that of levels of time (present, past, future) but that of *Aktionsarten* (kinds of action) or aspects (points of view)."

F. Blass, A. Debrunner, and R. W. Funk, *A Greek Grammar of the New Testament and Other Early Christian Literature* (Chicago: University of Chicago, 1961), 166.

PRESENT: "*durative* (*linear* or *progressive*) ... the action is represented as durative (in progress) and either as timeless ... or as taking place in present time."

AORIST: "*punctiliar* (*momentary*) ... the action is conceived as a point with either the beginning or the end of the action emphasized."

PERFECT: "*perfective* ... a condition or state as the result of a past action is designated."

Verbal Aspect Cont	Verbal Aspect Diagrams

3. Aspect (Viewpoint)

Today, experts argue for "verbal aspect" as the main feature expressed by tense-forms. Verbal aspect refers to the *viewpoint* from which an action or state is portrayed. The focus is not on the type of action as it occurs in reality, but on the writer's choice of how to portray it.

A. Internal Viewpoint

Both present and imperfect tense-forms convey *internal* aspect (also called *imperfective aspect*), which views an action *from within*, usually unfolding or as a state. The imperfect tense-form adds the idea of *remoteness*, normally in terms of time. *I am loosing* (or *I loose*) in the present, becomes *I was loosing* in the imperfect.

B. External Viewpoint

The aorist tense-form conveys *external* aspect (also called *perfective aspect*), which views an action *from the outside*, as a whole or in summary. It also has a sense of remoteness, usually translated in past time in the indicative mood, e.g., *I loosed*. While the significance of the future tense-form is disputed, we will treat it as external in aspect for a future action or state. So *I loosed* in the aorist, becomes *I will loose* in the future tense-form.

C. A Third Viewpoint?

Some scholars regard the perfect tense-form as an additional viewpoint, called "stative" aspect. However, we will follow the alternative view, which treats the perfect tense-form as *internal* in viewpoint like the present, but in some *intensified* sense. The pluperfect is like the imperfect with an element of *heightened remoteness*. These differences are often too subtle to translate. So we will opt for *I loose* for the perfect and *I was loosing* for the pluperfect, but remain aware of the author's intent as shown by the context.

NB: The stative aspect approach to the perfect, along with traditional approaches, would render the perfect as *I have loosed*, while the pluperfect would be *I had loosed*. Our approach acknowledges these possible translations for the perfect and pluperfect, but they are not our "starting point" glosses. Instead they may be translated these ways depending on the verb lexeme and context.

See Constantine R. Campbell, *Basics of Verbal Aspect in Biblical Greek* (Grand Rapids: Zondervan, 2008), for more on these issues.

TENSE-FORMS: VIEWPOINT AND TRANSLATION

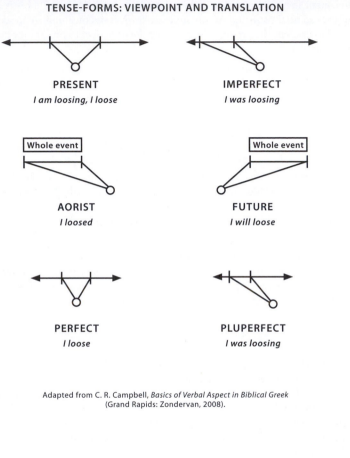

Adapted from C. R. Campbell, *Basics of Verbal Aspect in Biblical Greek* (Grand Rapids: Zondervan, 2008).

32. IMPERFECT TENSE-FORM

Imperfect Tense-Form

The imperfect tense-form is closely related to the present tense-form. The form of the imperfect is always based on the present stem. They both express internal aspect. Both the present and imperfect view an action from *within*. However, the imperfect presents the action or state as remote in some way from the speaker (usually remote in time; i.e., past time).

MEANING

Unlike the present, the imperfect exists only in the indicative mood. It usually depicts a process as progressing in the past from the viewpoint of the author. Such actions may be prolonged, repeated, or begun in the past. The imperfect can also indicate a state. For now, translate the imperfect indicative active as *I was loosing*.

FORM

The imperfect tense-form consists of three parts:

augment + present stem + personal endings
(may include a connecting vowel).

e.g., ἔ λυ ον

RULES FOR AUGMENTATION

An augment is the *epsilon* placed in front of the verb stem of imperfect and aorist verbs. Augments are used only in the indicative mood and indicate *remoteness* (usually past time).

If a verb begins with a **consonant**, the augment is simply added at the beginning (e.g., ἔγραφον, ἔβαλλον).

If a verb begins with a **short vowel**, the addition of the augment usually lengthens the vowel (ἤκουον, ἤγειρον).

Verbs beginning with a **diphthong** either lengthen the first letter (ηὐχαρίστουν) or remain unchanged (εὑρίσκω in the aorist).

Imperfect Active Indicative of λύω

Sg	**1st**	ἔλυον	I was loosing
	2nd	ἔλυες	you were loosing
	3rd	ἔλυεν	he/she/it was loosing
Pl	**1st**	ἐλύομεν	we were loosing
	2nd	ἐλύετε	you were loosing
	3rd	ἔλυον	they were loosing

RULES FOR AUGMENTATION

SHORT VOWELS

$$\varepsilon + \alpha = \eta$$
$$\varepsilon + \varepsilon = \eta$$
$$\varepsilon + o = \omega$$

DIPHTHONGS

$\varepsilon + \alpha\iota = \eta$	$\varepsilon + \alpha\upsilon = \eta\upsilon$
$\varepsilon + \varepsilon\iota = \eta$	$\varepsilon + \varepsilon\upsilon = \eta\upsilon$ OR $\varepsilon\upsilon$
$\varepsilon + o\iota = \varphi$	

UNCHANGED

η, ι, υ, ω

Exercises

1. Parse   (Tense, Voice, Mood, Pers, Num, Gk, Eng):

ἔβαλλεν

ἐλέγομεν

ἐγείρετε

ἐπίστευον

2. Translate into Greek:

she was healing

you (pl) were finding

I was carrying

they were teaching

33. Imperfect Tense-Form: εω Verbs

Imperfect Tense-Form: εω Verbs	Imperfect Active Indicative of ποιέω	Exercises
Imperfect contract verbs present a new challenge because they undergo changes at the beginning *and* at the end of the verb stem. However, these changes follow the same rules learned in earlier lessons. There is room for some confusion since *epsilon* is involved at both ends of the verb stem. So, take some time to review these rules (Lessons 29 and 32). The imperfect conjugation of ποιέω highlights most of these changes. Again, it will be simpler to learn the rules and how they are applied, than committing a new paradigm to memory. In the imperfect, every personal ending begins with a short vowel. So there is contraction and the formation of a new diphthong in each line. Also note the absence of a final *nu* for the third person singular.	**Sg** **1st** ἐποίουν — I was doing **2nd** ἐποίεις — you were doing **3rd** ἐποίει * — he/she/it was doing **Pl** **1st** ἐποιοῦμεν — we were doing **2nd** ἐποιεῖτε — you were doing **3rd** ἐποίουν — they were doing * Note the absence of ν	1. Form the imperfect active indicative of: 1st person plural of ἀκολουθέω 2nd person plural of ποιέω 3rd person plural of κρατέω 2. Parse: ἐζήτουν ἐφωνεῖτε ἐλαλοῦμεν

34. Compound Verbs

Compound Verbs	Rules for Augmenting Compound Verbs	Exercises

Compound Verbs

A compound verb is a verb formed by the addition of a preposition before the verb stem (e.g., ἐκβάλλω). Some of these were listed in Vocabs #7 and #8. They require no new vocab and minimal new learning.

One Verb; Two Parts

In the vocabulary lists, a space is left between the preposition and the verb stem to show the distinction between the two parts. Compound verbs do not have this space in lexicons or in the NT.

The verb διακονέω (*I serve*) highlights the importance of knowing where the preposition ends and the stem begins. It could easily be misread as δια + κονέω. In fact, the verb stem is ἀκονέω. The final *alpha* of the preposition has already been elided in the formation of the present tense-form.

Meaning: Sum of the Parts?

The meaning of a compound verb is not necessarily the sum of its two parts. It is the contemporary, first-century usage that determines the meaning, not a word's origin or history.

Some verbs are a sum of the two parts: e.g., ἐκβάλλω often translates as *I cast* (βάλλω) *out* (ἐκ).

Sometimes prepositions intensify the meaning of the verb.

Sometimes the addition of the preposition creates a very different meaning.

Forming the Imperfect

The main difficulty arises from the addition of an augment in forming imperfect and aorist tense-forms. This means changes occur in the middle of a word, not just at its beginning or end.

Since the augment affects the verbal part of a compound verb, the imperfect is formed by adding the augment to the front of the verb's stem, not the front of the preposition.

Rules for Augmenting Compound Verbs

The letters on either side of an augment determine the effect of the augment on a compound verb. Remember that the augment is added to the beginning of the *verb stem*, not the whole verb. You should be aware of four variations:

1. **Between two consonants**

   προσ φέρω   →   προσέφερον

2. **Before a vowel**

   δι ακονέω   →   διηκόνουν

3. **After a vowel**

   παρα καλέω   →   παρεκάλουν

   An exception

   περι πατέω   →   περιεπάτουν

4. **After ἐκ**

   ἐκ βάλλω   →   ἐξέβαλλον

Exercises

1. Form the imperfect active indicative of:

   2nd person singular of διακονέω

   3rd person singular of ἐκβάλλω

   1st person singular of ὑπάγω

2. Parse:

   παρεκάλεις

   ἀπέστελλες

   διακονεῖ

35. εἰμί, The Verb I Am (To Be)

εἰμί, The Verb I Am (To Be)	Present Active Indicative of εἰμί	Exercises

εἰμί, The Verb I Am (To Be)

An extremely important verb in the Greek NT is εἰμί, *I am (to be)*. This verb doesn't help us to learn other verbs' forms, but is important enough to pay it special attention. The verb εἰμί has only three tense-forms (present, imperfect, and future) and one voice—the active.

PRESENT TENSE-FORM

The present tense-form of the verb *I am* always begins with ε. Note the presence of a circumflex accent over the 2nd person singular (*see right*).

IMPERFECT TENSE-FORM

The imperfect tense-form always begins with η.

1. SUBJECT AND PREDICATE

As a verb that serves to equate two things (*Jesus is Lord*) or place something in a larger set (*Jesus was a Jew*), the verb *to be* does not have a direct object in the accusative case. Instead, the second noun is known as the "predicate" of the subject, and takes the same case, usually the nominative:

e.g., Luke 9:35

This is my Son
οὗτός (nom.) ἐστιν ὁ υἱός (nom.) μου.

2. YOU ARE (εἶ) AND IF (εἰ)

The Greek words for *you are* and *if* are very similar. The circumflex over the second person singular form of εἰμί is what distinguishes them (εἶ). This is one of the few occasions when it is essential to remember the placement of an accent mark.

Present Active Indicative of εἰμί

Sg	**1st**	εἰμί		I am
	2nd	εἶ		you are
	3rd	ἐστίν		he/she/it is
Pl	**1st**	ἐσμέν		we are
	2nd	ἐστέ		you are
	3rd	εἰσίν		they are

IMPERFECT ACTIVE INDICATIVE Of εἰμί

Sg	**1st**	ἤμην		I was
	2nd	ἦς		you were
	3rd	ἦν		he/she/it was
Pl	**1st**	ἦμεν*		we were
	2nd	ἦτε		you were
	3rd	ἦσαν		they were

*or ἤμεθα

Exercises

1. Translate into English:

καὶ φωνὴ ἐγένετο (came) ἐκ τῶν οὐρανῶν· σὺ (you sg) εἶ ὁ υἱός μου (my) ὁ ἀγαπητός (beloved) (Mark 1:11)

καὶ ἦν ἐν τῇ ἐρήμῳ (Mark 1:13)

Καὶ εὐθὺς ἦν ἐν τῇ συναγωγῇ αὐτῶν ἄνθρωπος ἐν πνεύματι ἀκαθάρτῳ (unclean spirit) (Mark 1:23)

ὁ Πέτρος λέγει αὐτῷ· Σὺ (you sg) εἶ ὁ Χριστός. (Mark 8:29)

36. First Aorist Tense-Form

First Aorist Tense-Form

The aorist is the tense-form most often used in the New Testament, just beating out the present in its frequency.

Meaning

The aorist tense-form expresses the external viewpoint. It also conveys remoteness, often expressed as past time in the indicative mood. The aorist presents an action or state in summary, viewed as a whole from the outside.

Form

Greek has two aorist tense-forms, which are formed differently but mean the same thing. The *first* aorist is formed by the addition of an augment to the aorist stem, characteristic σα, and distinctive personal endings. In the case of λύω, present and aorist stems are the same (λυ).

e.g., ἐ λύ σα μεν

Translation

Translate the aorist tense-form with the simple past tense in English (*I loosed, I made*). Over time you will become more aware of the effect of context on its meaning.

Contract Verbs

Forming contract verbs in the aorist tense-form is very straightforward. The εω verbs lengthen the ε to η when the σα is added (except καλέω, which does not lengthen the ε). Since σ is a consonant, the personal endings are not affected. You do not need to memorize this paradigm, but you should note the changes.

Mute Endings

Some verbs do combine with the aorist *sigma* in ways that require the learning of some new rules. The stems of some verbs end with a "mute" consonant. These combine with σ to form a new consonant.

First Aorist Active of λύω

Sg	**1st**	ἔλυσα	I loosed
	2nd	ἔλυσας	you loosed
	3rd	ἔλυσεν	he/she/it loosed
Pl	**1st**	ἐλύσαμεν	we loosed
	2nd	ἐλύσατε	you loosed
	3rd	ἔλυσαν	they loosed

First Aorist Active Indicative of ποιέω

Sg	**1st**	ἐποίησα	I did
	2nd	ἐποίησας	you did
	3rd	ἐποίησεν	he/she/it did
Pl	**1st**	ἐποιήσαμεν	we did
	2nd	ἐποιήσατε	you did
	3rd	ἐποίησαν	they did

Rules for Mute Endings

κ, γ, χ + σ = ξ   E.g., ἀνοίγω → ἤνοιξα

π, β, φ + σ = ψ   E.g., γράφω → ἔγραψα

τ, δ, θ + σ = σ   E.g., πειθώ → ἔπεισα

Exercises

1. Form the first aorist active indicative:

   2nd person plural of ποιέω

   1st person plural of παρακαλέω

   2nd person singular of γράφω

   3rd person plural of πιστεύω

2. Parse (from Mark 1):

   ἠκολούθησαν

   ἐκάλεσεν

   ἐθεράπευσεν

Vocab #9

37. Verb Roots and Stems

Verb Roots and Stems

Studying the aorist tense-forms means confronting one of the biggest headaches in learning Greek. For most students, mastery of irregular verbs comes only with enormous patience and effort.

For a range of reasons, most verbs do not simply follow λύω. This lesson provides an overview of the main sources of irregularity.

Present Stem and Verbal Root

The easiest way to enter into Greek verbs is via the present tense-form. This is the form provided in lexicons and vocab lists. With a regular verb like λύω, or even ποιέω, the rules of formation are straightforward.

Unpredictable or irregular verbs offer a bewildering range of exceptions. It is tempting to assume that each exception is some kind of variation on the present stem. In fact, there is a more basic "root" than the present stem. For a verb like λύω, the root remains constant and so λυ can be observed across all its tense-forms (*see far right*).

Stems Ending in Mutes

Vocab #9 introduces two groups of verbs (like βαπτίζω and κηρύσσω). The aorist tense-form is built on the underlying verbal root, which differs from the present stem and cannot be deduced from the present stem. Once this root is known, the various forms of the verb are more predictable. For βαπτίζω, the aorist form follows the rules of dental mutes (δ + σα = σα).

The verbal root of some verbs is the key to their formation. An awareness of the verbal root will minimize learning the variations.

Irregular Verbs

However, these do not exhaust the possible variations. Most of the remainder fall into one of four categories:

Liquid Stems

Certain letters (λ, μ, ν, and ρ) are known as "liquids." Verbs ending in these letters will not accept a σ to form the aorist, and so have no σ in their ending. They follow the first aorist endings otherwise.

Second Aorists

Some verb stems do not accept the addition of σ to form the aorist tense-form. So they take what is called a *second* aorist tense-form. These have the same endings as the imperfect, but are built on the aorist stem instead of the present stem.

Completely Different Stems

Some verbs have present and aorist tense-forms built on different roots. They bear no resemblance to each other, but they have the same meaning.

Other Irregularities

Some verbs have present and aorist tense-forms that are recognizably related, but somewhat unpredictable.

Table of Principal Parts

Mastery of these variations will take patience and hard work for anyone wanting to read and translate the Greek New Testament. As you continue through this grammar you will be introduced to the table of *Principal Parts*, which summarizes the most common and significant variations.

Examples

Verbal root	Present stem	Aorist stem
Regular Verbs		
λυ	λύω	ἔλυσα
ποιε	ποιῶ	ἐποίησα
βαπτιδ	βαπτίζω	ἐβάπτισα
κηρυκ	κηρύσσω	ἐκήρυξα
Liquid Stems		
ἐγειρ	ἐγείρω	ἤγειρα
Second Aorists		
βαλ	βάλλω	ἔβαλον
Different Stems		
mixed	ἔρχομαι	ἦλθον
Other Irregularities		
λαβ	λαμβάνω	ἔλαβον

38. Future Tense-Form

Future Tense-Form	Future Active Indicative of λύω	Examples

The future tense-form is used to refer to events and states occurring in the future. Of the Greek tense-forms this has the most consistent usage in terms of time reference. It is used much less frequently than the present and aorist tense-forms.

Meaning

The future tense-form is closely related to the aorist tense-form. We will assume that the future tense-form presents an external viewpoint, portraying a future event as a whole (though the verbal aspect of the future tense-form is contested). In Mark's Gospel, the tense-form is used more than 120 times, to communicate promises, questions, commands, etc.

To express this external viewpoint in English we will translate the future tense-form *I will loose*.

Form

The form of the future active indicative requires little new learning. Unlike the aorist, there is no augment. Like the aorist, the future tense-form adds a *sigma* to the end of the verbal stem. This stem is usually the same as the aorist, but there are enough exceptions to require learning some distinctive future stems.

The personal endings are the same as the present tense-form. Rules for the addition of *sigma* are the same as we have learned before for contract and mute endings.

E.g., λυ σ ομεν

Future Active Indicative of λύω

Sg	1st	λύσω	I will loose
	2nd	λύσεις	you will loose
	3rd	λύσει	he/she/it will loose
Pl	1st	λύσομεν	we will loose
	2nd	λύσετε	you will loose
	3rd	λύσουσιν	they will loose

Examples

Promises
He **will baptize** you with the Holy Spirit.

General Truths
If a house is divided, how **will** it **stand**?

Questions
How **will** you **understand** all the parables?

Convictions
If I touch his clothes, I **will be healed.**

Commands
You **shall love** your neighbour as yourself.

Exercises

1. Form the future active indicative 1st person plural of:

γράφω

ἀκούω

ἄγω

κρατέω

πράσσω

πείθω

2. Translate (from Mark):

βαπτίσει (1:8)

ποιήσω (1:17)

θεραπεύσει (3:2)

39. Adjectives

We return now to the world of nouns and noun-related words. Adjectives are words that modify or qualify nouns (e.g., *big, long, old, second*); thus they have case, number, and gender.

Usage

Adjectives usually occur with a noun to provide more information about the noun (e.g., the *beloved* disciple, a *rich young* ruler). The adjective will agree with the noun it qualifies in case, number, and gender. However, an adjective can be used on its own, in which case it functions as a noun. Often in translation a word will need to be supplied (i.e., *person, one, thing*, etc.).

> E.g., ὁ ἀγαπητός, *the beloved* (Mark 1:11)
>
> ὁ ἅγιος τοῦ θεοῦ, *the holy one of God* (1:24)

Form

In order to qualify a noun of any case, number, and gender, adjectives have endings for each gender. They are listed in a lexicon by their three nominative singular endings: masculine, feminine, and neuter: ἀγαθός, ή, όν, *good*. Rarely, an adjective is listed by two endings, when the masculine and feminine are the same. E.g., ἀκάθαρτος, ον.

Two types

There are two types of adjective formation, with different endings, for the singular feminine forms. These two types reflect whether the adjective stem ends in a consonant or in a vowel (or *rho*). Adjectives with a consonant stem follow the pattern of λόγος in the masculine (2nd declension), γραφή in the feminine (1st declension), and ἔργον (2nd declension) in the neuter.

Agreement

The pattern followed is determined by the ending of the adjective, not the ending of the noun with which it agrees. So, an adjective and noun may agree but have different endings.

> E.g., ἡ δικαία διδαχή (*the righteous teaching*).

Adjectives: Consonant Stem Like ἀγαθός, ή, όν

Sg	**Nom**	ἀγαθός	ἀγαθή	ἀγαθόν
	Gen	ἀγαθοῦ	ἀγαθῆς	ἀγαθοῦ
	Dat	ἀγαθῷ	ἀγαθῇ	ἀγαθῷ
	Acc	ἀγαθόν	ἀγαθήν	ἀγαθόν
Pl	**Nom**	ἀγαθοί	ἀγαθαί	ἀγαθά
	Gen	ἀγαθῶν	ἀγαθῶν	ἀγαθῶν
	Dat	ἀγαθοῖς	ἀγαθαῖς	ἀγαθοῖς
	Acc	ἀγαθούς	ἀγαθάς	ἀγαθά

Adjectives: Vowel or ρ Stem ἅγιος, α, ον

Sg	**Nom**	ἅγιος	ἁγία	ἅγιον
	Gen	ἁγίου	ἁγίας	ἁγίου
	Dat	ἁγίῳ	ἁγίᾳ	ἁγίῳ
	Acc	ἅγιον	ἁγίαν	ἅγιον
Pl	**Nom**	ἅγιοι	ἅγιαι	ἅγια
	Gen	ἁγίων	ἁγίων	ἁγίων
	Dat	ἁγίοις	ἁγίαις	ἁγίοις
	Acc	ἁγίους	ἁγίας	ἅγια

1. Write out in full the declension for δίκαιος, αἰώνιος and ὀλίγος.

2. Express the following in Greek. (Hint: work out the noun first, since the article and the adjective must agree with it):

   the beloved brother

   the sufficient day

   a good garment

   the holy Sabbath

   an unclean heart

   a new teaching

   the strong sound

   a good child

🔒

Vocab #10

40A. PARTICIPLES

Participles	Present Active Masculine Participle of λύω	Exercises

Participles are one of the scariest parts of the Greek language. The variety of forms is intimidating. NT writers use well over 6,000 participles. Mark employs over 550. So, participles cannot be avoided by anyone wanting to read and translate the Greek New Testament.

For the time being we will be concerned only with the *masculine* gender, *active* voice, and *present* and *aorist* tense-forms. These represent the majority of participles in Mark 1 (34 of 48).

HALF VERB, HALF ADJECTIVE

Participles are verbal adjectives. Strictly speaking, they lack mood, but computer search programs tend to treat *participle* in the category of mood. This hybrid nature means they have some characteristics of the verb and some of the adjective. They are built on a verb stem and have tense-forms and voice.

Participles are never augmented. Like adjectives, they agree with the noun they modify in case, number, and gender. This flexibility accounts for their frequency in the NT, and their difficulty.

3RD DECLENSION ENDINGS

One factor that adds to the difficulty of learning participles is their 3rd declension endings. Textbooks often postpone introducing the participle until 3rd declensions nouns have been learned. But this unnecessarily delays translation, since participles are crucial to understanding the New Testament. We will learn participle forms now and leave 3rd declension nouns until later.

Present Active Masculine Participle of λύω

Sg	Nom	λύων	loosing
	Gen	λύοντος	loosing
	Dat	λύοντι	loosing
	Acc	λύοντα	loosing
Pl	Nom	λύοντες	loosing
	Gen	λυόντων	loosing
	Dat	λύουσιν	loosing
	Acc	λύοντας	loosing

Exercises

1. Translate the following from Mark 1, and identify their tense-form, case, and number:

κηρύσσων (1:4)

ἐσθίων (1:6)

λέγων (1:15)

παράγων (1:16)

διδάσκων (1:22)

κρατήσας (1:31)

ἔχοντας (1:32)

ἐκβάλλων (1:39)

παρακαλῶν (1:40)

Participles *cont.*	1st Aorist Active Masculine Participle of λύω	Exercises

TRANSLATING PARTICIPLES

Our simplified approach will take a lot of the fear out of walking into a page full of participles.

For now, we will translate any participle as an English *-ing* word, regardless of tense-form, case, and number. Translation of the active voice is simply a matter of determining the root verb and adding *–ing* to an English gloss.

Remember that the author's choice of tense-form is important because it signifies verbal aspect. At an intermediate level of Greek translation (e.g., in a second year of Greek study), you should learn to reflect the difference between the internal viewpoint of the present participle and the external viewpoint of the aorist participle. For now, translate each tense-form as *–ing*.

This may sound overly simplistic. Some textbooks encourage first-year students to translate in a way that sounds more like English versions of the New Testament. But our approach safeguards some important grammatical insights. The *–ing* ending will remind us that the participle is always dependent on a finite verb in the context.

TWO TYPES

1. ADVERBIAL PARTICIPLES

These are by far the more common, and have no article. They function to modify or add information to the finite verb in the context.

E.g., *and he preached, saying* (λέγων) (Mark 1:7)

2. ADJECTIVAL PARTICIPLES

These are nearly always preceded by the article. An adjectival participle functions to qualify a noun that follows. More often it is used without a noun, as a noun substitute (substantive).

E.g., ὁ βαπτίζων *the baptizing one* (Mark 1:4)

1st Aorist Active Masculine Participle of λύω

Sg	**Nom**	λύσας	loosing
	Gen	λύσαντος	loosing
	Dat	λύσαντι	loosing
	Acc	λύσαντα	loosing
Pl	**Nom**	λύσαντες	loosing
	Gen	λυσάντων	loosing
	Dat	λύσασιν	loosing
	Acc	λύσαντας	loosing

Exercises

1. Translate:

ἦλθεν ὁ Ἰησοῦς εἰς τὴν Γαλιλαίαν κηρύσσων τὸ εὐαγγέλιον τοῦ θεοῦ (Mark 1:14)

καὶ εὐθὺς τοῖς σάββασιν εἰσελθὼν εἰς τὴν συναγωγὴν ἐδίδασκεν (Mark 1:21)

Καὶ ἔρχεται πρὸς αὐτὸν λεπρὸς παρακαλῶν αὐτὸν . . . καὶ λέγων (Mark 1:40)

41. PERSONAL PRONOUNS: 1ST AND 2ND PERSON

Personal Pronouns: 1st and 2nd Person	Personal Pronoun	Examples

Personal Pronouns: 1st and 2nd Person

Pronouns were introduced in Lesson 23, where we explored third person pronouns. Now we add the first and second person pronouns in order to complete the set.

FIRST AND SECOND PERSON

In Mark, the first (*I, we*) and second person (*you*) pronouns are confined largely to reported speech. They are more common in the epistles where the reader is addressed as the second person. Note the variation in the singular forms of the genitive, dative, and accusative, where an epsilon can occur at the front of the word.

Since Greek can imply person in the verb ending, the nominative form is not necessary, but it is often used for **emphasis**.

E.g., Mark 1:8 *I baptized (ἐγὼ ἐβάπτισα) you in water,
he will baptise you with the Holy Spirit*

Matt 5:13 *You are (ὑμεῖς ἐστε) the salt of the earth*

Personal Pronoun

		1st person	2nd person
Sg	Nom	ἐγώ	σύ
	Gen	μου	σοῦ
	Dat	μοι	σοί
	Acc	με	σέ
Pl	Nom	ἡμεῖς	ὑμεῖς
	Gen	ἡμῶν	ὑμῶν
	Dat	ἡμῖν	ὑμῖν
	Acc	ἡμᾶς	ὑμᾶς

Alternative Forms

Gen	ἐμοῦ
Dat	ἐμοί
Acc	ἐμέ

Vocab #11

Examples

2ND PERSON DIRECT SPEECH (GOSPEL)

If your (σου) right eye causes you (σε) to sin, tear it out and throw it away from you (σοῦ); it is better for you (σοι) to lose one of your (σου) members than for your (σου) whole body to be thrown into hell. And if your (σου) right hand causes you (σε) to sin, cut it off and throw it away from you (σοῦ); it is better for you (σοι) to lose one of your (σου) members than for your (σου) whole body to go into hell.

Matt 5:29–30

1ST PERSON (EPISTLE)

For through the law I (ἐγὼ) died to the law, so that I might live to God. I have been crucified with Christ; and it is no longer I (ἐγὼ) who live, but it is Christ who lives in me (ἐμοὶ). And the life I now live in the flesh I live by faith in the Son of God, who loved me (με) and gave himself for me (ἐμοῦ).

Gal 2:19–20

42A. Marking the Text for Translation

Marking the Text for Translation		Examples

You are encouraged to adopt certain conventions for marking Greek forms in the companion book, *Reading Biblical Greek Workbook*. The order of the steps outlined below reflects the nature of the Greek language and its translation. These instructions are also found in the introduction to *Reading Biblical Greek Workbook*.

1. Double Underline Finite Verbs

Finite verbs include the indicative, imperative, subjunctive, and optative, and exclude the infinitive and the participle.

2. Single Underline Other Verbal Forms

Identify and mark infinitives and participles.

3. Bracket Prepositional Phrases

Place brackets around any preposition and its object that follows (including words that modify the object, of the same case). This makes the next step much easier, saving confusion over the function of noun cases.

4. Mark Subject, Object, Genitive, Indirect Object.

Use the following symbols:

→ Subject; i.e., it will precede the main verb in English.

← Object; i.e., it will follow the main verb in English.

of Genitive often translates as *of*.

2/4 Indirect object often translates *to* or *for*.

5. Place Vertical Line Between Clauses

Unlike English, most Greek clauses begin with a conjunction (*and, but, then*). These function like English punctuation, and serve as a guide to the beginning and end of clauses — the basic unit of meaning. There should be only one finite verb between these lines.

6. Bracket Other Clauses and Phrases

After following these steps there may be groups that are left over. These will be related to the main clause in some way, usually adverbially or adjectivally. We will learn more about relative clauses, subordinate clauses (subjunctive and infinitive), and participial phrases later.

7. Place Square Brackets Around Direct Speech

Technically, direct speech, or everything contained within speech marks in an English translation, is the direct object of a verb of speaking or thinking. I.e., *Jesus said x.* Here x could equal = *I am the way, the truth and the life.* The sentence in direct speech has its own grammar with main verb, subject, etc. It helps to mark off clearly the words enclosed in direct speech. We will learn more about Greek conventions for indicating speech.

Marking Mark 1:16–17

| Καὶ παράγων (παρὰ τὴν θάλασσαν)

of ←
τῆς Γαλιλαίας εἶδεν Σίμωνα καὶ

← ← *of*
Ἀνδρέαν τὸν ἀδελφὸν Σίμωνος

ἀμφιβάλλοντας (ἐν τῇ θαλάσσῃ:) |

→ 2/4
ἦσαν γὰρ ἁλιεῖς. | καὶ εἶπεν αὐτοῖς

→
ὁ Ἰησοῦς: [δεῦτε (ὀπίσω μου,) | καὶ

← ←
ποιήσω ὑμᾶς γενέσθαι ἁλιεῖς

of
ἀνθρώπων.]

42B. Translating Greek into English

Translating Greek into English

When it comes to rendering Greek into English there are three broad approaches to translation. Each has strengths and weaknesses.

There is no shortage of good translations of the Bible in English. One reason for learning New Testament Greek is to enable us to make judgments about the text rather than taking the translators' word for it. This is not to say we stand in judgment of experienced and capable translators, since any translation involves interpretation, and they inevitably face and make decisions. Learning Greek enables us to be more aware of the alternatives they faced and the decisions they made. It can alert us to original ambiguities that have been "translated out" and interpretations that have been "translated in" our English versions.

Formal Equivalence

This approach aims for "accuracy." In seeking to preserve the original meaning there is the tendency to translate Greek words consistently with the same English words and maintain the Greek word order where possible. The RV and NASB (which are more "literal" than the ESV, NRSV, NIV, and HCSB) will seem stilted and awkward at points. They tend to be unsuitable for public reading of Scripture but useful for study purposes. The ESV, NRSV, NIV, and HCSB highlight different choices made by translators in order to be faithful to the Greek, and accessible for English readers.

Dynamic Equivalence

Other versions will seek to convey the original meaning by reproducing the sense as appropriately as possible. This may mean idiomatic Greek expressions are translated by very different English words, in an attempt to better capture the original meaning. The GNB was an attempt to adopt this approach. Sometimes the associations, carried by a word or phrase, are lost (e.g., *Son of Man*).

Paraphrase

This approach is more concerned with readability and contemporary "relevance" than the other approaches. Paraphrases will tend to take more liberties with the original language. Unfortunately, many of the connections and associations of the original are lost. The Living Bible exemplifies this approach. While they have little place in a college or seminary, most young children begin reading the Bible from appropriate paraphrases.

1st Year Greek

Our aim for this year will be to provide literal translations of Greek phrases and sentences. The goal is to become competent at identifying the original Greek forms. While it may be necessary to change the word order to make sense in English, don't be concerned if your translations are not idiomatic, or sound a little wooden. In later study you should strive for a smoother, more idiomatic, approach.

Examples

English Versions of Mark 1:30–31

Greek

ἡ δὲ πενθερὰ Σίμωνος κατέκειτο πυρέσσουσα, καὶ εὐθὺς λέγουσιν αὐτῷ περὶ αὐτῆς. καὶ προσελθὼν ἤγειρεν αὐτὴν κρατήσας τῆς χειρός· καὶ ἀφῆκεν αὐτὴν ὁ πυρετός, καὶ διηκόνει αὐτοῖς.

New American Standard Bible

Now Simon's mother-in-law was lying sick with a fever; and immediately they spoke to Him about her. And he came to her and raised her up, taking her by the hand, and the fever left her, and she waited on them.

New International Version

Simon's mother-in-law was in bed with a fever, and they immediately told Jesus about her. So he went to her, took her hand and helped her up. The fever left her and she began to wait on them.

Good News Bible

Simon's mother-in-law was sick in bed with a fever, and as soon as Jesus arrived, he was told about her. He went to her, took her by the hand, and helped her up. The fever left her, and she began to wait on them.

New Living Translation

Now Simon's mother-in-law was sick in bed with a high fever. They told Jesus about her right away. He went to her bedside, and as he took her by the hand and helped her to sit up, the fever suddenly left, and she got up and prepared a meal for them.

You are now ready to begin regular translation of Mark, using the companion book, *Reading Biblical Greek Workbook: A Reading & Translation Guide to Mark 1–4.*

Reading Biblical Greek Workbook: Class 1:1–3; Home 1:4–5

43A. Conjunctions

Conjunctions	Examples

Conjunctions are words used to join together paragraphs, clauses, and phrases. Examples in English are words like *and, but, for, or*. Greek makes much more use of conjunctions than English. In fact, any clause lacking a conjunction is a notable exception (called *asyndeton*).

Though often small, these words are very helpful. As boundary markers between units of meaning in a language, they clarify the beginning and end of clauses. They serve as punctuation, setting the limits for where the subject, object, etc., will be found. Also, conjunctions define the relationship between two clauses. One clause may be connected to or contrasted with the preceding clause. Or it may give an alternative, an explanation, or draw an inference from the previous clause.

Two Types

There are two basic kinds of connection created:

Coordination
When two items of equal syntactical significance are joined they are coordinated by the conjunction.

Subordination
A subordinating conjunction joins a secondary or dependent idea to a clause as an explanation, condition, cause, etc.

Coordinating Conjunctions

		Frequency in Mark 1–3
καί	and, also, but	201
δέ	and, but	12
γάρ	for, since	7
ἀλλά	but, rather	8
οὖν	then, therefore	0
ἤ	or, than	3

Subordinating Conjunctions

ὅτι	(see section 43b)	17
εἰ	if, whether	6
ὡς	as, like	3
καθώς	as, just as	1

Vocab #12

1. Below are some of the relationships expressed by conjunctions. There is no need to learn them now. Look up an English translation and note the words used to convey the force of the conjunction.

Connection
Mark 1:15 "The time is fulfilled, *καὶ* the kingdom of God has come near; repent, *καὶ* believe in the good news."

Contrast
Mark 2:17 "Those who are well have no need of a physician, *ἀλλ'* those who are sick; I have come to call not the righteous *ἀλλὰ* sinners."

Alternative
Mark 3:4 "Is it lawful to do good *ἢ* to do harm on the sabbath, to save life *ἢ* to kill?"

Explanation
Mark 1:22 They were astounded at his teaching, *γὰρ* he taught them as one having authority, and not as the scribes.

Condition
Mark 3:2 They watched him to see *εἰ* he would cure him on the sabbath

Comparison
Mark 1:22 They were astounded at his teaching, for he taught them *ὡς* one having authority, and not *ὡς* the scribes.

43B. THE CONJUNCTION ὅτι

The Conjunction ὅτι	Examples	Exercises
This little conjunction is very common. For reading and translation you need to be aware of three possible meanings:		1. How does your English version translate ὅτι in the following?
		1:34
" … "	" … "	1:37
ὅτι is used to introduce direct speech, when something someone said or thought is directly recorded. Called ὅτι *recitative*, it simply becomes inverted commas (quotation marks) in English. The content of direct speech is, grammatically, the direct object of a verb (i.e., *He says X*).	UBS5 and NA28 have two different conventions for indicating direct speech:	1:40
	A. CAPITAL LETTER FOLLOWING ὅτι:	2:8
	καὶ λέγων ὅτι Πεπλήρωται ὁ καιρός	2:10
	and saying, "The time is fulfilled." (Mark 1:15)	2:12
	B. SEMI-COLON:	3:11
	καὶ φωνὴ ἐγένετο ἐκ τῶν οὐρανῶν· σὺ εἶ ὁ υἱός μου (Mark 1:11)	
"THAT"	"THAT"	3:21
ὅτι may signal a *dependent* or *indirect statement*, translated by "that." This is common after verbs of mental or sense perception (*I think, believe, judge, see, feel,* etc.). This use may also introduce a clause, which functions as the direct object of a verb of speech or thought.	When he returned to Capernaum after some days, it was reported that (ὅτι) he was at home. (Mark 2:1)	3:22
		3:30
Often when Greek recalls something said, heard, thought, sensed, or felt in the past, it will preserve the *original tense-form of the verb* heard or thought by the person when they experienced the process. *She thought that she is lost …*, in Greek, will be translated, *She thought that she was lost*. Unlike English, the Greek tense-form reflects the original thought: *I am lost*.		4:41
		2. Compare your results with a different English version.
"BECAUSE"	"BECAUSE"	
The most common use of ὅτι is *causal*. "Because" will usually work as a translation. Here it functions to introduce an adverbial clause, introducing a subordinate clause that explains the cause of the main verb.	and he would not permit the demons to speak, because (ὅτι) they knew him. (Mark 1:34)	

44. Charting the Syntax of a Passage

Charting the Syntax of a Passage	Examples

One of the most fruitful disciplines in analyzing the meaning of a passage is to draw a sentence syntax diagram. The steps involved follow on from the marking of the text (see Lesson 42A), and work most effectively with computer texts.

A syntax diagram forces the reader to move beyond words to see how they contribute to phrases and clauses, and how they in turn contribute to paragraphs and discourses.

This is a skill that takes considerable time to develop. To do this from the Greek text requires a good understanding of the language. You are not expected to do so right away, but you should practice the skill to be ready for your second year of Greek study. Some basic steps are worth outlining:

1. Divide into clauses.

2. Identify independent and dependent clauses.

3. Place independent clauses at the left margin.

4. Indent dependent clauses under their verb or noun.

You may begin by drawing some flow diagrams of English text. Don't worry if you don't catch on immediately. But persevere, for it is a task that pushes you to read texts more carefully. Eventually, you will want to diagram every Greek text that you seek to study carefully.

Charting the Syntax of Mark 1:16–18 (NRSV)

↓As Jesus passed along the Sea of Galilee,
←he saw Simon and his brother Andrew
↳casting a net into the sea—
for they were fishermen.

And Jesus said to them,
    "Follow me
    and I will make you fish for people."
And ↓immediately they left their nets
and followed him

Reading Biblical Greek Workbook: Class 1:6–8; Home 1:9–11

45. Imperative Mood

Imperative Mood

To this point we have confined our attention to the indicative mood (the participle is not a mood). The imperative mood is used for *commands* and *requests*.

Form

Note the conjugation of the present and aorist active, especially the absence of the first person (the subjunctive mood is used for bossing yourself about!). Apart from the second person singular it is quite regular.

The 2nd person plural of the present imperative (λύετε) is the same as the indicative. Context normally resolves any ambiguity.

The same rules apply for the formation of the imperative of contract verbs as apply in the indicative.

Translation

The present tense-form usually conveys general instruction, while the aorist is used for specific commands. The present can also be used for specific commands when verbs of coming, going, raising, etc., are used.

The third person takes some getting used to, since *Let her/them loose* sounds awkward and is ambiguous in English. The third person is used by Jesus: *if anyone wants to follow me, let them take up their cross.*

Negating Verbs

Verbs in the *indicative* mood are negated by οὐ (οὐκ, οὐχ). Verbs outside the indicative mood, including the *participle* and the *imperative*, are negated by μή.

Present Active Imperative of λύω

Sg	**1st**		
	2nd	λῦε	Loose!
	3rd	λυέτω	Let him /her loose
Pl	**1st**		
	2nd	λύετε	Loose!
	3rd	λυέτωσαν	Let them loose

Aorist Active Imperative of λύω

Sg	**1st**		
	2nd	λῦσον	Loose!
	3rd	λυσάτω	Let him /her loose
Pl	**1st**		
	2nd	λύσατε	Loose!
	3rd	λυσάτωσαν	Let them loose

Vocab #13

Exercises

1. Translate into Greek:

   Speak! (you sg)

   Heal my house! (you sg)

   Believe in the gospel! (you pl)

   Let them serve!

2. Parse:

   ποιεῖτε

   ὕπαγε

   ἀκολούθει

3. Translate:

   ἑτοιμάσατε τὴν ὁδὸν κυρίου (Mark 1:3)

   μετανοεῖτε καὶ πιστεύετε ἐν τῷ εὐαγγελίῳ (Mark 1:15)

   σοὶ λέγω, ἔγειρε ἆρον (lift up) τὸν κράβαττόν (mattress) σου καὶ ὕπαγε εἰς τὸν οἶκόν σου. (Mark 2:11)

46. Passive Voice

Voice was briefly introduced in Lesson 27. So far, we have seen verbs only in the active voice. We now turn to the passive voice.

The passive voice conveys a process that affects or is done *to* the subject of the verb, rather than *by* the subject. In the active voice of the verb *I find,* the subject does the finding.

εὑρίσκει τὸν ἀδελφόν.

He finds the brother.

When the passive is used, the subject is found.

εὑρίσκεται ὑπὸ τοῦ ἀδελφοῦ.

He is found by the brother.

Agent and Instrument

Greek distinguishes between the person performing the action of a passive verb and the instrument used to effect it. The personal agent is expressed by ὑπό + genitive of the agent. The instrument is expressed by the dative case of the thing used.

E.g., *He is healed by Jesus with a word.*

θεραπεύεται ὑπὸ τοῦ Ἰησοῦ λόγῳ.

Verbs with a middle or passive lexical form

Some verbs are entered in the lexicon under their middle or passive voice only. They will require special attention later on.

Contract Verbs

Verbs ending in εω will again undergo contraction with the addition of the passive endings. These follow the same rules as for the active voice.

Present Passive Indicative of λύω

Sg	**1st**	λύομαι	I am loosed
	2nd	λύῃ	you are loosed
	3rd	λύεται	he/she/it is loosed
Pl	**1st**	λυόμεθα	we are loosed
	2nd	λύεσθε	you are loosed
	3rd	λύονται	they are loosed

Imperfect Passive Indicative of λύω

Sg	**1st**	ἐλυόμην	I was being loosed
	2nd	ἐλύου	you were being loosed
	3rd	ἐλύετο	he/she/it was being loosed
Pl	**1st**	ἐλυόμεθα	we were being loosed
	2nd	ἐλύεσθε	you were being loosed
	3rd	ἐλύοντο	they were being loosed

Exercises

1. Express the following in Greek:

he is trusted

you (pl) were being followed

I am encouraged

you (sg) are being called

she was being cleansed

2. Parse and translate:

βαλλόμεθα

ἐδιδάσκου

θεραπεύονται

ὑπήγοντο

προσεφερόμην

3. Translate:

καὶ ἐβαπτίζοντο ὑπ᾽ αὐτοῦ ἐν τῷ Ἰορδάνῃ ποταμῷ (Mark 1:5)

47. Middle Voice

Middle Voice

The third and final voice to be introduced is the middle voice. The significance of the middle voice has been a matter of recent debate. Traditionally it was thought that by the time of the New Testament the distinction between the middle voice and the other voices was disappearing. But more recently, especially for so-called *deponent* verbs (verbs without active voice forms), grammarians are urging that the middle voice be given fresh appreciation.

The middle voice can convey a *reflexive* element. This use emerges most clearly with a lexeme like *I dress* (ἐνδύω), where the middle implies a process carried out on oneself:

Active	Middle	Passive
I dress	*I dress myself*	*I am dressed*

However, the middle voice is very broad and can behave like the active voice at one end of the spectrum and the passive voice at the other. In all, the middle voice expresses *subject affectedness*, stressing the involvement of the subject.

Forms – Indicative Mood

The forms of the middle and passive voices are the same in the present and imperfect, so these have already been learned. In some contexts, you might argue that a middle voice is intended rather than a passive, but the usual assumption is that this form is chosen to indicate the passive voice.

There is no such ambiguity in the future and first aorist, which have separate forms for the middle voice. The future is formed by inserting σ after the verb stem, before the present middle endings. The aorist middle is formed simply by insertion of the characteristic σα for ο and ε in the Imperfect Middle/Passive, with the exception of the 2nd person singular.

Forms – Imperative Mood

There are no imperfect or future tense-forms in the imperative mood. The present and aorist forms are given to the right. Subject affectedness is not always translatable, so the middle voice can be translated as a *sort-of active*. The difference between the present and aorist is too subtle to translate, so the forms are translated the same way.

Middle/Passive Indicative of λύω

Present	Imperfect
λύομαι	ἐλυόμην
λύῃ	ἐλύου
λύεται	ἐλύετο
λυόμεθα	ἐλυόμεθα
λύεσθε	ἐλύεσθε
λύονται	ἐλύοντο

Middle Indicative of λύω

Future	1st Aorist
λύσομαι	ἐλυσάμην
λύσῃ	ἐλύσω
λύσεται	ἐλύσατο
λυσόμεθα	ἐλυσάμεθα
λύσεσθε	ἐλύσασθε
λύσονται	ἐλύσαντο

Middle Imperative of λύω

Present	1st Aorist	English
λύου	λῦσαι	Loose! (you sg)
λυέσθω	λυσάσθω	Let him/her loose
λύεσθε	λύσασθε	Loose! (you pl)
λυέσθωσαν	λυσάσθωσαν	Let them loose

Exercises

1. Form the 1st aorist middle indicative 3rd person sg of:

γράφω

δοκέω

παρακαλέω

ἀνοίγω

θεραπεύω

☑

Reading Biblical Greek Workbook: Class 1:12–15;
Home 1:16–18

48. Verbs with Middle Lexical Forms

Verbs with Middle Lexical Forms

An important group of verbs are listed in the lexicon by their middle (e.g., δέχομαι) or passive form (e.g., δέομαι). These have traditionally been called *deponent* verbs, defined as *middle or passive in form but active in meaning*. Deponent verbs were treated as though active in voice despite their middle or passive voice forms.

Recent scholarly revision of our understanding of the middle voice suggests this is a misnomer, taken over from the study of Latin. In Latin, a deponent verb *lays aside* its active form and takes a middle or passive form for its active meaning. But in Greek, these verbs never had active forms. The middle or passive forms *are* the original forms of such verbs.*

Since lexicons list these verbs under their middle or passive form, they appear in the vocab lists in this form. We will keep in mind the middle's expression of *subject affectedness*, even when this is not translatable. We will thus tend to translate middle verbs as "sort-of active":

> Present Indicative: *I receive, you receive, we receive,* etc.
>
> Present Imperative: *Receive! Let him/her receive,* etc.

A few verbs have very different meanings in active and middle forms (e.g., ἄρχω *I rule*; ἄρχομαι *I begin*).

* See Constantine R. Campbell, *Advances in the Study of Greek: New Insights for Reading the New Testament* (Grand Rapids: Zondervan, 2015), ch. 4, for more discussion of the middle voice and the now-rejected category of deponency.

Middle Indicative of δέχομαι

Present	Imperfect
δέχομαι	ἐδεχόμην
δέχῃ	ἐδέχου
δέχεται	ἐδέχετο
δεχόμεθα	ἐδεχόμεθα
δέχεσθε	ἐδέχεσθε
δέχονται	ἐδέχοντο

Middle Indicative of δέχομαι

Future	1st Aorist
δέξομαι	ἐδεξάμην
δέξῃ	ἐδέξω
δέξεται	ἐδέξατο
δεξόμεθα	ἐδεξάμεθα
δέξεσθε	ἐδέξασθε
δέξονται	ἐδέξαντο

Middle Imperative of δέχομαι

Present	1st Aorist
δέχου	δέξαι
δεχέσθω	δεξάσθω
δέχεσθε	δέξασθε
δεχέσθωσαν	δεξάσθωσαν

Exercises

1. Express the following in Greek:

   you (sg) are greeting

   they worked

   he is beginning

   you (pl) are praying

   I reckoned

2. Parse:

   ἥψατο

   ἐλογίσασθε

   ἠσπάσαντο

   ἐδεξάμεθα

Vocab #14

49. The Verb ἔρχομαι

The Verb ἔρχομαι	Forms of ἔρχομαι	Exercises

The Verb ἔρχομαι

An important middle-only verb is ἔρχομαι. Forms of this verb occur 40 times in Mark 1:1–4:34, so they require attention. The verb's complex morphology is challenging, and provides a preview of some of the irregularities we must cover (compound, 2nd aorist etc.). The present tense-form of ἔρχομαι translates as *I go* or *I come*.

Principal Parts

Pres Act	Fut Act	Aor Act	Perf Act	Eng
ἔρχομαι	ἐλεύσομαι	ἦλθον	ἐλήλυθα	I come, go

Present Tense-Form

The first principal part indicates that it is a verb listed under its middle form. These take a middle or passive ending in their dictionary form but are translated as sort-of active. Remember that they convey *subject affectedness*, even if that is not translatable.

Since the imperfect is based on the present stem, its form can be inferred.

Future Tense-Form

The future tense-form is built on a different stem. Like the present and imperfect it takes a middle form. It will conjugate following the middle endings, but translate as sort-of active.

Forms of ἔρχομαι

Present Indicative

ἔρχομαι	I am coming
ἔρχῃ	you are coming
ἔρχεται	he/she/it is coming
ἐρχόμεθα	we are coming
ἔρχεσθε	you are coming
ἔρχονται	they are coming

Imperfect Indicative

ἠρχόμην	I was coming
ἤρχου	you were coming
ἤρχετο	he/she/it was coming
ἠρχόμεθα	we were coming
ἤρχεσθε	you were coming
ἤρχοντο	they were coming

Exercises

1. Use the table opposite to parse the following forms of ἔρχομαι from Mark 1–2:

ἔρχεται (1:7)

ἤρχοντο (1:45)

ἔρχονται (2:3)

ἤρχετο (2:13)

50. Future Tense-Form: Middle and Passive

Future Tense-Form: Middle & Passive

The indicative mood of the future tense-form is used to depict a process or state expected to occur, or wished for, at some time in the future. We will translate it by a simple future, i.e., *I will loose* (active and middle), *I will be loosed* (passive).

FORM
Like the active voice, the distinctive feature of the future middle is the *sigma* (σ) placed after the stem; θη is added to the passive. Endings are the same as the present tense-form in all voices.

CHANGES CAUSED BY ADDITIONS
Contract verbs ending in εω undergo lengthening of ε to η before σ and θησ.

In the passive voice, the addition of θησ causes mutes, except dentals, to change to the aspirated form.

E.g., ἀνοίγω → ἀνοιχθήσομαι

Dentals form σθ rather than double *thēta*.

Some verbs (e.g., γράφω) add the passive ending without the θ (i.e., γραφήσομαι). The principal parts indicate the most frequent and important variations. Verbs ending in liquids (λ, μ, ν, ρ) undergo changes that will be dealt with in Lesson 52.

Vocab #15

FUTURE OF λύω

Indicative Mood

		Middle	Passive
Sg	1st	λύσομαι	λυθήσομαι
	2nd	λύσῃ	λυθήσῃ
	3rd	λύσεται	λυθήσεται
Pl	1st	λυσόμεθα	λυθησόμεθα
	2nd	λύσεσθε	λυθήσεσθε
	3rd	λύσονται	λυθήσονται

FUTURE ACTIVE OF εἰμί

ἔσομαι
ἔσῃ
ἔσται
ἐσόμεθα
ἔσεσθε
ἔσονται

RULES FOR MUTES + θησ

κ or γ or χ + θ = χθ
π or β or φ + θ = φθ
τ or δ or θ + θ = σθ

Exercises

1. Form the future middle indicative 1st person plural of:

γράφω

ἀκούω

ἄγω

κρατέω

πράσσω

πείθω

2. Form the future passive indicative 2nd person singular of:

πειράζω

φωνέω

ἄγω

γράφω

κηρύσσω

Reading Biblical Greek Workbook: Class 1:19–20; Home 1:21–24

51. Aorist Passive

Aorist Passive

Remember that the passive voice is used to indicate that the process of the verb is done *to* the verb's subject rather than *by* its subject (see Lesson 46). Note that in all moods, the addition of θ to the verb stem follows the same rules as for the future passive.

Indicative

The aorist passive form consists of:

augment + verb stem + distinctive θη + personal endings

The aorist indicative is translated by a simple past in the passive.

> E.g., *I was loosed* or *they were loosed*.

Imperative

These forms follow a familiar pattern, except in the 2nd person singular. The passive should be translated as *be loosed* or *let him/them be loosed*. Remember that the aorist imperative normally expresses specific commands.

2nd Aorist Verbs

The principal parts show that 2nd aorist verbs in the active voice change to a stem that accepts these same passive endings. Some verbs drop the θ (e.g., ἐγράφην).

Passive Lexical Form Verbs

Those verbs listed under their passive form in the vocabulary lists (e.g., βούλομαι, φοβέομαι) should be translated by the active voice in all moods, though an element of passivity will sometimes be apparent.

γινώσκω and -βαίνω

The 2nd aorist **active** of these verbs follow a very similar pattern to the 1st aorist passive, so these are introduced here. ἔγνων substitutes the long ω sound for η in ἐλύθην and –ἔβην.

Aorist Passive Indicative

Sg	**1st**	ἐλύθην
	2nd	ἐλύθης
	3rd	ἐλύθη
Pl	**1st**	ἐλύθημεν
	2nd	ἐλύθητε
	3rd	ἐλύθησαν

1st Aorist Passive Imperative

Sg	**2nd**	λύθητι
	3rd	λυθήτω
Pl	**2nd**	λύθητε
	3rd	λυθήτωσαν

Aorist Active of γινώσκω & -βαίνω

Sg	**1st**	ἔγνων	(ἀν)έβην
	2nd	ἔγνως	(ἀν)έβης
	3rd	ἔγνω	(ἀν)έβη
Pl	**1st**	ἔγνωμεν	(ἀν)έβημεν
	2nd	ἔγνωτε	(ἀν)έβητε
	3rd	ἔγνωσαν	(ἀν)έβησαν

Exercises

1. From the principal-parts table (p. 125), identify the passive form of those verbs that take a 2nd aorist active form.

2. From the principal-parts table, list the aorist passive forms that drop the θ.

3. Parse the following (Mark 1, 2):

καθαρίσθητι (1:41)

ἐκαθαρίσθη (1:42)

ἠκούσθη (2:1)

ἠγέρθη (2:12)

4. Parse the following (Mark):

ἀνέβησαν (4:7)

ἔγνω (5:29)

ἐπέγνωσαν (6:33)

ἀνέβη (6:51)

ἐγίνωσκεν (15:10)

52. Liquid Stem Verbs

Liquid Stem Verbs	Exercises

We turn now to a set of verbs whose forms require special attention due to the nature of their lexical stem.

Liquid stems is a shorthand way of referring to a group of verbs whose stems end with one of the following consonants:

λ   μ   ν   ρ

In the future and first aorist tense-forms these behave in a certain way because Greek doesn't accept a *sigma* after these consonants. As a result, they have the following characteristics:

> There is **no σ** before the endings.
>
> The future stem is usually **shorter** than the present stem (often drops a vowel or λ).
>
> The future has endings like the *present of εω verbs* (N.B., ἐγεροῦμεν, ἐγερεῖτε).
>
> The stem (aorist) may *change in other ways* (e.g., ἀγγέλλω).
>
> For some verbs (e.g., βάλλω) these rules apply for the future but not for the aorist, since they take a second aorist form (ἔβαλον).

Distinguishing Present and Future

The future indicative endings of liquid stem verbs are the same as the present indicative endings. The difference between the present and future *stem* makes it possible to distinguish them in most cases, despite the absence of a *sigma*.

However, μένω and κρίνω are examples of verbs for which the stem is the same in both tense-forms. The future forms, however, are identified by a **circumflex**. You will need to remember this difference in accentuation to know the difference between present and future forms.

Present	Future	1st Aorist
Indicative Mood		
ἐγείρω	ἐγερῶ	ἤγειρα
ἐγείρεις	ἐγερεῖς	ἤγειρας
ἐγείρει	ἐγερεῖ	ἤγειρεν
ἐγείρομεν	ἐγεροῦμεν	ἠγείραμεν
ἐγείρετε	ἐγερεῖτε	ἠγείρατε
ἐγείρουσιν	ἐγεροῦσιν	ἤγειραν
Imperative Mood		
ἔγειρε		ἔγειρον
ἐγειρέτω		ἐγειράτω
ἐγείρετε		ἐγείρατε
ἐγειρέτωσαν		ἐγειράτωσαν
κρίνω		
κρίνω	κρινῶ	ἔκρινα
κρίνεις	κρινεῖς	ἔκρινας
κρίνει	κρινεῖ	ἔκρινεν
κρίνομεν	κρινοῦμεν	ἐκρίναμεν
κρίνετε	κρινεῖτε	ἐκρίνατε
κρίνουσιν	κρινοῦσιν	ἔκριναν

1. Consult the principal parts table and list all the *liquid stems*.

2. Parse the following:

ἐγερεῖτε

μενεῖ

ἔσπειρας

ἀράτω

κρίνεις

ἐμείναμεν

φωνήσομεν

σπερεῖτε

ἀποκτενῶ

Vocab #16

Reading Biblical Greek Workbook: Class 1:25–28; Home 1:29–31

53A. 2ND AORIST TENSE-FORM

2nd Aorist Tense Form	2ND AORIST ACTIVE INDICATIVE	Exercises

2nd Aorist Tense Form

We learned the 1st aorist forms in Lessons 36 and 51. The 2nd aorist is an alternate set of aorist forms that have the exact same meaning as the 1st aorist forms.

The 2nd aorist is therefore translated the same way as the more common 1st aorist. It is usually found with verbs that do not welcome the addition of σα with their stem (e.g., βάλλω). There are a negligible number of verbs with both a 1st and 2nd aorist form.

MEANING

The indicative mood should be translated, like the 1st aorist, by a simple past tense in English (*I threw, he threw*). In every mood, we will try to reflect the external (perfective) aspect of the aorist, viewing the action as a whole.

FORM

In the indicative mood it is convenient to think of the verb in three parts (ignoring compounds). The 2nd aorist indicative is made up of:

augment (ἐ)

2nd aorist stem (e.g. βαλ-)

imperfect endings.

N.B. The 2nd aorist and imperfect indicatives are distinguished only by the stem (βαλ instead of βαλλ).

2ND AORIST ACTIVE INDICATIVE

βάλλω

Sg	**1st**	ἔβαλον
	2nd	ἔβαλες
	3rd	ἔβαλεν
Pl	**1st**	ἐβάλομεν
	2nd	ἐβάλετε
	3rd	ἔβαλον

Exercises

1. From the table of principal parts, **list** the present active indicative of those verbs that take the second aorist.

2. **Translate** the following from Mark 1 (use the principal-parts table):

   εἶδεν (1:10)

   εἶπεν (1:17)

   προσένεγκε (1:44)

2nd Aorist Tense-Form: Outside the Indicative

Outside the indicative mood (subjunctive, imperative, participle, infinitive) there is no augment. Again the aorist stem is used.

The endings will be the same as the **present** tense-form (unlike the indicative mood, which uses imperfect endings for the 2nd aorist). So, the 2nd aorist and present tense-forms of some verbs are distinguished only by the stem.

E.g., Imperative βάλλε (pres) βάλε (2nd aor).

2ND AORIST OF ἔρχομαι

The aorist of ἔρχομαι is built on yet another stem, ἐλθ. It is a second aorist. This means it borrows the imperfect active endings to show person and number, but is understood as an aorist.

2ND AORIST ACTIVE IMPERATIVE

Sg	**2nd**	βάλε
	3rd	βαλέτω
Pl	**2nd**	βάλετε
	3rd	βαλέτωσαν

PARTICIPLE

Pres Active Masculine	2nd Aorist Active Masculine
βάλλων	βαλών
βάλλοντος	βάλοντος
etc.	etc.

2ND AORIST ACTIVE INDICATIVE ἔρχομαι

ἦλθον	I came
ἦλθες	you came
ἦλθεν	he/she/it came
ἤλθομεν	we came
ἤλθετε	you came
ἦλθον	they came

Exercises

1. Using the aorist column of the table of principal parts, conjugate in full the 2nd aorist active imperative of:

ἄγω

λαμβάνω

2. Decline in full the masculine 2nd aorist active participle of βάλλω.

3. Use the table to the left to parse the following forms and compounds of ἔρχομαι from Mark 1. For compounds, simply place the meaning of the preposition after *I go* or *come* in the appropriate tense of the verb:

1:9	ἦλθεν	
1:20	ἀπῆλθον	I go from
1:24	ἦλθες	
1:25	ἔξελθε	
1:26	ἐξῆλθεν	
1:29	ἦλθον	
1:35	ἀπῆλθεν	
1:38	ἐξῆλθον	

☑

Reading Biblical Greek Workbook: Class 1:32–34; Home 1:35–37

54a. Participles: Feminine and Neuter

Participles — Feminine & Neuter	Exercises

Present Tense-Form

Not all the participles in Mark 1 are masculine. To the right are the declensions for the feminine and neuter participles in the active voice. Other than the new paradigm, these do not represent new learning. For now, they are also translated as simple -ing words.

Gender

The gender of *adverbial* participles varies according to the gender of the noun to which it is linked in the clause or sentence.

E.g., in Mark 1:30, Peter's *mother-in-law* is the subject (nominative) of the main verb. So the participle describing her action/state is nominative, singular, and feminine: ἡ δὲ πενθερὰ Σίμωνος κατέκειτο πυρέσσουσα.

The gender of an *adjectival* participle will depend on the "gender" of the person or thing named by the participle. In some instances, it will qualify a noun, with which it agrees.

> E.g., Matt 3:7 τῆς μελλούσης ὀργῆς
> *the coming anger*

Adjectival participles are often used with an article but no noun, and function in place of a noun. You will need to consider the context when reading and translating.

> E.g., Mk 1:32 τοὺς κακῶς ἔχοντας: Lit.
> *the having badly people* (i.e. *the sick*).

The participle is masculine because it implies *people* who are unwell. Since ἄνθρωπος is grammatically masculine, the participle is too.

Participle of εἰμί (the verb I am)

The present active participle endings are the same as the participle of the verb *I am*. There are no separate aorist forms for the participle of εἰμί. We will simply translate these as *being*.

> E.g., Mk 2:26 τοῖς σὺν αὐτῷ οὖσιν =
> to those **being** with him

Feminine & Neuter Participles Present Active

		Feminine	Neuter
Sg	Nom	λύουσα	λῦον
	Gen	λυούσης	λύοντος
	Dat	λυούσῃ	λύοντι
	Acc	λύουσαν	λῦον
Pl	Nom	λύουσαι	λύοντα
	Gen	λυουσῶν	λυόντων
	Dat	λυούσαις	λύουσιν
	Acc	λυούσας	λύοντα

Participle of εἰμί (being)

Masculine	Feminine	Neuter
ὤν	οὖσα	ὄν
ὄντος	οὔσης	ὄντος
ὄντι	οὔσῃ	ὄντι
ὄντα	οὖσαν	ὄν
ὄντες	οὖσαι	ὄντα
ὄντων	οὐσῶν	ὄντων
οὖσιν	οὔσαις	οὖσιν
ὄντας	οὔσας	ὄντα

Exercises

1a. Identify the case, number, gender, and tense of these participles in Mark 1:

πυρέσσουσα (v. 30)

ἔχοντας (v. 32)

κηρύσσων (v. 39)

1b. Account for the gender in each instance.

2. Form the present active feminine participle (sg nom) of:

μαρτυρέω

ἀνοίγω

γράφω

κατοικέω

πειράζω

Vocab #17

Participles — Feminine & Neuter		Exercises

1ST AORIST TENSE-FORM

There are also *aorist* feminine and neuter participles that require attention.

FORM

First, it is best to think of the participle as made up of three pieces:

- the verb stem
- the distinctive participle bit
- the endings

Note that for both present and aorist participles the masculine and neuter are the same except in nominative and accusative cases. Masculine and neuter participles share 3rd declension noun endings. The feminine has a distinctive middle section and endings like δόξα (i.e., 1st declension).

As we would expect, the first aorist is formed by substituting σα for the ο and ου sounds.

TRANSLATION

Remember the simplistic principle we are applying (at this stage) to participles in the active voice. Simply turn them into an *-ing* word. In the case of a substantival participle, supply the necessary word according to its gender.

E.g., ἡ βαπτίζουσα implies *the baptizing* (woman)

But check the context for another word that may be grammatically feminine.

LEARNING

You are not expected to learn these forms immediately. Aim first for recognition, then work toward memorization. The translation exercises should help to reduce anxiety.

FEMININE & NEUTER PARTICIPLES: AORIST ACTIVE

		Feminine	Neuter
Sg	**Nom**	λύσασα	λῦσαν
	Gen	λυσάσης	λύσαντος
	Dat	λυσάσῃ	λύσαντι
	Acc	λύσασαν	λῦσαν
Pl	**Nom**	λύσασαι	λύσαντα
	Gen	λυσασῶν	λυσάντων
	Dat	λυσάσαις	λύσασιν
	Acc	λυσάσας	λύσαντα

1a. Identify the case, gender, number, and tense-form of these participles in Mark 1:

σπαράξαν (v. 26)

φωνῆσαν (v. 26)

κρατῆσας (v. 31)

1b. Account for the gender in each instance.

2. Form the 1st aorist active feminine participle (sg nom) of:

μαρτυρέω

ἀνοίγω

γράφω

κατοικέω

πειράζω

☑

Reading Biblical Greek Workbook: Class 1:38–39; Home 1:40–43

55. Demonstrative Pronouns

Demonstrative Pronouns

We studied personal pronouns in Lessons 23 and 41, but they are not the only type of pronoun. *This* (οὗτος) and *that* (ἐκεῖνος) are *demonstrative* pronouns (*He said **this** to them*), which are often used as *adjectives* (*Jesus healed **this** man*) in both Greek and English.

Demonstratives point to the particular thing intended (e.g., **this** word, **that** word). Originally the distinction between the two demonstrative pronouns seems to have been proximity (οὗτος) vs remoteness (ἐκεῖνος), but this should not be pressed in NT contexts.

In English, the plural of *this* is *these*, and the plural of *that* is *those*. Note also the neuter nominative and accusative singular endings for ἐκεῖνος.

The declension of οὗτος is unique. It has the same endings as ἐκεῖνος, the same initial letters as the article, and follows the strange rule that when there is an ο or ω in the ending, there is an ο in the stem. And when there is an α or η in the ending, there is an α in the stem.

Vocab #18

Demonstrative οὗτος

		Masculine	Feminine	Neuter
Sg	Nom	οὗτος	αὕτη	τοῦτο
	Gen	τούτου	ταύτης	τούτου
	Dat	τούτῳ	ταύτῃ	τούτῳ
	Acc	τοῦτον	ταύτην	τοῦτο
Pl	Nom	οὗτοι	αὗται	ταῦτα
	Gen	τούτων	τούτων	τούτων
	Dat	τούτοις	ταύταις	τούτοις
	Acc	τούτους	ταύτας	ταῦτα

Demonstrative ἐκεῖνος

		Masculine	Feminine	Neuter
Sg	Nom	ἐκεῖνος	ἐκείνη	ἐκεῖνο
	Gen	ἐκείνου	ἐκείνης	ἐκείνου
	Dat	ἐκείνῳ	ἐκείνῃ	ἐκείνῳ
	Acc	ἐκεῖνον	ἐκείνην	ἐκεῖνο
Pl	Nom	ἐκεῖνοι	ἐκεῖναι	ἐκεῖνα
	Gen	ἐκείνων	ἐκείνων	ἐκείνων
	Dat	ἐκείνοις	ἐκείναις	ἐκείνοις
	Acc	ἐκείνους	ἐκείνας	ἐκεῖνα

Exercises

1. Parse the following (from Mark 1):

ἐκείναις (v. 9)

τοῦτο (v. 27)

ὅλην (v. 28)

ὅλη (v. 33)

τοῦτο (v. 38)

56A. ADJECTIVE POSITIONS AND SPECIAL USES OF αὐτός

Adjective Positions & Special Uses of αὐτός	Adjective Positions	Examples

	ATTRIBUTIVE POSITION	IDENTICAL ADJECTIVE: αὐτός IN ATTRIBUTIVE POSITION

When an adjective is used with an article and noun, the adjective may be placed in different positions relative to its article and noun. Greek distinguishes two positions, the *attributive* and *predicative* positions, which impact meaning and translation.

1st attributive position
Article — Adjective — Noun

E.g., ὁ ἀγαθὸς ἄνθρωπος ἐκ τοῦ ἀγαθοῦ θησαυροῦ τῆς καρδίας προφέρει τὸ ἀγαθόν

καὶ πάλιν ἀπελθὼν προσηύξατο **τὸν αὐτὸν λόγον** εἰπών.

And again he went away and prayed, saying **the same words** (lit. "word") (Mark 14:39)

ATTRIBUTIVE POSITION

Most adjectives are placed in the *attributive* position, in one of two constructions (*see right*). Note that the article immediately precedes the adjective in both patterns. These constructions serve to *attribute* a quality (adjective) to the noun.

The good person out of the good treasure of the heart produces good (Luke 6:45)

οὐ γάρ ἐστιν διαστολὴ Ἰουδαίου τε καὶ Ἕλληνος, ὁ γὰρ **αὐτὸς κύριος** πάντων

2nd attributive position
Article — Noun — Article — Adjective

For there is no distinction between Jew and Greek; **the same Lord** is Lord of all (Rom 10:12)

PREDICATIVE POSITION

The alternative position, the *predicative*, can also be expressed in two ways (*see right*). Translation sometimes requires the addition of the (implied) verb *to be*, to complete the sense. In these constructions, something is *predicated* of the noun.

E.g., Ὁ νικῶν οὐ μὴ ἀδικηθῇ ἐκ **τοῦ θανάτου τοῦ δευτέρου**

EMPHASIZING PRONOUN: αὐτός IN PREDICATIVE POSITION

Whoever conquers will not be harmed by **the second death** (Rev 2:11)

αὐτός WITH NOUNS

The third person personal pronoun is used in two distinctive ways when qualifying a noun. Rather than substituting for a noun, αὐτός is used to qualify a noun in one of two ways, depending on which position it takes.

PREDICATIVE POSITION

αὐτὸς Δαυὶδ εἶπεν ἐν τῷ πνεύματι τῷ ἁγίῳ

David himself, by the Holy Spirit, declared (Mark 12:36)

1st predicative position
Adjective — Article — Noun

E.g., μακάριος ὁ δοῦλος ἐκεῖνος

IDENTICAL ADJECTIVE (ATTRIBUTIVE)

In the attributive position, αὐτός is translated by *same*. So ὁ αὐτὸς κύριος and ὁ κύριος ὁ αὐτός should both be rendered, *The same Lord*.

Blessed is that **slave** (Luke 12:43)

Αὐτὸς γὰρ ὁ Ἡρῴδης ἀποστείλας ἐκράτησεν τὸν Ἰωάννην

EMPHASIZING PRONOUN (PREDICATIVE)

In the predicative position, αὐτός serves to add emphasis to the person or thing named. So αὐτὸς ὁ κύριος and ὁ κύριος αὐτός both translate as *The Lord himself*.

2nd predicative position
Article — Noun — Adjective

E.g., οὗτοι οἱ λόγοι πιστοὶ

For **Herod himself** had sent men who arrested John (Mark 6:17)

These words are trustworthy (Rev 22:6)

56b. Words That "Take" the Predicative Position

Words That "Take" the Predicative Position	Examples	Exercises
One of the distinctive features of both demonstrative pronouns οὗτος and ἐκεῖνος is the position in which they are placed, relative to their article and noun.	**οὗτος**	1. Express the following in Greek:
Both οὗτος and ἐκεῖνος "take" the predicative position. This means that they are not placed between the article and the noun it qualifies, where an article is present. Despite this, they should be translated as though in the attributive position.	οὐκ οἴδατε **τὴν παραβολὴν ταύτην** …;	this Sabbath
	Do you not understand **this parable**? (Mark 4:13)	those tongues
E.g., ἐν ἐκείναις ταῖς ἡμέραις translates *In those days*.	**ἐκεῖνος**	that day
	καὶ τότε νηστεύσουσιν ἐν **ἐκείνῃ τῇ ἡμέρᾳ**	the whole crowd
An adjective from the vocabulary, ὅλος, also prefers the predicative position (ὅλη ἡ πόλις, *the whole city*). Unlike the demonstratives it declines like ἀγαθός, ή, όν.	and then they will fast on **that day** (Mark 2:20)	these clothes
Later we will meet 3rd declension adjectives for *all, every* (πᾶς, ἅπας), which also "take" the predicative position.	**ὅλος**	the whole desert
	Καὶ ἦλθεν κηρύσσων εἰς τὰς συναγωγὰς αὐτῶν εἰς **ὅλην τὴν Γαλιλαίαν**	
	So he went into **all of Galilee**, preaching in their synagogues (Mark 1:39)	2. Translate:
	πᾶς	Καὶ ἐγένετο ἐν ἐκείναις ταῖς ἡμέραις ἦλθεν Ἰησοῦς ἀπὸ Ναζαρὲτ τῆς Γαλιλαίας (Mark 1:9)
	… καὶ πῶς **πάσας τὰς παραβολὰς** γνώσεσθε;	Καὶ ἦλθεν κηρύσσων εἰς τὰς συναγωγὰς αὐτῶν εἰς ὅλην τὴν Γαλιλαίαν καὶ τὰ δαιμόνια ἐκβάλλων. (Mark 1:39)
	Then how will you understand **all the parables**? (Mark 4:13)	
	ἅπας	
	ὁ λαὸς γὰρ **ἅπας** ἐξεκρέματο αὐτοῦ ἀκούων	
	for **all the people** were spellbound by what they heard (Luke 19:48)	☑
		Reading Biblical Greek Workbook: Class 1:44–45; Home 2:1–4

57. Reflexive Pronoun

Reflexive Pronoun

The next type of pronoun to explore is the reflexive pronoun. The usage of the reflexive pronoun is easily confused with the emphasizing pronoun (i.e. αὐτός in predicative position). Like the emphasizing pronoun it translates as *himself, herself, itself*. Unlike the emphasizing pronoun the reflexive pronoun refers back to *an antecedent*, usually the subject, from a different part of the sentence. Therefore, it never takes the nominative case. *Myself* (1st), *yourself* (2nd) and *himself, herself, itself* (3rd) render the singular reflexive into English.

Singular Reflexive Pronoun

This pronoun is formed by adding personal prefixes to αὐτός.

ἐμαυτοῦ	of myself
σεαυτοῦ	of yourself
ἑαυτοῦ, ης, ου	of himself, herself, itself

N.B. The 1st and 2nd persons have no neuter form.

Examples

John 5:30	I am able to do nothing from myself (ἐμαυτοῦ)
Mark 12:31	Love your neighbor as yourself (σεαυτόν).
Mark 15:31	He is not able to save himself (ἑαυτόν).

Plural Reflexive Pronoun

The third person plural form is used for all 1st, 2nd, and 3rd person plurals (i.e., there are no separate plural forms for 1st and 2nd person).

ἑαυτῶν	of ourselves
	of yourselves
	of themselves

Examples

2 Cor 4:5	For we do not preach ourselves (ἑαυτούς)
Mark 13:9	Watch yourselves (ἑαυτούς)
Mark 9:10	They kept the matter to themselves (ἑαυτούς)

1st Person Singular

Masculine & Feminine

Sg	Nom	
	Gen	ἐμαυτοῦ
	Dat	ἐμαυτῷ
	Acc	ἐμαυτόν

2nd Person Singular

Masculine & Feminine

Sg	Nom	
	Gen	σεαυτοῦ
	Dat	σεαυτῷ
	Acc	σεαυτόν

3rd Person Singular

Sg	Nom			
	Gen	ἑαυτοῦ	ἑαυτῆς	ἑαυτοῦ
	Dat	ἑαυτῷ	ἑαυτῇ	ἑαυτῷ
	Acc	ἑαυτόν	ἑαυτήν	ἑαυτό

1st, 2nd, 3rd Person Plural

Pl	Nom			
	Gen	ἑαυτῶν	ἑαυτῶν	ἑαυτῶν
	Dat	ἑαυτοῖς	ἑαυταῖς	ἑαυτοῖς
	Acc	ἑαυτούς	ἑαυτάς	ἑαυτά

Exercises

1. Classify (personal or reflexive) each of the following pronouns from Mark 1. Identify whether it is 1st, 2nd, or 3rd person. Parse for case, number, and gender:

μοῦ (v. 2)

σοῦ (v. 2)

ἐγώ (v. 8)

ὑμᾶς (v. 8)

Σύ (v. 11)

σοί (v. 11)

ἡμῖν (v. 24)

ἡμᾶς (v. 24)

σέ (v. 24)

ἑαυτούς (v. 27)

μέ (v. 40)

σεαυτόν (v. 44)

Vocab #19

58. Relative Pronoun

The relative pronoun works as a shorthand way of referring back to a noun previously mentioned or implied. It is translated "who," "that," or "which."

A relative pronoun agrees in number and gender with its antecedent. However, its *case will be determined by the pronoun's role* in its own relative clause.

In form, relative pronouns are very similar to the endings of the definite article (like ἐκεῖνος). An accent distinguishes the forms that might otherwise be confused with the article. While the lexical form appears as ὅς, ἥ, ὅ (with acute accents), grave accents will more often appear in the Greek text of the NT.

While it is the smallest of words, the relative pronoun can present great difficulties (e.g., Mark 1:7 in NRSV). In both English and Greek it is helpful to reconstruct the two sentences that have been joined by the relative pronoun.

E.g., ἰδοὺ ἀποστέλλω τὸν ἄγγελόν μου πρὸ προσώπου σου, ὃς κατασκευάσει τὴν ὁδόν σου·(Mark 1:2)

can be construed as two sentences.

A. See, I send my messenger before your face.

B. The messenger will prepare your way.

Since τὸν ἄγγελόν is masculine, singular, the relative pronoun is too. But while τὸν ἄγγελόν is the object of ἀποστέλλω in A, it is the subject of κατασκευάσει in B. So the relative pronoun is nominative.

οὗτός ἐστιν ὁ υἱός μου ὁ ἀγαπητός, ἐν ᾧ εὐδόκησα (Matt 3:17)

A. This is my son, the beloved.   Masc, Sg (like υἱός)

B. I am well pleased in the son.   Dat (after ἐν)

Most relative pronouns introduce a relative clause, which is adjectival in function since it qualifies the antecedent. Sometimes the antecedent of the relative pronoun is only implied.

ὃς γὰρ οὐκ ἔστιν καθ᾽ ἡμῶν, ὑπὲρ ἡμῶν ἐστιν. (Mark 9:40)

for, who(ever) is not against us is for us.

Translate the relative pronoun by "who," "that," or "which," depending on the sense of the clause. "Who" inflects in English (whose, to whom, whom).

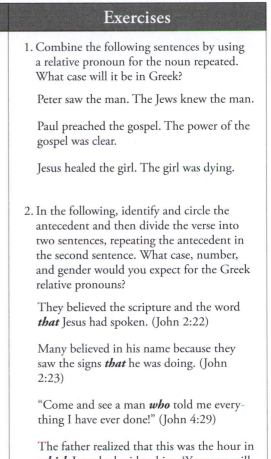

		Masc	Fem	Neut
Sg	**Nom**	ὅς	ἥ	ὅ
	Gen	οὗ	ἧς	οὗ
	Dat	ᾧ	ᾗ	ᾧ
	Acc	ὅν	ἥν	ὅ
Pl	**Nom**	οἵ	αἵ	ἅ
	Gen	ὧν	ὧν	ὧν
	Dat	οἷς	αἷς	οἷς
	Acc	οὕς	ἅς	ἅ

Vocab #20

Exercises

1. Combine the following sentences by using a relative pronoun for the noun repeated. What case will it be in Greek?

   Peter saw the man. The Jews knew the man.

   Paul preached the gospel. The power of the gospel was clear.

   Jesus healed the girl. The girl was dying.

2. In the following, identify and circle the antecedent and then divide the verse into two sentences, repeating the antecedent in the second sentence. What case, number, and gender would you expect for the Greek relative pronouns?

   They believed the scripture and the word ***that*** Jesus had spoken. (John 2:22)

   Many believed in his name because they saw the signs ***that*** he was doing. (John 2:23)

   "Come and see a man ***who*** told me everything I have ever done!" (John 4:29)

   The father realized that this was the hour in ***which*** Jesus had said to him, 'Your son will live.' (John 4:53)

   "Is not this Jesus, the son of Joseph, ***whose*** father and mother we know?" (John 6:42)

Reading Biblical Greek Workbook: Class 2:5–7; Home 2:8–9

59. Participles: Middle and Passive Voices

Participles: Middle & Passive Voices

Middle Voice

We return now to the participle, and its middle and passive voices in particular. The middle voice of the participle should be translated as "kind of active." Verbs listed under their middle form are often translated like active voice participles, but they also convey subject affectedness.

Both the present and aorist middle participles decline like ἀγαθός (endings like λόγος, ἀρχή, and ἔργον). The second aorist is formed from the verb stem and present endings.

Passive Voice

Our simple principle of making an *–ing* word from the verb's root needs a little adjustment. The passive participle should be translated *being loosed*, with care not to imply any sense of time (at this stage). With an article, the translation will be *the being loosed one*.

The forms of the present passive are exactly the same as the middle. For the 1st aorist there is a separate passive form. It follows the same general pattern as λύων (present active) and λύσας (aorist active). Apart from the first line, the distinctive θε is substituted for o and σα. The feminine substitutes θει for ου.

The 2nd aorist passive of βάλλω is βληθείς. By using a different stem, it is able to take the same endings as the 1st aorist. See the Principal Parts for other second aorist stems.

Participles: Present Middle / Passive

Masculine	Feminine	Neuter
λυόμενος	λυομένη	λυόμενον
λυομένου	λυομένης	λυομένου
λυομένῳ	λυομένη	λυομένῳ
λυόμενον	λυομένην	λυόμενον
λυόμενοι	λυόμεναι	λυόμενα
λυομένων	λυομένων	λυομένων
λυομένοις	λυομέναις	λυομένοις
λυομένους	λυομένας	λυόμενα

1st Aorist Middle

λυσάμενος	λυσαμένη	λυσάμενον
λυσαμένου	λυσαμένης	λυσαμένου etc.

2nd Aorist Middle

βαλόμενος	βαλομένη	βαλόμενον
βαλομένου	βαλομένης	βαλομένου etc.

Aorist Passive

λυθείς	λυθεῖσα	λυθέν
λυθέντος	λυθείσης	λυθέντος
λυθέντι	λυθείσῃ	λυθέντι
λυθέντα	λυθεῖσαν	λυθέν
λυθέντες	λυθεῖσαι	λυθέντα
λυθέντων	λυθεισῶν	λυθέντων
λυθεῖσι(ν)	λυθείσαις	λυθεῖσι(ν)
λυθέντας	λυθείσας	λυθέντα

Exercises

1. Identify the tense, voice, number, gender, and case of the following:

   N.B. You will not know whether or not some are listed under their middle form in a lexicon.

   ἐξομολογούμενοι (1:5)

   σχιζομένους (1:10)

   πειραζόμενος (1:13)

   γενομένης (1:32)

   δαιμονιζομένους (1:32)

   σπλαγχνισθείς (1:41)

   ἐμβριμησάμενος (1:43)

   αἰρόμενον (2:3)

   διαλογιζόμενοι (2:6)

2. Express the following in Greek using the nominative, singular, masculine of:

   being greeted (pres)

   being received (aor)

   being reckoned (pres)

60A. PERFECT TENSE-FORM: INDICATIVE MOOD

Perfect Tense-Form: Indicative Mood

We return now to the indicative mood. The perfect tense-form is the fifth of six key tense-forms and is often used for significant theological statements (e.g., John 19:30, *It is finished*).

MEANING

Traditionally the perfect has been understood as describing a present state resulting from a past action. It would then be translated as *I have loosed, he has loosed*.

However, we regard the perfect as a "type of present," sharing its internal (imperfective) aspect. It is normally more emphatic or prominent than the present tense-form.

TRANSLATION

Be aware that the normal convention is to translate the perfect as *I have loosed*, though it is often translated like a present anyway in English versions of the NT (e.g., γέγραπται *It is written*; τετέλεσται *It is finished*).

We will translate the perfect like the present, except where the context requires otherwise. It should therefore be translated as *I loose*, though it may also be translated *I have loosed* (in line with traditional approaches) if the lexeme and context suggest as much. Occasionally it will be best to translate the perfect like an aorist (e.g., ἀπέσταλκεν *he sent*).

FORM

The active voice is best thought of as having four parts:

reduplication +	stem +	κα +	endings
λε	λυ	κα	μεν

The middle/passive voice has only three parts:

reduplication +	stem +	endings
λε	λυ	μεθα

Perfect Indicative of λύω

Active	Middle / Passive
λέλυκα	λέλυμαι
λέλυκας	λέλυσαι
λέλυκεν	λέλυται
λελύκαμεν	λελύμεθα
λελύκατε	λέλυσθε
λελύκασιν	λέλυνται
(λέλυκαν *)	

* αν ending used 9 times of 32 in the NT

N.B. the absence of a connecting vowel

Vocab #21

Exercises

1. Consult the principal parts table and list:

   a. Verbs with no perfect active

   b. Verbs that reduplicate irregularly in the perfect active

   c. Verbs that end in other than κα in the perfect active

2. Find the perfect verb forms in the following verses. How is each one rendered in the English version you use?

   Mark 1:2

   Mark 6:14

   John 1:34

   John 3:18

   John 17:7

   Acts 7:35

   Romans 3:10

   Hebrews 11:28

Perfect Tense-Form: Indicative Mood *cont.*

1. Consonants at the beginning of a verb stem are duplicated at the front, with an *epsilon* (ε) added to separate the two consonants (λέλυκα). *Aspirated* consonants (φ; χ; θ) are duplicated in their corresponding de-aspirated forms (π, κ, τ), e.g., πεφίληκα.

2. Vowels or diphthongs at the beginning of words undergo *lengthening of the first vowel*. (This means that they begin the same way as aorist and imperfect tense-forms; e.g. ἦρκα).

   Verb stems beginning with two consonants (e.g. ἔγνωκα) or σ, ζ, or ξ (e.g. ἔσταλκα) often *reduplicate only the epsilon*.

   N.B. The epsilon is **not** an augment, so it still appears with verbs outside the indicative mood (i.e., participles, infinitive).

3. Compound verbs nearly always reduplicate between the preposition and the verbal part of the word as in the addition of augments in the indicative, e.g., ἐκβέβληκα.

VERB STEMS IN THE PERFECT

For the majority of verbs, the stem will be the same as the present stem. Some will be the same as the aorist (or verb) stem. But there are enough irregularities to make learning principal parts necessary.

Regular contract verbs ending in εω always lengthen the ε to η before the addition of endings (except καλέω). This is still true in the passive voice because there are no connecting vowels with which to coalesce.

Perfect Indicative of ποιέω

Active	Middle / Passive
πεποίηκα	πεποίημαι
πεποίηκας	πεποίησαι
πεποίηκεν	πεποίηται
πεποιήκαμεν	πεποιήμεθα
πεποιήκατε	πεποίησθε
πεποιήκασιν	πεποίηνται

Exercises

1. Give the perfect active indicative 1st singular of:

   μισέω

   πράσσω

   γινώσκω

   εἰσέρχομαι

   καλέω

   γίνομαι

   κράζω

2. Give the perfect middle passive indicative 1st singular of:

   βάλλω

   ἀνοίγω

   παραγγέλλω

   γράφω

☑

Reading Biblical Greek Workbook: Class 2:10–12; Home 2:13–15

61. Perfect Non-Indicative

Perfect Non-Indicative

First the good news. The perfect is only rarely found in the imperative and subjunctive moods. We need not be concerned with these rare instances here.

Only the infinitive (two voice-forms) and the participle need to be mastered. Again the distinctive reduplication and κ endings make recognition relatively easy.

THE PARTICIPLE

There had to be some bad news. At first sight the forms of the participle are bewildering. This complexity of the participle is mitigated by the fact there are only active and middle/passive voices.

Like some adjectives and pronouns that we will meet later, the active participle endings are a mixture of 3rd declension (masculine and neuter) endings and 1st declension (feminine) endings (like ἡμέρα). It should translate as *loosing* (traditionally: *having loosed*).

The perfect middle/passive is the same as the present middle/passive except for reduplication and the absence of the connecting vowel. It translates *being loosed* (traditionally: *having been loosed*).

PERFECT ACTIVE PARTICIPLES

Masculine	Feminine	Neuter
λελυκώς	λελυκυῖα	λελυκός
λελυκότος	λελυκυίας	λελυκότος
λελυκότι	λελυκυίᾳ	λελυκότι
λελυκότα	λελυκυῖαν	λελυκός
λελυκότες	λελυκυῖαι	λελυκότα
λελυκότων	λελυκυιῶν	λελυκότων
λελυκόσι(ν)	λελυκυίαις	λελυκόσι(ν)
λελυκότας	λελυκυίας	λελυκότα

PERFECT MIDDLE / PASSIVE PARTICIPLE

Masculine	Feminine	Neuter
λελυμένος	λελυμένη	λελυμένον
λελυμένου	λελυμένης	λελυμένου
λελυμένῳ	λελυμένῃ	λελυμένῳ
λελυμένον	λελυμένην	λελυμένον
λελυμένοι	λελυμέναι	λελυμένα
λελυμένων	λελυμένων	λελυμένων
λελυμένοις	λελυμέναις	λελυμένοις
λελυμένους	λελυμένας	λελυμένα

Exercises

1. Translate from Mark:

γέγραπται (1:2)

ἐνδεδυμένος (1:6)

ἤγγικεν (1:15)

ἐσπαρμένον (4:15)

πεποίηκεν (5:19)

γέγονεν (5:33)

σέσωκεν (5:34)

ἐγήγερται (6:14)

ἐξελήλυθεν (7:29)

βεβλημένον (7:30)

βέβληται (9:42)

ἠκολουθήκαμεν (10:28)

Reading Biblical Greek Workbook: Class 2:16–18; Home 2:19–20

62. Verbs Like δύναμαι

Verbs Like δύναμαι

A new verb pattern?

The verb δύναμαι is used six times in Mark 1:1–3:9. It is representative of two other verbs—κάθημαι (see Mark 2:6, 14) and κεῖμαι.

Most lexicons will list these verbs in this form as the present active indicative of the verb. As such they are unlike any verbs we have met so far.

δύναμαι	I am able
κάθημαι	I sit, sit down
κεῖμαι	I lie, recline

However, it helps to think of these as being like perfect passives in form.

Form

Their forms lack connecting vowels, but the endings are the same as perfect and pluperfect middle/passive endings. Their present endings follow the perfect middle/passive of λύω. Their imperfect endings follow the pluperfect middle/passive. Similarly, compare the participle with λυόμενος.

Meaning

These verbs translate like normal present tense-forms.

Indicative of δύναμαι, κάθημαι, κεῖμαι

Present Active	Imperfect Active
δύναμαι	ἐδυνάμην
δύνασαι	ἐδύνασο
δύναται	ἐδύνατο
δυνάμεθα	ἐδυνάμεθα
δύνασθε	ἐδύνασθε
δύνανται	ἐδύναντο

Present Active Participle: δύναμαι, κάθημαι, κεῖμαι

Masculine	Feminine	Neuter
δυνάμενος	δυναμένη	δυνάμενος
δυναμένου	δυναμένης	δυναμένου
etc.		

Exercises

1. Using the table opposite, translate the following:

δύνασαι (1:40)

δυνάμενοι (2:4)

καθήμενοι (2:6)

δύναται (2:7)

καθήμενον (2:14)

δύνανται (2:19)

Vocab #22

63. Pluperfect Tense-Form

Pluperfect Tense-Form

The pluperfect is the only indicative tense-form left to introduce. It does not require the same attention as the perfect, as it is far less frequent (86 instances in the NT). The pluperfect occurs only in the indicative mood, and its endings follow familiar patterns. You should become familiar with the similarities to, and differences from, the perfect.

MEANING

The traditional view of the pluperfect is that it is like the perfect, but one step further into the past. While the perfect is understood to indicate a past event with ongoing consequences, the pluperfect indicates action in the past that may have had ongoing implications for some time but no longer does in the present. It would then be translated as *I had loosed*.

Again, however, we take a different approach. Just as we regard the perfect is a "type of present," the pluperfect is a "type of imperfect," sharing its internal (imperfective) aspect, only with more remoteness than the imperfect.

TRANSLATION

Be aware that the normal convention is to translate the pluperfect as *I had loosed*. We however will translate it like the imperfect, except where context requires otherwise. Occasionally, however, it will be best to translate the pluperfect as *I had loosed* (in line with traditional approaches).

FORMS

The pluperfect may be distinguished from the perfect by an *epsilon* augment prior to the reduplication, though this is frequently dropped. The active has a characteristic *kappa* (κ) with endings like the aorist passive, except that ει is substituted for η. The passive endings have the same first consonant as the perfect middle/passive but then resemble the imperfect mid/pass most of all.

οἶδα (I know)

The verb οἶδα is an "old" perfect, reaching back into very early Greek, and—even according to traditional analyses—is understood like a present. Similarly, the pluperfect of οἶδα is treated like an aorist.

PLUPERFECT INDICATIVE OF λύω

Active	Middle / Passive
(ἐ)λελύκειν	(ἐ)λελύμην
(ἐ)λελύκεις	(ἐ)λέλυσο
(ἐ)λελύκει	(ἐ)λέλυτο
(ἐ)λελύκειμεν	(ἐ)λελύμεθα
(ἐ)λελύκειτε	(ἐ)λέλυσθε
(ἐ)λελύκεισαν	(ἐ)λέλυντο

οἶδα (I know)

οἶδα (perf)	*I know* (pres)
ᾔδειν (pluperf)	*I knew* (aor)
εἰδέναι (inf)	*to know*
εἰδῶ (subj)	*I might know*
PARTICIPLE	
εἰδώς, υἶα, ός, ότος	*knowing*

Exercises

1. Form:

   the pluperfect active of θεραπεύω

   the pluperfect mid/pass of δέω

2. Parse and translate the following verbs:

   Mark

   ᾔδεισαν (1:34)

   ᾔδει (9:6)

   πεποιήκεισαν (15:7)

   Luke

   ᾠκοδόμητο (4:29)

   ἐπεποίθει (11:22)

   ἐβέβλητο (16:20)

   John

   ἀπεληλύθεισαν (4:8)

   ἐληλύθει (7:30)

   εἰρήκει (11:13)

Reading Biblical Greek Workbook: Class 2:21–22; Home 2:23–25

64. οὐ AND μή IN NEGATION

οὐ and μή in Negation	οὐ and μή in Questions	Exercises

οὐ and μή in Negation

Greek has a sophisticated system of *negation*. First, verbs are negated in different ways. Both οὐ (or οὐκ or οὐχ) and μή are adverbs. They are usually translated by *not* in English. While οὐ is used to negate verbs in the indicative mood, μή is used in all other moods and participles.

They are also often found in compounds, like οὐδέ, οὔτε, μηδέ, μήτε (*and not, neither, nor*), and οὐκέτι, μηκέτι (*no longer*).

INDICATIVE

I am **not** (οὐκ εἰμί) worthy to stoop down and untie the thong of his sandals. (Mark 1:7)

IMPERATIVE

Do not be astonished (μὴ θαυμάζετε) at this (John 5:28)

PARTICIPLE

ADVERBIAL

And **not being able** (μὴ δυνάμενοι) to carry him because of the crowd, they removed the roof. (Mark 2:4)

ADJECTIVAL

The one not honoring (ὁ μὴ τιμῶν) the Son does not honor the Father who sent him. (John 5:23)

εἰ μή - EXCEPT, UNLESS

Second, you will meet the phrase εἰ μή (lit. *if not*). This may be translated as *except* or *unless* to fit the context.

οὐ and μή in Questions

Third, οὐ (οὐχί) and μή (μήτι) may also be used in questions (with ;). The presence of either affects the way questions are understood.

A. ORDINARY QUESTIONS (. . . ;)

Ordinary questions simply conclude with a question mark (;).

ἦλθες ἀπολέσαι ἡμᾶς;
Did you come to destroy us? (Mark 1:24)

B. μή . . . ;

μή (or μήτι) at the beginning of a question implies:

i) a *hesitant* question, or
ii) a question expecting *no* as an answer.

Your choice will depend on the context.

μὴ καὶ ὑμεῖς θέλετε αὐτοῦ μαθηταὶ γενέσθαι;
Do you also want to become his disciples?
(John 9:27)

μή τις ἤνεγκεν αὐτῷ φαγεῖν;
Surely no one has brought him something to eat?
(John 4:33)

C. οὐ . . . ;

οὐ (or οὐκ, οὐχ, οὐχί) in a question implies a question expecting **yes** as an answer.

οὐχ οὗτός ἐστιν ὃν ζητοῦσιν ἀποκτεῖναι;
Is not this the man whom they are trying to kill?
(John 7:25)

Exercises

1. Look up the following questions in your English Bible. What Greek constructions would you expect?

   Mark 2:7, 9; 4:38; 6:3 (2x); 8:12; 14:37

2. Look up these questions in John's gospel. What Greek construction would you expect?

   John 4:29, 33; 6:42; 7:42, 52; 9:8, 10, 12, 40

N.B. In some sentences οὐ or μή is used to negate a verb, rather than affect the nature of the question. When affecting a question, they occur at the beginning of a sentence or clause.

ἴδε τί ποιοῦσιν τοῖς σάββασιν ὃ οὐκ ἔξεστιν;

Look, why are they doing what is **not** lawful on the sabbath? (Mark 2:24)

Here, οὐκ negates the verb ἔξεστιν, but does not affect the way the question is construed.

65. Subjunctive Mood

Subjunctive Mood

We have studied the indicative and imperative moods. The second most frequent mood, after the indicative, is the subjunctive mood.

The underlying meaning of the subjunctive mood is *potential* or *probability*. This "kernel" of meaning is not always apparent in particular uses. In some contexts, the mood functions like a future tense-form, in others like an imperative.

Just as with the active voice, the present middle subjunctives simply lengthen the vowel sound at the beginning of the present indicative personal endings. Remember that *iōtas* become subscript.

The aorist active and middle forms use the same endings as the present active and middle, with a *sigma* inserted between stem and endings. The aorist passive uses the same endings as the active, but inserts a *thēta* between stem and endings, rather than a *sigma*. The aorist has no augment in the subjunctive.

The Untranslatable Particle ἄν

This tiny Greek word is often found with the subjunctive. It is not directly translatable, but serves to amplify the sense of indefiniteness.

E.g., *who* (ὅς) + ἄν = *whoever*

Vocab #23

Present Subjunctive of λύω

Active	Middle / Passive
λύω	λύωμαι
λύῃς	λύῃ
λύῃ	λύηται
λύωμεν	λυώμεθα
λύητε	λύησθε
λύωσιν	λύωνται

1st Aorist Subjunctive of λύω

Active	Middle	Passive
λύσω	λύσωμαι	λυθῶ
λύσῃς	λύσῃ	λυθῇς
λύσῃ	λύσηται	λυθῇ
λύσωμεν	λυσώμεθα	λυθῶμεν
λύσητε	λύσησθε	λυθῆτε
λύσωσιν	λύσωνται	λυθῶσιν

Subjunctive of εἰμί

ὦ
ᾖς
ᾖ
ὦμεν
ἦτε
ὦσιν

Exercises

1. Form the present active subjunctive:

   1st person singular of ἐγείρω

   3rd person singular of μισέω

   2nd person plural of σῴζω

   1st person singular of ζητέω

   3rd person plural of δέχομαι

2. Form the aorist passive subjunctive:

   3rd person singular of κηρύσσω

   2nd person plural of βάλλω

   1st person plural of ἀκούω

   2nd person singular of θεραπεύω

   3rd person plural of ἄγω

3. Parse:

   ἀνοίχθης

   αἴρωμεν

   ὦσιν

   βάλωμαι

   ἔλθη

Reading Biblical Greek Workbook: Class 2:26–28; Home 3:1–3

66A. USES OF THE SUBJUNCTIVE

Uses of the Subjunctive	Examples	Exercises
While the inherent meaning of the subjunctive can be a little vague, there are eight key functions that are very clear. The first four functions occur in independent clauses, i.e., clauses that could stand alone as sentences. The subjunctive provides the main verb for the clause.		1. Which of the constructions opposite would you expect to find in the Greek of: What must I do **to be saved**? (Acts 16:30)
1. HORTATORY: SUBJUNCTIVE ALONE IN 1ST PERSON PLURAL The "hortatory" subjunctive is used to urge or invite others (usually companions) to join in an action; i.e. *Let us…* It serves as a kind of 1st person imperative. The subjunctive reflects the possibility of refusal.	1. ἄγωμεν εἰς τὴν Ἰουδαίαν πάλιν. **Let us go** to Judea again. (John 11:7) ἀλλὰ ἄγωμεν πρὸς αὐτόν. But **let us go** to him. (John 11:15)	**Whoever keeps** the whole law, yet stumbles in one point, has become guilty of all. (Jas 2:10) **Do not seal up** the words of the prophecy of this book. (Rev 22:10)
2. DELIBERATIVE: SUBJUNCTIVE ALONE IN 1ST PERSON IN A QUESTION The "deliberative" subjunctive is used for someone thinking "aloud" about what he/she/they should do in certain circumstances. *What shall I …* may reflect a speaker's genuine quandary or it may be just a rhetorical device.	2. τί εἴπω; πάτερ, σῶσόν με ἐκ τῆς ὥρας ταύτης; what **shall I say**? Father, save me from this hour? (John 12:27)	Do not be anxious, saying, "What **should we eat**?" (Matt 6:31) Therefore God highly exalted him…**that** at the name of Jesus every knee **should bend**. (Phil 2:9, 10)
3. PROHIBITION: μή + AORIST SUBJUNCTIVE This is used to forbid someone from performing an action. The majority of these employ the 2nd person subjunctive.	3. μὴ θαυμάσῃς ὅτι εἶπόν σοι· δεῖ ὑμᾶς γεννηθῆναι ἄνωθεν. **Do not be astonished** that I said to you, "You must be born from above." (John 3:7)	**… let us eat and drink** (1 Cor 15:32) **I will not** at all **fail** nor **will I ever leave** you. (Heb 13:5)
4. EMPHATIC FUTURE NEGATIVE: οὐ μή + AORIST SUBJUNCTIVE The "emphatic future negative" rules out a future event in the strongest terms, by denying even the possibility of it happening; i.e., *in no way shall … , will not possibly …, definitely will not …*	4. καὶ τὸν ἐρχόμενον πρὸς ἐμὲ οὐ μὴ ἐκβάλω ἔξω and anyone who comes to me **I will never drive away** (John 6:37) ὁ ἀκολουθῶν ἐμοὶ οὐ μὴ περιπατήσῃ ἐν τῇ σκοτίᾳ, The one who follows me **will never walk** in darkness. (John 8:12)	It is better for him that a millstone **should be tied** round his neck. (Matt 18:6) **Whenever I am weak**, then I am strong. (2 Cor 12:10)

Uses of the Subjunctive *cont.*	Examples	Exercises

More often the subjunctive is used in clauses subordinated to the main clause of a sentence.
 	
5. **Purpose clause:** ἵνα (or ὅπως) + **Subjunctive**
 	
The most common use of the subjunctive, this will usually be translated as a purpose clause: *that he/she might ... , in order to ... , to ...* However, there is some overlap with result or consequence, especially when God is involved leading to a translation like *so that,* or *with the result that ...*
 	
6. **Noun clause:** ἵνα + **Subjunctive**
 	
On rare occasions ἵνα might also introduce a whole clause that functions as though it were a noun. The clause may function as subject, or object, or be explaining another noun or pronoun more fully.
 	
7. **Indefinite Clauses**
 	
  A. **Person: Relative Pronoun** + ἄν + **Subjunctive**
 	
  When ὅς or ὅστις precedes the particle and subjunctive, the indefiniteness is best translated by "whoever" or "whatever."
 	
  B. **Time:** ὅταν + **Subjunctive and** ἄχρι **or** ἕως + (ἄν) + **Subjunctive**
 	
  Phrases like this refer to a future time that is not definitely fixed. ὅταν is a compound of ὅτε ἄν and is rendered in English by "whenever." Both ἄχρι ἄν and ἕως + (ἄν) translate as "until."
 	
8. **Conditions**
 	
  (see 3rd class Conditions in the next lesson)
	5. οὐ γὰρ ἀπέστειλεν ὁ θεὸς τὸν υἱὸν εἰς τὸν κόσμον **ἵνα κρίνῃ** τὸν κόσμον, ἀλλ᾽ **ἵνα σωθῇ** ὁ κόσμος δἰ αὐτον
	For God did not send his son into the world **to judge** the world, but **that the world might be saved** through him (John 3:17)
	
	δόξασόν σου τὸν υἱόν, **ἵνα** ὁ υἱὸς **δοξάσῃ** σέ
	glorify your Son **so that** the Son **may glorify** you (John 17:1)
	
	6. ἐμὸν βρῶμά ἐστιν **ἵνα ποιήσω** τὸ θέλημα τοῦ πέμψαντός με
	My food is **to do** the will of him who sent me (John 4:34)
	
	συμφέρει ὑμῖν **ἵνα** ἐγὼ **ἀπέλθω.**
	it is to your advantage **that I go away.** (John 16:7)
	
	7a. **ὃς** δ᾽ **ἂν πίῃ** ἐκ τοῦ ὕδατος
	but **whoever drinks** of the water (John 4:14)
	
	ὅ τι ἂν λέγῃ ὑμῖν ποιήσατε.
	Do **whatever he says** to you. (John 2:5)
	
	7b. ὁ δὲ χριστὸς **ὅταν ἔρχηται** οὐδεὶς γινώσκει πόθεν ἐστίν.
	but **when** the Messiah **comes,** no-one will know where he is from (John 7:27)
	
	οὐ μὴ ἀλέκτωρ φωνήσῃ **ἕως** οὗ **ἀρνήσῃ** με τρίς.
	a cock shall not crow **until you deny** me three times (John 13:38)
		1. Find subjunctives in the following verses in Mark, and classify them according to the categories opposite:
		
		1:38
		
		1:38
		
		2:10
		
		2:20
		
		3:12
		
		3:14
		
		3:14
		
		3:29
		
		3:35
		
		4:12
		
		4:15
		
		4:22
		
		4:22
		
		4:32
		
		4:35
		
		☑
		
		Reading Biblical Greek Workbook: Class 3:4–6; Home 3:7–9

67A. Conditions

Conditions	Examples	Exercises
Conditional sentences make an "*if x, then y*" kind of statement; e.g., *If we we say we have no sin, (then) we deceive ourselves* (1 John 1:8).	**FIRST CLASS: CONDITIONS OF "FACT"**	1. Identify the class(es) of condition with:

Conditional sentences make an "*if x, then y*" kind of statement; e.g., *If we we say we have no sin, (then) we deceive ourselves* (1 John 1:8).

PROTASIS AND APODOSIS

Conditional statements are divided into two parts. The technical name for the first part (*if . . .*) is the *protasis*. The second half (*then . . .*) is known as the *apodosis*.

THREE MAIN CLASSES

Greek can generate different types of conditions by verbal mood, tense-form, and the choice of particles in either half of the sentence. These affect how the protasis is understood from the point of view of the speaker. "Fact" and "contrary to fact" are not descriptions of reality so much as how the speaker chooses to portray the situation.

FIRST CLASS: CONDITIONS OF "FACT"

First class conditions assume that the protasis is true.

Protasis	Apodosis
εἰ + indicative (any tense)	negate with οὐ any mood, any tense

---

FIRST CLASS: CONDITIONS OF "FACT"

PRESENT

εἰ ἀλήθειαν λέγω, διὰ τί ὑμεῖς οὐ πιστεύετέ μοι;
If I tell the truth, why do you not believe me?
(John 8:46)

PAST

εἰ ἐμὲ ἐδίωξαν, καὶ ὑμᾶς διώξουσιν·
If they persecuted me, they will persecute you.
(John 15:20)

---

1. Identify the class(es) of condition with:

   ἄν in the apodosis?

   εἰ in the protasis?

   ἐάν in the protasis?

   a present indicative in the protasis?

   a subjunctive in the protasis?

Conditions *cont.*	Examples	Exercises
SECOND CLASS: "CONTRARY TO FACT"	**SECOND CLASS: "CONTRARY TO FACT"**	**1.** Classify and translate these conditions in Mark:

SECOND CLASS: "CONTRARY TO FACT"

In second class conditions, the protasis is assumed to be false, and the apodosis contains ἄν.

N.B. imperfect often translates as present in the protasis.

Protasis	Apodosis
εἰ + indicative	ἄν + indicative
(aorist or imperfect); negate with μή	(same tense-form as protasis)

Examples — SECOND CLASS: "CONTRARY TO FACT"

PRESENT

εἰ γὰρ ἐπιστεύετε Μωϋσεῖ, ἐπιστεύετε **ἄν** ἐμοί·
If you believed Moses (but you don't), you would believe me. (John 5:46)

PAST

εἰ ἦς ὧδε οὐκ **ἄν** ἀπέθανεν ὁ ἀδελφός μου·
if you had been here (but you weren't), my brother would not have died. (John 11:21)

Exercises

1:40

3:26

3:27

3:28

14:29

14:35

THIRD CLASS: FUTURE CONDITIONS

Third class conditions express statements that will or may occur in the future, or are generally true, or are hypothetical. Thus the subjunctive is a key feature of these conditions.

Protasis	Apodosis
ἐάν + subjunctive;	any mood, any tense
negate with μή	

Examples — THIRD CLASS: FUTURE CONDITIONS

ἐάν τις τὸν λόγον μου **τηρήσῃ**, οὐ μὴ γεύσηται θανάτου εἰς τὸν αἰῶνα.
If anyone **keeps** my word, he will never taste death. (John 8:52)

οὐκ εἶπόν σοι ὅτι **ἐὰν πιστεύσῃς** ὄψῃ τὴν δόξαν τοῦ θεοῦ;
Did I not tell you that **if you believed**, you would see the glory of God? (John 11:40)

ἐὰν ἐγὼ **δοξάσω** ἐμαυτόν, ἡ δόξα μου οὐδέν ἐστιν
If I glorify myself, my glory is nothing. (John 8:54)

68. Adverbs

Adverbs	Examples	Exercises

Adverbs

Adverbs are a part of speech we have not yet addressed directly. They are to verbs what adjectives are to nouns: adverbs qualify verbs (e.g., The boy ran quickly).

In English adverbs are often formed by adding –*ly* to the end of an adjective. But there are many irregularities: true → truly; good → well.

Mastery of the adverb endings greatly extends vocabulary. In Greek, many adverbs are formed from the "stem" of an adjective.

The final two letters (ος or ης) of the lexicon form of the adjective (masc nom sg) are replaced by ως:

| ἀληθής | *true* | δίκαιος | *righteous* |
| ἀληθῶς | *truly* | δικαιῶς | *righteously* |

Not all Greek adverbs are formed this way. You have already learned some adverbs as vocabulary items, such as εὐθύς, νῦν, πάλιν, ὧδε. You will encounter many more.

Different adverbs function in different ways:

Adverbs of place answer the question, *where?*

time	*when?*
manner	*how?*
degree	e.g., *more, greater*

Interrogative adverbs introduce questions.

Examples

Καὶ **εὐθὺς** τὸ πνεῦμα αὐτὸν ἐκβάλλει εἰς τὴν ἔρημον.
And the Spirit **immediately** drove him out into the wilderness. (Mark 1:12)

ἃ γὰρ ἂν ἐκεῖνος ποιῇ, ταῦτα καὶ ὁ υἱὸς **ὁμοίως** ποιεῖ.
for whatever the Father does, the Son does **likewise.** (John 5:19)

καὶ ἦν **ἐκεῖ** ἄνθρωπος ἐξηραμμένην ἔχων τὴν χεῖρα.
and a man was **there** who had a withered hand. (Mark 3:1)

πῶς δύναται Σατανᾶς Σατανᾶν ἐκβάλλειν;
How can Satan cast out Satan? (Mark 3:23)

Exercises

1. Translate the following from Mark, and identify the verb being qualified:

ἐσχάτως (5:23)

καλῶς (7:37)

οὕτως (10:43)

ἀληθῶς (14:70)

Vocab #24

Reading Biblical Greek Workbook: Class 3:10 – 12; Home 3:13 – 15

69A. 3RD DECLENSION NOUNS: MASCULINE AND FEMININE

3rd Declension Nouns: Masculine & Feminine	Exercises

We now return to complete our study of the Greek noun system. We have already studied first and second declension nouns. The third declension simply gathers together all of the leftover noun forms. Learning this declension provides a significant advance in vocabulary.

ENDINGS

The participle takes third declension endings, which means that we have already learned most of the forms. The nominative singular forms vary, but the remaining forms should be familiar.

THE NOUN STEM

The nominative singular form is rarely a guide to discerning the noun stem. Therefore, the stem of a third declension noun should be found by taking ος off the genitive form.

The third declension masculine and feminine nouns are divided into two main groups, according to whether the stem ends in a consonant or vowel.

CONSONANT STEM ENDING

Many third declension nouns whose stems end in a consonant follow the same pattern as ἀστήρ (*see right*). The same endings are added to the noun stem (see the genitive singular). Both masculine and feminine nouns are found in this category. There are three important words that follow a variation on this declension: three "family" words, father (πατήρ), mother (μήτηρ), and daughter (θυγάτηρ), all of which drop the ε in the stem at certain points.

FORMING THE DATIVE PLURAL

The vocabulary list contains a number of nouns for which the addition of -σιν to form the dative plural affects final consonants. These follow rules we have already seen.

STEMS ENDING IN A CONSONANT

Sg	Nom	ἀστήρ	πατήρ
	Gen	ἀστέρος	πατρός
	Dat	ἀστέρι	πατρί
	Acc	ἀστέρα	πατέρα
Pl	Nom	ἀστέρες	πατέρες
	Gen	ἀστέρων	πατέρων
	Dat	ἀστράσιν	πατράσιν
	Acc	ἀστέρας	πατέρας

RULES FOR THE DATIVE PLURAL

κ, γ, χ	+	σιν	=	ξιν
π, β, φ	+	σιν	=	ψιν
τ, δ, θ, ν	+	σιν	=	σιν
αντ	+	σιν	=	ασιν
εντ	+	σιν	=	εισιν
οντ	+	σιν	=	ουσιν

Exercises

1. Form the dative plural of:

    γυνή

    νύξ

    πούς

    μήτηρ

2. Parse the following 3rd declension nouns from Mark:

    πατέρα (1:20)

    χεῖρα (1:41)

    Σίμωνι (3:16)

    εἰς τὸν αἰῶνα (3:29)

    μήτηρ (3:31)

    νύκτα (4:27)

🔒

Vocab #25

3rd Declension Nouns: Masculine & Feminine *cont.*		Exercises
VOWEL STEM ENDING	**STEMS ENDING IN A VOWEL**	

Vowel Stem Ending / Stems Ending in a Vowel

Nouns like πόλις and βασιλεύς are quite different from ἀστήρ. Their noun stems end with a vowel rather than a consonant.

Words like πόλις are always feminine. Words like βασιλεύς are always masculine. In form, they differ only in accusative singular and dative plural. Both have the same plural nominative and accusative form.

		Feminine	Masculine
Sg	**Nom**	πόλις	βασιλεύς
	Gen	πόλεως	βασιλέως
	Dat	πόλει	βασιλεῖ
	Acc	πόλιν	βασιλέα
Pl	**Nom**	πόλεις	βασιλεῖς
	Gen	πόλεων	βασιλέων
	Dat	πόλεσιν	βασιλεῦσιν
	Acc	πόλεις	βασιλεῖς

Exercises

1. Parse the following 3rd declension nouns from Mark:

ἄφεσιν (1:4)

γραμματεῖς (1:22)

πόλις (1:33)

πόλιν (1:45)

γραμματέων (2:6)

ἀρχιερέως (2:26)

ἱερεῖς (2:26)

θλίψεως (4:17)

Reading Biblical Greek Workbook: Class 3:16–19; Home 3:20–22

70. 3rd Declension Nouns: Neuter

3rd Declension Nouns: Neuter	Neuter Nouns	Exercises

3rd Declension Nouns: Neuter

To complete the third declension nouns, we need to become familiar with two groups of neuter nouns. As with all neuter nouns:

a) nominative and accusative forms are the same
b) nominative and accusative plural forms end with an α sound

> i.e., τέλε + α = τέλη

c) plural neuter nouns take a singular verb

It is important to learn these nouns under their lexical form. From σῶμα, ατος, το one can determine the stem to which endings are added and the gender of the noun.

τέλος seems to depart significantly from the pattern. Originally the stem was τέλες, and once the *sigma* is dropped the endings make more sense. Note that, words like τέλος, ους, το are easily confused with the λόγος, ου, ὁ group.

3rd Declension Adjectives

It is appropriate to turn to two types of third declension adjectives at this point. They follow the third declension noun formations (the feminine does not have a separate first declension form). They are most like the neuter nouns, and thus fall into two types:

πλείων (*more*) represents a group of comparative adjectives. While the form is best learned now, the meaning will be explored in the next section. The masculine/feminine endings resemble ἀστήρ, while the neuter endings resemble σῶμα.

ἀληθής is most like γένος, especially in the neuter.

Neuter Nouns

		Type 1	Type 2
Sg	Nom	σῶμα	τέλος
	Gen	σώματος	τέλους
	Dat	σώματι	τέλει
	Acc	σῶμα	τέλος
Pl	Nom	σώματα	τέλη
	Gen	σωμάτων	τελῶν
	Dat	σώμασιν	τέλεσιν
	Acc	σώματα	τέλη

Adjectives

Type 1		Type 2	
Masc/Fem	Neut	Masc/Fem	Neut
πλείων	πλεῖον	ἀληθής	ἀληθές
πλείονος	πλείονος	ἀληθοῦς	ἀληθοῦς
πλείονι	πλείονι	ἀληθεῖ	ἀληθεῖ
πλείονα	πλεῖον	ἀληθῆ	ἀληθές
πλείονες	πλείονα	ἀληθεῖς	ἀληθῆ
πλειόνων	πλειόνων	ἀληθῶν	ἀληθῶν
πλείοσιν	πλείοσιν	ἀληθέσιν	ἀληθέσιν
πλείονας	πλείονα	ἀληθεῖς	ἀληθῆ

Exercises

1. Parse and translate the following 3rd declension nouns from Mark:

ὕδατι (1:8)

πνεύματι (1:8)

πνεῦμα (1:10)

πνεύμασι (1:27)

πνεύματα (3:11)

ὄρος (3:13)

ὄνομα (3:16)

θέλημα (3:35)

ὦτα (4:23)

Vocab #26

3rd Declension Pronouns: τίς

We have studied various types of pronouns (personal, demonstrative, reflexive, and relative pronouns). Now we turn to two more types of pronouns that follow the third declension adjectives in their formation.

Form

The form of τίς follows third declension formations, and most resembles πλεῖων.

Meaning

τίς can have a wide range of meanings. Its two main uses are distinguished by accents, as seen below.

Interrogative Pronoun τίς, τί, τίνος

First, the interrogative pronoun always has an acute accent on the first syllable (τίς, τίνων, etc.), and is used in questions to ask *who?*, *which person?*, *what thing?*, or even *why?* (i.e., *what [reason]?*).

Indefinite Pronoun τις, τι, τινός

Second, the indefinite pronoun (*anyone, someone, something, a certain person or thing*) is used to refer generally to a person or thing without naming or specifying them.

It will normally have *no accent* at all (τις). However, there are *three possible exceptions* to this:

1. Sometimes the second syllable is accented (τινός, τινὸς)

2. The first syllable can carry a grave accent (τὶς, τὶ)

3. Rarely, the first syllable may have an acute accent (τίς), thus making it indistinguishable from the interrogative pronoun, apart from context (e.g. John 12:47).

ὅστις

By compounding the relative and indefinite pronouns, Greek can form an *indefinite relative* pronoun ὅστις, which means *whoever*. However, by the time of the NT, this form has come to overlap significantly with the normal relative pronoun, often showing no real distinction. In other instances, its indefiniteness *is* clearly observed.

Interrogative and Indefinite Pronouns*

		Masculine / Feminine	Neuter
Sg	Nom	τίς	τί
	Gen	τίνος	τίνος
	Dat	τίνι	τίνι
	Acc	τίνα	τί
Pl	Nom	τίνες	τίνα
	Gen	τίνων	τίνων
	Dat	τίσιν	τίσιν
	Acc	τίνας	τίνα

*The accents here are for the interrogative

Indefinite Relative Pronoun ὅστις

		Masc	Fem	Neut
Sg	Nom	ὅστις	ἥτις	ὅτι
Pl	Nom	οἵτινες	αἵτινες	ἅτινα

Vocab #27

Exercises

1. Find, parse, and classify examples of τις, τίς and ὅστις in these verses in Mark:

1:24

2:6

2:18

3:33

4:20

4:23

5:31

7:5

8:23

8:29

11:13

12:9

12:13

15:14

15:35

Reading Biblical Greek Workbook: Class 3:23 – 26; Home 3:27 – 30

72. Adjectives of 3rd and 1st Declensions

Adjectives of 3rd & 1st Declensions	3rd and 1st	Exercises

A small number of adjectives take third declension endings for their masculine and neuter forms, and first declension endings for the feminine. While most other adjectives follow second and first declensions (2 – 1 – 2), these are 3 – 1 – 3.

πᾶς

The word πᾶς is very common and is usually translated by *every* (when followed by single noun) or *all* (with a plural noun). Sometimes *everyone*, *everything* or *the whole* will be appropriate.

The feminine forms follow δόξα. Usage will mostly fall into three basic categories:
  a. As an adjective, with noun and article, in the predicative position
  b. As an adjective, with noun only
  c. As a noun substitute, with πᾶς on its own

εἷς

The word εἷς, *one*, needs no plural. It can be used to mean *alone* or *only* (Mark 2:7), or as a noun substitute (*one* man). The feminine follows ὥρα. Be careful not to confuse it with the prepositions εἰς or ἐν.

οὐδείς

The word εἷς may be found in a compound word with οὐ (indicative) or μή (other moods) to mean *no one* or *nothing*. The endings follow the declension of εἷς, but note the *epsilon* in the feminine.

N.B. In Greek, *two negatives do not cancel each other out*. In English, *I did not give it to no-one* means *I gave it to someone*. The same literal Greek sentence means the opposite, *I gave it to no-one* or *I did not give it to anyone*.

πᾶς, πᾶσα, πᾶν, παντός (ALL, EVERY)

Sg	Nom	πᾶς	πᾶσα	πᾶν
	Gen	παντός	πάσης	παντός
	Dat	παντί	πάσῃ	παντί
	Acc	πάντα	πᾶσαν	πᾶν
Pl	Nom	πάντες	πᾶσαι	πάντα
	Gen	πάντων	πασῶν	πάντων
	Dat	πᾶσιν	πάσαις	πᾶσιν
	Acc	πάντας	πάσας	πάντα

εἷς, μία, ἕν, ἑνός (ONE)

Nom	εἷς	μία	ἕν
Gen	ἑνός	μιᾶς	ἑνός
Dat	ἑνί	μιᾷ	ἑνί
Acc	ἕνα	μίαν	ἕν

οὐδείς (NO-ONE, NOTHING)

Indicative			Other moods		
οὐδείς	οὐδεμία	οὐδέν	μηδείς	μηδεμία	μηδέν
οὐδενός	-εμιᾶς	-ενός	etc.		
οὐδενί	-εμιᾷ	-ενί	etc.		
οὐδένα	-εμίαν	-έν	etc.		

Exercises

1. Parse and translate πᾶς from Mark:

   1:5

   1:32, 37

   2:13

   4:1

   4:13

   5:5

   5:20

   5:33

   6:33

   7:18

2. Express in Greek:

   one hand

   one word

   one woman

   one prophet

πολύς and μέγας	1st & 2nd Declension	Exercises

πολύς and μέγας

Two remaining adjectives require a little special attention. They are addressed at this point because the noun stem is derived from the genitive (as also happens with third declension adjectives).

πολύς (*much* sg; *many* pl) and μέγας (*great*) need little explanation in English.

Their form is very much like ἀγαθός, ή, όν, except for the masculine and neuter nominative and accusative. That is, apart from those forms, they follow second and first declension endings (2–1–2).

1st & 2nd Declension

πολύς (MUCH, MANY)

Sg	**Nom**	πολύς	πολλή	πολύ
	Gen	πολλοῦ	πολλῆς	πολλοῦ
	Dat	πολλῷ	πολλῇ	πολλῷ
	Acc	πολύν	πολλήν	πολύ
Pl	**Nom**	πολλοί	πολλαί	πολλά
	Gen	πολλῶν	πολλῶν	πολλῶν
	Dat	πολλοῖς	πολλαῖς	πολλοῖς
	Acc	πολλούς	πολλάς	πολλά

μέγας (GREAT)

Sg	**Nom**	μέγας	μεγάλη	μέγα
	Gen	μεγάλου	μεγάλης	μεγάλου
	Dat	μεγάλῳ	μεγάλη	μεγάλῳ
	Acc	μέγαν	μεγάλην	μέγα
Pl	**Nom**	μεγάλοι	μεγάλαι	μεγάλα
	Gen	μεγάλων	μεγάλων	μεγάλων
	Dat	μεγάλοις	μεγάλαις	μεγάλοις
	Acc	μεγάλους	μεγάλας	μεγάλα

Exercises

1. Translate these phrases from Mark:

ἐθεράπευσεν πολλούς (1:34)

οὐδεὶς βάλλει οἶνον (2:22)

παραβολαῖς πολλαῖς ἐλάλει αὐτοῖς (4:33)

ἐφοβήθησαν φόβον μέγαν (4:41)

κράξας φωνῇ μεγάλῃ λέγει (5:7)

δαιμόνια πολλὰ ἐξέβαλλον (6:13)

οὐδεὶς ἀγαθός (10:18)

οἱ μεγάλοι αὐτῶν (10:42)

οὐκ ἀποκρίνῃ οὐδέν (14:60)

οὐδενὶ οὐδὲν εἶπαν (16:8)

2. Express in Greek:

great works

every person

he ate nothing

much hardship

all sinners

many days

everything

the whole crowd

Reading Biblical Greek Workbook: Class 3:31–32; Home 3:33–35

74. The Infinitive

The Infinitive

The infinitive is a verbal noun. As the name implies, the infinitive is the most general form of the verb; it does not express a subject, like the finite verbs do, but just the verbal idea.

The infinitive is *indeclinable* (i.e., no case or number), but it is considered *neuter*.

The so-called articular infinitive adds the singular neuter article to underscore the noun side of the infinitive. This article declines as required.

Meaning

The infinitive is usually translated by placing *to …* in front of the verb (e.g., λύειν = *to loose*). The present tense-form expresses internal (imperfective) aspect; the aorist expresses external (perfective) aspect. We will translate both present and aorist infinitives as *to loose* (or *to be loosed* in the passive voice).

Form

The infinitive has no augment. Nearly all infinitives end in αι (except the present and 2nd aorist active).

> The present is built from present stem endings.
>
> The 1st aorist is built from the verbal root and aorist endings.
>
> The 2nd aorist combines the verbal root and present endings.
>
> The infinitive is negated by μή.

Accusative of Respect

Technically, the infinitive does not have a subject. In some contexts, however, a noun in the **accusative** will function like a subject. You will need to decide from the context whether an accusative noun with an infinitive is the subject or object of the verbal process implied. E.g. δοξάζειν τὸν θεόν in Mark 2:12 implies there was a 'glorifying' process *with respect to* God, but did someone *glorify God* OR did *God glorify*? From the context, we can infer that Jesus's miracle caused *all the people to glorify God*.

Present

Active	Middle /Passive
λύειν	λύεσθαι

1st Aorist

Active	Middle	Passive
λῦσαι	λύσασθαι	λυθῆναι

2nd Aorist

Active	Middle	Passive
βαλεῖν	βαλέσθαι	βληθῆναι

Perfect

Active	Middle /Passive
λελυκέναι	λελύσθαι

εἰμί

εἶναι

Common Constructions

Infinitive alone

ὥστε + infinitive

τό + infinitive

Preposition + neuter article + infinitive

Exercises

1. Express the following in Greek:

to call (aorist)

to be made (present)

to baptize (aorist)

to be thrown (present)

to preach (aorist)

Vocab #28

75. Uses of the Infinitive

Uses of the Infinitive

As a verbal noun, the infinitive may function as a noun, adjective, or adverb.

The noun and adjective functions are listed below, but our focus will be on the *adverbial* functions.

As a Noun

Subject

ῥαββί, καλόν ἐστιν ἡμᾶς ὧδε **εἶναι**

Rabbi, it is good for us **to be** here (…to be here is good) (Mark 9:5)

Object

τῷ υἱῷ ἔδωκεν ζωὴν **ἔχειν** ἐν ἑαυτῷ

he has granted the Son also **to have** life in himself (John 5:26)

In Apposition

Τοῦτο γάρ ἐστιν θέλημα τοῦ θεοῦ, ὁ ἁγιασμὸς ὑμῶν, **ἀπέχεσθαι** ὑμᾶς ἀπὸ τῆς πορνείας

For this is the will of God, your sanctification: **that you abstain** from fornication (1 Thess 4:3)

Reported Speech

ἤρξαντο παρακαλεῖν αὐτὸν **ἀπελθεῖν**

they began to beg Jesus **to leave** (Mark 5:17)

As an Adjective

Explanatory or Epexegetical

δέδωκα ὑμῖν τὴν ἐξουσίαν **τοῦ πατεῖν** ἐπάνω ὄφεων

I have given you authority **to tread** on snakes (Luke 10:19)

As an Adverb

1. Complement

Some verbs in Greek (and in English) are incomplete and need the infinitive to fill them out. The subject of both verb and infinitive will tend to be nominative. The most common are: ἄρχομαι, βούλομαι, δύναμαι, ζητέω, θέλω, μέλλω, ὀφείλω.

ἤρξατο διδάσκειν παρὰ τὴν θάλασσαν:

he **began to teach** beside the sea (Mark 4:1)

2. Purpose

The goal or intention of a process can be expressed by τοῦ + infinitive, εἰς τό + infinitive, πρὸς τό + infinitive, or the infinitive alone. This answers the question "why?" regarding the action expressed by the finite verb. The translation *to loose* carries this implication, but *in order to loose* makes it clearer.

ἐξῆλθεν ὁ σπείρων **σπεῖραι**

A sower went out **to sow** (Mark 4:3)

3. Result

The result or consequence of the process as expressed by the finite verb is indicated by ὥστε + infinitive. It answers the question, "what resulted?" from the process of the finite verb, in terms of its effects. Translate *so that, with the result that.*

συνέρχεται πάλιν [ὁ] ὄχλος, **ὥστε μὴ δύνασθαι** αὐτοὺς μηδὲ ἄρτον φαγεῖν

the crowd came together again, **so that** they **could not** even eat (Mark 3:20)

4. Cause

The cause of a process answers "why?" by indicating its ground or reason. This is expressed in Greek by διὰ τό + infinitive. Translate *because* followed by an appropriate finite expression.

διὰ τὸ μὴ ἔχειν ῥίζαν ἐξηράνθη

and **since** it **had no** root, it withered away (Mark 4:6)

5. Time

The articular infinitive preceded by a range of prepositions may be used to answer the question "when?" regarding the process of a finite verb.

a. **Before:** πρὸ τοῦ OR πρίν (ἤ) + infinitive

ὁ πατὴρ ὑμῶν ὧν χρείαν ἔχετε **πρὸ τοῦ** ὑμᾶς **αἰτῆσαι** αὐτόν.

your Father knows what you need **before** you **ask** him (Matt 6:8)

b. **While, as, when:** ἐν τῷ + infinitive

ἐν τῷ σπείρειν ὃ μὲν ἔπεσεν παρὰ τὴν ὁδόν

as he sowed, some seed fell on the path (Mark 4:4)

c. **After:** μετὰ τό + infinitive

μετὰ τὸ ἐγερθῆναί με προάξω ὑμᾶς

after I am **raised up**, I will go before you (Mark 14:28)

☑

Reading Biblical Greek Workbook: Class 4:1–3; Home 4:4–6

76. Contract Verbs αω

Contract Verbs αω

We have long been familiar with the εω contract verbs. Verbs ending in αω follow similar principles and require only the learning of some new rules of contraction.

Aorist, Future, Perfect, & Pluperfect

Lengthening α to η

In the case of future (add σ or θ), aorist (add σ or θ), and perfect (add κ, etc.) tense-forms, verbs ending in αω behave the same as those ending in εω; *alpha* lengthens to *ēta* before these letters are added. Since the present and verb stems are the same, there is no need to worry about, e.g., second aorists (*see* Principal Parts).

Present & Imperfect

New Rules of Contraction

For the present and imperfect tense-forms some contractions will differ from εω verbs. In some cases, no contraction is necessary. However, *alpha* will combine with some vowels differently. Rules of contraction are:

α + o, ω, ου = ω   γεννῶμεν

α + ε, η = α   γεννᾶτε

α + ει, η = ᾳ   γεννᾶν

N.B. Present indicative and subjunctive forms are indistinguishable.

Two Exceptions

1. The present active infinitive is γεννᾶν (rather than γεννᾷν, as the rules would suggest).

2. For the important verb ζάω, η replaces α in the contracted forms.

γεννάω

Present Indicative & Subjunctive

Active	Middle / Passive
γεννῶ	γεννῶμαι
γεννᾷς	γεννᾷ
γεννᾷ	γεννᾶται
γεννῶμεν	γεννώμεθα
γεννᾶτε	γεννᾶσθε
γεννῶσιν	γεννῶνται

Imperfect Indicative

Active	Middle / Passive
ἐγέννων	ἐγεννώμην
ἐγέννας	ἐγεννῶ
ἐγέννα	ἐγεννᾶτο
ἐγεννῶμεν	ἐγεννώμεθα
ἐγεννᾶτε	ἐγεννᾶσθε
ἐγέννων	ἐγεννῶντο

Present

Imperative		Infinitive	
Active	Middle / Passive	Active	Middle / Passive
γέννα	γεννῶ	γεννᾶν	γεννᾶσθαι
γεννάτω	γεννάσθω		
γεννᾶτε	γεννᾶσθε		
γεννάτωσαν	γεννάσθωσαν		

Exercises

1. For the verb ἀγαπάω, form:

   aorist active indicative

   imperfect middle/passive

   present active imperative

   future passive indicative

   present active subjunctive

   present active (fem) participle

2. For the verb ζάω, form:

   present mid/pass indicative

   imperfect active indicative

3. Parse the following verbs from Mark:

   ἐπετίμησεν (1:25)

   ὅρα (1:44)

   ἠρώτων (4:10)

   ἐπηρώτα (5:9)

   ζήσῃ (5:23)

   τιμᾷ (7:6)

   πλανᾶσθε (12:24)

   ἀγαπήσεις (12:30)

   ἐγεννήθη (14:21)

77. CONTRACT VERBS οω

Contract Verbs οω

Verbs in οω require more new learning than the αω verbs. They follow the same principles as εω and αω verbs and represent a smaller pool of vocabulary. However, the present indicative and subjunctive of οω verbs *do* differ in form.

AORIST, FUTURE, PERFECT, & PLUPERFECT

LENGTHENING ο TO ω

When consonants (σ, θ, κ, etc.) are added to the verb stem, *omicron* lengthens to *ōmega* rather than *ēta* (*see* Principal Parts).

PRESENT & IMPERFECT

NEW RULES OF CONTRACTION

Naturally the omicron at the end of the verb stem will combine in distinctive ways when various vowels are added. These rules of contraction are:

ο	+	long vowel (η, ω)	=	ω
ο	+	short vowel (ε, ο), ου	=	ου
ο	+	ι (incl. ει, οι, η)	=	οι

N.B. Present indicative and subjunctive do differ at points.

AN EXCEPTION
1. Present active infinitive is φανεροῦν (rather than φανεροῖν, as the rules would suggest).

φανερόω

PRESENT

Indicative		Subjunctive	
Active	**Middle / Passive**	**Active**	**Middle / Passive**
φανερῶ	φανεροῦμαι	φανερῶ	φανερῶμαι
φανεροῖς	φανεροῖ	φανεροῖς	φανεροῖ
φανεροῖ	φανεροῦται	φανεροῖ	φανερῶται
φανεροῦμεν	φανερούμεθα	φανερῶμεν	φανερώμεθα
φανεροῦτε	φανεροῦσθε	φανερῶτε	φανερῶσθε
φανεροῦσιν	φανεροῦνται	φανερῶσιν	φανερῶνται

IMPERFECT INDICATIVE

Active	**Middle / Passive**
ἐφανέρουν	ἐφανερούμην
ἐφανέρους	ἐφανεροῦ
ἐφανέρου	ἐφανεροῦτο
ἐφανεροῦμεν	ἐφανερούμεθα
ἐφανεροῦτε	ἐφανεροῦσθε
ἐφανέρουν	ἐφανεροῦντο

PRESENT

Imperative		Infinitive	
Active	**Middle / Passive**	**Active**	**Middle / Passive**
φανέρου	φανεροῦ	φανεροῦν	φανεροῦσθαι
φανερούτω	φανερούσθω		
φανεροῦτε	φανεροῦσθε		
φανερούτωσαν	φανερούσθωσαν		

Exercises

1. For the verb πληρόω, form:

   aorist active indicative

   imperfect middle/passive

   present active imperative

   future passive indicative

   present active subjunctive

   present active (fem) participle

2. Parse the following verbs from Matthew and Mark:

   ἐδικαιώθη (Matt 11:19)

   δικαιωθήσῃ (Matt 12:37)

   πεπλήρωται (Mark 1:15)

   φανερωθῇ (Mark 4:22)

   πληρωθῶσιν (Mark 14:49)

   σταύρωσον (Mark 15:13)

   σταυρωθῇ (Mark 15:15)

   σταυροῦσιν (Mark 15:24)

Vocab #29

Reading Biblical Greek Workbook: Class 4:7–9; Home 4:10–13

78A. PRAGMATICS OF PARTICIPLES

Pragmatics of Participles	Examples	Exercises
We are familiar with the distinction between adjectival (usually preceded by the article) and adverbial participles. Now we turn to the way adverbial participles qualify or modify the main verb. English versions of the NT rarely leave participles as *-ing* words. They make decisions about the relationship between a participle and the verb it qualifies. ## DEMYSTIFYING THE PROCESS It's worth being familiar with technical terms used by grammars. But we must be sensitive to the interpretative decisions being made. To label a participle "causal," for example, might make one think that the participle carries that meaning in its form, but this is not the case. The participle *form* contributes only lexical information (root meaning) and aspect; causality can by inferred only from the *context*. ## VARIOUS RELATIONSHIPS The relationship between an adverbial participle and its main verb may be understood in terms of: ### I. TEMPORAL RELATIONSHIP — HAVING, AFTER, AS, WHEN, BEFORE I.e., Relative time—the process described by the participle may have occurred *before*, at the *same time as* (or overlapping with), or *after* the main verb. Aspect is the key contributor to these temporal relationships. The aorist (external, or perfective, aspect) may be used for *events or actions that precede the main verb or occur after the main verb*. The present participle (internal, or imperfective, aspect) is preferred for *overlapping or simultaneous action*, or even an *event yet to take place*. The perfect (internal, or imperfective, aspect) *parallels the present* in temporal reference. Nevertheless, these temporal relationships are not the core meaning of participles. Verbal aspect is core, and this is often expressed through temporal relationships. As such, we will occasionally find aorist participles that occur at the same time as the main verb (e.g., with participles of attendant circumstance) and present participles that precede the main verb (with verbs of coming, going, etc.). Allow context to be your guide.	1. καὶ **ἀνοίξας** τὸ στόμα αὐτοῦ ἐδίδασκεν αὐτοὺς λέγων· and **having opened** his mouth, he was teaching them, saying (Matt 5:2) καὶ **ἐλθὼν** ἐκεῖνος ἐλέγξει τὸν κόσμον and **after he has come**, that one will convict the world (John 16:8)	1. Find adverbial participles in Mark 1:1–15. Identify the main verb they coordinate with. Choose the most likely relationship between them (ignore v. 6 and v. 13; these are periphrastic participles).

Pragmatics of Participles *cont.*	Examples	Exercises
2. Causal Relationship — because A participle may be used to indicate the cause of an action or event. **3. Concessive Relationship — although** In this case the participle concedes an exception, or admits an alternative point, and could be translated *although* or *despite*. Sometimes particles like καίπερ, καὶ γε, and καίτοι are used to make this clearer. **4. Conditional — if** A clause containing a participle may function as the protasis in a conditional-sounding sentence. **5. Instrumental — by** A participle may indicate the instrument, manner, or means by which an action takes place. **6. Purpose — in order to** A participle may be used to show the purpose or intended result of an action. Occasionally the rare future participle is used (e.g., Matt 27:49). **N.B.** The wide range of possibilities should serve as a caution against prematurely rendering a participle in a particular way.	2. οἱ πατριάρχαι **ζηλώσαντες** τὸν Ἰωσὴφ ἀπέδοντο εἰς Αἴγυπτον **because** the patriarchs **were jealous** of Joseph, they sold him to Egypt (Acts 7:9) 3. εἰ οὖν ὑμεῖς πονηροὶ **ὄντες** οἴδατε δόματα ἀγαθὰ διδόναι **although you are** evil, you know how to give good gifts (Matt 7:11) 4. ἐξ ὧν **διατηροῦντες** ἑαυτοὺς εὖ πράξετε **if you keep** yourselves from such things, you will do well (Acts 15:29) 5. **ἁψάμενος** τοῦ ὠτίου ἰάσατο αὐτόν. **by touching** the ear, he healed him (Luke 22:51) 6. ἀνέστη **ἐκπειράζων** αὐτόν he stood up **in order to test** him (Luke 10:25)	1. Decide the most likely relationship between the participles below and their main verb. Compare with an English version. ὢν (Matt 1:19) πιστεύοντες (Matt 21:22) βαπτίζοντες, διδάσκοντες (Matt 28:19, 20) πειράζοντες (Mark 8:11) ἔχοντες (Mark 8:18) ἰδόντες (Mark 9:15)
The Genitive Absolute	**The Genitive Absolute**	
Occasionally a participle describes action which is clearly related to the action of the main verb but which has no formal grammatical link to it. The subject of the participle is not the subject of the main verb. The participial phrase will be expressed in Greek by the genitive case. It is called the *genitive absolute* because it is *loosed* grammatically from the main verb's clause.	Καὶ εὐθὺς ἔτι **αὐτοῦ λαλοῦντος** παραγίνεται Ἰούδας And immediately, while (**Jesus is**) **speaking**, Judas arrives (Mark 14:43)	☑ *Reading Biblical Greek Workbook*: Class 4:14 – 17; Home 4:18 – 20

Periphrastic Participles	Examples	Exercises

Periphrastic Participles

Another key way that participles are used is within *periphrastic* constructions. Periphrastic constructions are a *roundabout* way of expressing the equivalent of finite verbal tense-forms, using a form of εἰμί (the auxiliary) together with a participle.

Periphrastic constructions may have a number of words between the auxiliary and the participle. Originally they seem to have been used to emphasize the continuous nature of an action, and this may account for the aorist participle being used very rarely (3x?) in this construction. But the continuous emphasis was largely lost by the time of the NT.

We have already met and translated a number of these in Mark's Gospel without necessarily being aware of their mechanics. They are relatively infrequent and involve a few simple principles. Most importantly, the translation ought to be equivalent to that of a finite tense-form (normally in the indicative mood, but sometimes in the subjunctive).

Some sentences will contain a form of εἰμί and a participle and yet these will not be examples of periphrasis. In a genuine periphrastic construction, only words that modify the participle will stand between it and its auxiliary (e.g., Mark 1:13).

The tense-form of the finite verb is determined by:

tense-form of εἰμί		tense-form of participle		tense-form of indicative translation
1. present	+	present	=	PRESENT
2. imperfect	+	present	=	IMPERFECT
3. future	+	present	=	FUTURE
4. present	+	perfect	=	PERFECT
5. imperfect	+	perfect	=	PLUPERFECT

A tip for remembering: If you assign numerical values, the combinations become simple equations: Pluperfect = −3; Perfect = −2; Imperfect = −1; Present = 0; Future = 1.

Examples

1. ὅ ἐστιν μεθερμηνευόμενον

   which **is interpreted** (Matt 1:23)

2. θεὸς ἦν ἐν Χριστῷ κόσμον **καταλλάσσων**

   God **was reconciling** the world in Christ (2 Cor 5:19)

3. ἀπὸ τοῦ νῦν ἀνθρώπους **ἔσῃ ζωγρῶν**

   from now on **you will be catching** people (Luke 5:10)

4. χάριτί **ἐστε σεσῳσμένοι**

   by grace **you are saved** (Eph 2:5)

5. οὐκ εἶχες ἐξουσίαν … εἰ μὴ **ἦν δεδομένον** σοι ἄνωθεν·

   you would not have authority … unless **it was given** to you from above (John 19:11)

Exercises

1. Choose the English tense to best render:

   future εἰμί + pres part

   impf εἰμί + perf part

   impf εἰμί + pres part

   pres εἰμί + perf part

   pres εἰμί + pres part

2. Find the periphrastic construction in these verses. Identify the tenses and give an English equivalent.

   Mark 1:6

   Mark 1:22

   Mark 1:33

   Mark 2:18

   Mark 5:41

   Mark 9:4

   Mark 10:32

   Mark 13:13

   John 2:17

☑

Reading Biblical Greek Workbook: Class 4:21–22; Home 4:23–25

80a. Three Key μι Verbs (ε, ο, α): Indicative and Participle

Three Key μι Verbs (ε, ο, α): Indicative and Participle

We have reached the final final category of verbs left to study. The so-called "μι–verbs" contain a characteristic μι formation in the present active indicative 1st singular.

There are three key μι–verbs to learn, together used (including compounds) over 1300 times in the NT. Luke makes especially frequent use of them in Luke–Acts. They represent verbs with stem endings ε, ο, and α.

Mastery of every variation of these three verbs is unrealistic at this stage. The vast majority of forms found in the New Testament require careful attention only to their principal parts, present active indicative and participle, and aorist active forms. The middle and passive voices are used very rarely. It is also worth being familiar with the perfect participle of ἵστημι (66x; see next page).

Study the principal parts for these verbs carefully. Note the *kappa* (κ) in the aorist active of τίθημι and δίδωμι, but not of ἵστημι.

The verb ἵστημι provides the biggest challenge. Note the *rough breathing* on the present and perfect of ἵστημι. The remaining principal parts are based on the verbal stem and follow paradigms we have learned already.

The two separate lines are for the *transitive* and *intransitive* forms. Intransitive verbs require no object (*I stand up*). Transitive verbs require an object as the process passes from subject to object in some way (*I cause to stand*).

For the present active indicative of μι–verbs, the stem vowel is lengthened for the singular, but remains short for the plural.

Present Active Indicative

τίθημι	δίδωμι	ἵστημι *
τίθης	δίδως	ἵστης
τίθησιν	δίδωσιν	ἵστησιν
τίθεμεν	δίδομεν	ἵσταμεν
τίθετε	δίδοτε	ἵστατε
τιθέασιν	διδόασιν	ἱστᾶσιν

*the NT also has forms of ἱστάνω

Present Active Participle of δίδωμι

Masculine	Feminine	Neuter
διδούς	διδοῦσα	διδόν
διδόντος	διδούσης	διδόντος
διδόντι	διδούσῃ	διδόντι
διδόντα	διδοῦσαν	διδόν
διδόντες	διδοῦσαι	διδόντα
διδόντων	διδουσῶν	διδόντων
διδοῦσιν	διδούσαις	διδοῦσιν
διδόντας	διδούσας	διδόντα

Exercises

1. Form the following (indicative):

Perf act 3rd sg of δίδωμι

1st aor act 2nd pl of τίθημι

Fut act 1st pl of ἵστημι

Perf pass 2nd sg of δίδωμι

1st aor pass 3rd pl of ἵστημι

Fut pass 2nd sg of τίθημι

2. Parse:

δώσουσιν

ἑστήκαμεν

ἐθήκατε

δεδόνται

τεθείκεν

3. Find, parse, and translate examples of τίθημι and δίδωμι in the following verses in Mark:

6:22

6:29

8:12

8:25

14:44

80b. Three Key μι Verbs (ε, ο, α): Other Moods, Aorist Forms

Three Key μι Verbs (ε, ο, α): Other Moods, Aorist Forms	τίθημι, δίδωμι, ἵστημι	Exercises

These three μι–verbs are used most often as aorist tense-forms. The Principal Parts provide the key to the indicative mood.

Some aspects of the formation of the subjunctive, imperative, infinitive, and participle cannot be inferred from the Principal Parts.

Present and Aorist Stems

The distinction between *present* (present, imperfect, etc.) and *verbal* (aorist) stems is crucial. The present has a kind of reduplication. The verbal stem is shorter.

	Present stem	Verbal stem
τίθημι	τιθε	θε
δίδωμι	διδο	δο
ἵστημι	ἱστα	στα

This observation helps to make sense of the forms of the aorist outside the indicative mood.

Perfect Active Participle

The perfect active participle of ἵστημι occurs enough times (66x) to warrant familiarity. There are two forms of the perfect participle. The most common is given to the right.

Aorist Active Subjunctive

θῶ	δῶ	στῶ
θῇς	δῷς	στῇς
θῇ	δῷ	στῇ
θῶμεν	δῶμεν	στῶμεν
θῆτε	δῶτε	στῆτε
θῶσιν	δῶσιν	στῶσιν

Aorist Active Imperative

θές	δός	στῆθι
θέτω	δότω	στήτω
θέτε	δότε	στῆτε
θέτωσαν	δότωσαν	στήτωσαν

Aorist Active Infinitive

θεῖναι	δοῦναι	στῆναι

Aorist Active Participle

θείς, θεῖσα, θέν	δούς, δοῦσα, δόν	στάς, στᾶσα, στάν
θέντος	δόντος	στάντος
etc.	etc.	etc.

Perfect Active Participle of ἵστημι

ἑστώς, στῶσα, ἑστός

ἑστηκότος, etc.

1. Find, parse and translate examples of τίθημι, δίδωμι, and ἵστημι (including compounds) in the following verses in Mark:

1:14

3:19

3:24

3:26

5:23

6:37

7:9

7:13

8:25

9:1

10:40

13:9

13:11

13:14

15:10

15:35

Vocab #30

Reading Biblical Greek Workbook: Class 4:26–29; Home 4:30–32

81. OTHER μι VERBS

Other μι Verbs

To round out our study of μι verbs, we turn to some other examples. These are less prominent than the three already learned, but require attention nonetheless.

ἀφίημι AND συνίημι

These two verbs together occur 169 times in the New Testament. The verb ἀφίημι has a wide range of meanings, including *I forgive*, *I leave*, and *I allow*, which makes it a significant word. The verb συνίημι means *I understand, I comprehend*.

Both verbs are compounds formed from the verb ἵημι (*to send, let flow*). This verb only occurs in compounds in the New Testament; looking at the present and verb stems will help you realize why this is fortunate.

The principal parts of ἀφίημι should be observed at this point. You don't need to learn them at this stage. They follow τίθημι very closely.

δείκνυμι, δεικνύω

The verb meaning *I show, display* occurs just over 30 times in the NT. Some of the forms follow the pattern of τίθημι. Others behave more like verbs ending in ω. E.g., the present infinitive δεικνύειν occurs, and also the genitive singular participial δεικνύοντος.

φημί

While this word (*I say*) is used 66 times in the New Testament, all but a few references are to the third person (sg and pl). The first person singular φημί is found only in 1 Corinthians.

ἀπόλλυμι

This is another word used frequently (90x), and in significant enough ways to deserve attention. Examine the principal parts. The verb means *I destroy* but in the middle voices (pres, fut, 2nd aor) and perfect active the meaning is *I perish*.

-ιημι VERBS

P A I 1st sg	Present stem	Verb stem
-ιημι	-ιε	-ε

Pres A	Fut A	Aor A	Perf A	Perf P	Aor P
ἀφίημι	ἀφήσω	ἀφῆκα	—	ἀφέωνται	ἀφέθην

N.B. ἀφέωνται (3rd pers pl) is the only perfect passive personal form in the New Testament.

δείκνυμι

Pres A	Fut A	Aor A	Perf A	Perf P	Aor P
δείκνυμι	δείξω	ἔδειξα	—	—	ἐδείχθην
δεικνύω					

NT FORMS OF φημί

Present:	φημί	φησίν	φασίν
	I say	he says	they say
Imperfect:		ἔφη	
		he said	

ἀπόλλυμι

Pres A	Fut A	Aor A	Perf A	Perf P	Aor P
ἀπόλλυμι	ἀπολέσω	ἀπώλεσα	ἀπόλωλα	---	---

Exercises

1. Using the principal parts and the table of μι verbs, parse and translate examples of ἀφίημι in Mark. Bear in mind the verb's wide range of meanings:

ἀφῆκαν (11:6)

ἤφιεν (11:16)

ἀφίετε (11:25)

ἀφέντες (12:12)

ἀφῇ (12:19)

ἀφεθῇ (13:2)

ἀφείς (13:34)

ἄφετε (14:6)

82. The μὲν ... δέ Construction

The μὲν ... δέ Construction	Examples	Exercises
Greek has the capacity for comparing or contrasting two ideas or things, using two small particles. These are used to structure a sentence, and δέ may appear at quite a distance from the original μέν. The participle μέν occurs first of the two, but it never is the first word of a clause. ### On one hand ... on the other ... The nature of the comparison in English is *on the one hand ... on the other* .... However, most of the time this will prove to be an unnecessarily awkward rendering. You will just need to be aware of the comparison or contrast, and translate as fitting (e.g., Mark 14:21, 38). ### Some ... others ... The construction can be used to express the idea of *some ... others* .... In this case the plural article or relative pronoun will precede the two particles (e.g., John 7:12).	**Mark 14:21** ὅτι ὁ **μὲν** υἱὸς τοῦ ἀνθρώπου ὑπάγει καθὼς γέγραπται περὶ αὐτοῦ, οὐαὶ **δὲ** τῷ ἀνθρώπῳ ἐκείνῳ δι᾽ οὗ ὁ υἱὸς τοῦ ἀνθρώπου παραδίδοται· *The son of man departs just as it is written concerning him.* **But** *woe to that person through whom the son of man is betrayed* **John 7:12** οἱ **μὲν** ἔλεγον ὅτι ἀγαθός ἐστιν, ἄλλοι [**δὲ**] ἔλεγον· οὔ, ἀλλὰ πλανᾷ τὸν ὄχλον. **Some** *were saying that he was good,* **others** *were saying, "No, but he deceives the the crowd."*	1. Find the μὲν ... δέ ... constructions in these verses in John and note how an English version translates them: 10:41 16:9, 10 16:22 19:24–25 19:32–33 20:30–31

83. The Optative Mood

The Optative Mood

There is one mood in the Greek verbal system left to explore.

Some first year Greek courses will opt to skip this mood, since there is no pressing need to learn this material at this stage. The optative does occur in the NT (approx. 70x), especially in Luke's Gospel and Romans. However, the optative mood should be learned later if not now, perhaps in a second year of Greek study.

Meaning

The optative conveys the underlying idea of the *possibility* of an action or process. It is often used to express a wish. By the time of the New Testament it is being supplanted by the closely-related (in meaning) subjunctive.

Forms

In the NT only present and aorist tense-forms occur. The forms are given at the right. There is no augment. Note the characteristic *iōta* and connecting *omicron*.

The mood follows the familiar pattern of the aorist adding the distinctive σα in the active and middle voices, and θε in the passive voice.

Three Uses

1. Expressing a wish or pronouncing a curse

2. Conveying an indirect question

3. Some conditions (all incomplete)

"No way"

The most frequent use of the optative mood in the NT is in an idiom found repeatedly in Romans (3:4, 6, 31; 6:2, 15; 7:7, 13; 9:14; 11:1, 11). The expression μὴ γένοιτο is often rendered *God forbid* or *may it never be*. It serves to express the very strong hope that a possibility never eventuates.

Present

Active	Middle / Passive
λύοιμι	λυοίμην
λύοις	λύοιο
λύοι	λύοιτο
λύοιμεν	λυοίμεθα
λύοιτε	λύοισθε
λύοιεν	λύοιντο

Aorist

Active	Middle	Passive
λύσαιμι	λυσαίμην	λυθείην
λύσαις	λύσαιο	λυθείης
λύσαι	λύσαιτο	λυθείη
λύσαιμεν	λυσαίμεθα	λυθείημεν
λύσαιτε	λύσαισθε	λυθείητε
λύσαιεν	λύσαιντο	λυθείησαν

Examples

1

Ὁ δὲ θεὸς τῆς ἐλπίδος **πληρώσαι** ὑμᾶς πάσης χαρᾶς
May the God of hope **fill** you with all joy (Rom 15:13)

μηκέτι εἰς τὸν αἰῶνα ἐκ σοῦ μηδεὶς καρπὸν **φάγοι.**
May no one ever **eat** from you again! (Mark 11:14)

νόμον οὖν καταργοῦμεν διὰ τῆς πίστεως; **μὴ γένοιτο·**
Do we then overthrow the law by this faith? **By no means!** (Rom 3:31)

2

ἀκούσας δὲ ὄχλου διαπορευομένου ἐπυνθάνετο τί **εἴη** τοῦτο.
When he heard a crowd going by, he asked what **was happening.** (Luke 18:36)

ἀνακρίνοντες τὰς γραφὰς εἰ **ἔχοι** ταῦτα οὕτως.
examining the Scriptures to see **whether** *these things were so.* (Acts 17:11)

3

διηπόρουν περὶ αὐτῶν τί ἂν **γένοιτο** τοῦτο.
...wondering what **might be going on** (Acts 5:24)

εἰ καὶ **πάσχοιτε** διὰ δικαιοσύνην, μακάριοι
Even if you **should suffer** *for righteousness, you are blessed!* (1 Pet 3:14)

Reading Biblical Greek Workbook: Class 4:33–34;
Home 4:35–41, reading this in your Greek New Testament.
Use a lexicon for any unlearned vocabulary.

ANSWERS TO EXERCISES

4. Alphabet

1a. *sigma* (σ, ς)
1b. *iōta* (i or y)
2a. *alpha, bēta, delta, epsilon, iōta, kappa, omicron, tau, upsilon*
2b. *ēta, thēta, xi, pi, rho, phi, chi, psi, ōmega*
2c. *gamma, ēta, nu, rho, chi*
3a. Survey says: *zēta, xi*
3b. Survey says: *ēta, chi, psi*

5. Vowels and Consonants

1. Underline vowels, circle mutes:

Καὶ ἐγένετο ἐν ἐκείναις ταῖς ἡμέραις ἦλθεν
Ἰησοῦς ἀπὸ Ναζαρὲτ τῆς Γαλιλαίας καὶ
ἐβαπτίσθη εἰς τὸν Ἰορδάνην ὑπὸ Ἰωάννου.
10 καὶ εὐθὺς ἀναβαίνων ἐκ τοῦ ὕδατος
εἶδεν σχιζομένους τοὺς οὐρανοὺς καὶ τὸ
πνεῦμα ὡς περιστερὰν καταβαῖνον εἰς
αὐτόν·

6. Letter Combinations

1. Circle diphthongs:

θησαυρόν	πνεύματος
προορίσας	ποιήσατε
Καφαρναοὺμ	δίκαιος
Καϊάφα	βασιλεία
γενεάν	Βόος
παισίν	χεῖρας
μετανοίας	σταυροῦ
νηστεύσας	δωρεάν
βουλεύσεται	

7. Other Sounds and Symbols

1. Match the Greek word:

gamma nasal	προσένεγκε
smooth breathing	αὐτόν
rough breathing	ἱερεῖ
iōta subscript	πλοίῳ
diaeresis	πρωΐ
semicolon	λέγων·
question mark	τοῦτο;
apostrophe	κατ' ἐξουσίαν

8. Accents

1. Count the number:
Acute 9; Grave 7; Circumflex 7

2. How many lack?
ἐν, μου, σου, σου

3. How many have two?
ἄγγελόν

14. The Article

1. Definite article—find and identify.

Verse	Form	Case	Number	Gender
1	τοῦ	Gen	Sg	Masc/Neut
2	τῷ	Dat	Sg	Masc/Neut
2	τῷ	Dat	Sg	Masc/Neut
2	τόν	Acc	Sg	Masc
2	τήν	Acc	Sg	Fem
3	τῇ	Dat	Sg	Fem
3	τήν	Acc	Sg	Fem
3	τάς	Acc	Pl	Fem
4	ὁ	Nom	Sg	Masc
4	τῇ	Dat	Sg	Fem
5	ἡ	Nom	Sg	Fem
5	οἱ	Nom	Pl	Masc
5	τῷ	Dat	Sg	Masc/Neut
5	τάς	Acc	Pl	Fem

15. Masculine Nouns

1. Find each word in Vocab #2 & Mark 1.

Form	Case	No.	Gend
ἄγγελον	Acc	Sg	Masc
ἀδελφόν	Acc	Sg	Masc
ἄνθρωπος	Nom	Sg	Masc
ἥλιος	Nom	Sg	Masc
καιρός	Nom	Sg	Masc
κυρίου	Gen	Sg	Masc
λόγον	Acc	Sg	Masc
οὐρανούς	Acc	Pl	Masc
ποταμῷ	Dat	Sg	Masc
τόπον	Acc	Sg	Masc
υἱοῦ	Gen	Sg	Masc
ἐρήμῳ	Dat	Sg	Fem
ὁδόν	Acc	Sg	Fem

18. Feminine Nouns

1. Find Vocab #3, identify:

Ἀρχή	Nom	Sg	Fem
διδαχῇ	Dat	Sg	Fem
συναγωγῇ	Dat	Sg	Fem
φωνή	Nom	Sg	Fem
ἁμαρτιῶν	Gen	Pl	Fem
βασιλεία	Nom	Sg	Fem
ἐξουσίαν	Acc	Sg	Fem
ἡμέραις	Dat	Pl	Fem
θύραν	Acc	Sg	Fem
μετανοίας	Gen	Sg	Fem
οἰκίαν	Acc	Sg	Fem
θάλασσαν	Acc	Sg	Fem

2. Write out the full declension:
βασιλεία follows ὥρα
φωνή follows ἀρχή
θάλασσα follows δόξα

20. Neuter Nouns

2. Work out the lexicon entry:

ἁμαρτία,	ας,	ἡ
οὐρανός,	ου,	ὁ
θάλασσα,	ης,	ἡ
ἄνθρωπος,	ου,	ὁ
ἔρημος,	ου,	ἡ
ἐξουσία,	ας,	ἡ
δαιμόνιον,	ου,	το
τόπος,	ου,	ὁ

3. Parse the following nouns:

Case	Number	Gender	Gk	Eng
Dat	Sg	Neut	πλοῖον	boat
Acc	Pl	Fem	συναγωγή	synagogue
Gen	Sg	Neut	πρόσωπον	face
Dat	Pl	Fem	ἡμέρα	day
Nom	Sg	Fem	φωνή	voice
Gen	Sg	Masc	υἱός	son
Acc	Sg	Fem	διδαχή	teaching
Acc	Sg	Fem	οἰκία	house

21. 1st Declension Masculine Nouns

1. Parse the following first declension masculine nouns from Mark 1:

Form	Case	Number	Gender
Ἠσαΐᾳ	Dat	Sg	Masc
προφήτῃ	Dat	Sg	Masc
Ἰωάννης	Nom	Sg	Masc
Ἰορδάνῃ	Dat	Sg	Masc
Ἰορδάνην	Acc	Sg	Masc
Ἰωάννου	Gen	Sg	Masc
Ἰωάννην	Acc	Sg	Masc
Ἀνδρέαν	Acc	Sg	Masc
Ἀνδρέου	Gen	Sg	Masc

23. Personal Pronouns: 3rd Person

1. Count, identify & compare:

Verse	Form	Case	Number	Gender	NRSV
3	αὐτοῦ	Gen	Sg	Masc	his
5	αὐτόν	Acc	Sg	Masc	him
5	αὐτοῦ	Gen	Sg	Masc	him
5	αὐτῶν	Gen	Pl	Masc	their
6	αὐτοῦ	Gen	Sg	Masc	his
7	αὐτοῦ	Gen	Sg	Masc	his
8	αὐτός	Nom	Sg	Masc	he
10	αὐτόν	Acc	Sg	Masc	him
12	αὐτόν	Acc	Sg	Masc	him
13	αὐτῷ	Dat	Sg	Masc	him
17	αὐτοῖς	Dat	Pl	Masc	to them
18	αὐτῷ	Dat	Sg	Masc	him
19	αὐτοῦ	Gen	Sg	Masc	his
19	αὐτούς	Acc	Pl	Masc	??
20	αὐτούς	Acc	Pl	Masc	them
20	αὐτῶν	Gen	Pl	Masc	their
20	αὐτοῦ	Gen	Sg	Masc	him

2. Find, parse, translate:

Acc	Sg	Masc	3rd	pers	pro	him (5:10)
Dat	Sg	Masc	3rd	pers	pro	to him x 2 (5:33)
Dat	Pl	Ma/Ne	3rd	pers	pro	to them (10:14)
N/A	Pl	Neut	3rd	pers	pro	them (10:14)
Dat	Pl	Fem	3rd	pers	pro	to them (16:6)
Acc	Sg	Masc	3rd	pers	pro	him (16:6)
Acc	Pl	Fem	3rd	pers	pro	them (16:8)

24. Other Uses of Case: Time

1. Identify, give case:

Matt 24:42	time when	Dative
1 Thess 2:9	time during	Genitive
Acts 21:7	time how long	Accusative
Rev 21:25	time during	Genitive
Acts 9:9	time how long	Accusative

25. Prepositions

1. Translate prepositional phrases:

in Isaiah the prophet	in the desert
toward him	in the Jordan river
in those days	out of the water
into him	from the heavens
into the desert	out of the synagogue
toward the door	from him
toward him	

28. Verbs Ending ω, Like λύω

1. Form the present active indicative:

ἔχετε	πιστευει
θεραπευομεν	φερεις

2. Parse:

Tense	Voice	Mood	Pers	No.	Gk	Eng
Pres	Act	Ind	2nd	Pl	ἄγω	I go
Pres	Act	Ind	3rd	Pl	βαλλω	I throw
Pres	Act	Ind	1st	Sg	ἐσθιω	I eat

3. Translate:
   we are believing
   he, she, it is writing
   you (sg) are raising

5. Find each of the verbs in Vocab #7:

Pre	Stem	End
ἄγ	ωμεν	
γέ	γραπ	ται
ἐ	δίδασκ	εν
ε	ἔγειρ	εν
ἐσθί	ων	
εὑρ	ον	
ἔχ	ων	
θέλ	ης	
ἐ	θεράπευ	σεν
λέγ	ων	
λῦ	σαι	
πιστεύ	ετε	
ἔ	φερ	ον

29. Contract Verbs in εω

1. Form the impf act ind:
   ἀκολουθοῦμεν
   ποιεῖτε
   κρατοῦσιν

2. Parse:

T	V	M	P	N	G	E
Pres	Act	Ind	1st	Sg	διακονέω	I serve
Pres	Act	Ind	2nd	Pl	φωνέω	I call
Pres	Act	Ind	2nd	Sg	ὑπάγω	I go away
Pres	Act	Ind	1st	Pl	λαλέω	I speak

3. Translate:
   See, I send my messenger before your face
   Jesus came from Nazareth of Galilee

32. Imperfect Tense-Form

1. Parse:

T	V	M	P	N	G	E
Impf	Act	Ind	3rd	Sg	βάλλω	I throw
Impf	Act	Ind	1st	Pl	λέγω	I say
Pres	Act	Ind	2nd	Pl	ἐγείρω	I raise
Impf	Act	Ind	1st	Sg	πιστεύω	I trust OR
"	"	"	3rd	Pl	"	"

2. Translate into Greek:

ἐθεράπευεν	εὑρίσκετε
ἔφερον	ἐδίδασκον

33. Imperfect Tense-Form: εω Verbs

1. Form the imperfect of:
   ἠκολουθοῦμεν
   ἐποιεῖτε
   ἐκράτουν

2. Parse:

Impf	Act	Ind	1st	Sg	ζητέω	I seek
		-or-	3rd	Pl		
Impf	Act	Ind	2nd	Pl	φωνέω	I call
Impf	Act	Ind	1st	Pl	λαλέω	I speak

34. Compound Verbs

1. Form the imperfect of:
   διηκόνεις
   ἐξέβαλλεν
   ὑπῆγον

2. Parse:

Impf	Act	Ind	2nd	Sg	παρακαλέω I urge
Impf	Act	Ind	2nd	Sg	ἀποστέλλω I send
Pres	Act	Ind	3rd	Sg	διακονέω I serve

35. εἰμί, The Verb I Am (To Be)

1. Translate:
   And a voice came from the heavens, "You are my Son, the beloved."

   And he was in the desert

   And immediately a man in an unclean spirit was in their synagogue

   Peter says to him, "You are the Christ."

36. First Aorist Tense-Form

1. Form:
   ἐποιήσατε
   παρεκαλέσαμεν
   ἔγραψας
   ἐπίστευσαν

2. Parse:

Aor	Act	Ind	3rd	Pl	ἀκολουθέω I follow
Aor	Act	Ind	3rd	Sg	καλέω I call
Aor	Act	Ind	3rd	Sg	θεραπεύω I heal

38. Future Tense-Form

1. Form:
   γράψωμεν
   ἀκούσομεν
   ἄξομεν
   κρατήσομεν
   πράξομεν
   πείσομεν

2. Translate:
   He will baptize
   I will make
   He will heal

39. Adjectives

2. Express the following in Greek:
   ὁ ἀγαπητὸς ἀδελφός
   ἡ ἱκανὴ ἡμέρα
   ἀγαθὸν ἱμάτιον
   τὸ ἅγιον σάββατον
   ἀκάθαρτος καρδία
   καινὴ διδαχή
   ἡ ἰσχυρὰ φωνή
   ἀγαθὸν παιδίον

40A. Participles

1. Translate, identify tense-form, case, number:

	T	C	N
preaching	Pres	Nom	Sg
eating	Pres	Nom	Sg
saying	Pres	Nom	Sg
going beside	Pres	Nom	Sg
teaching	Pres	Nom	Sg
holding	Aor	Nom	Sg
having	Pres	Acc	Pl
casting out	Pres	Nom	Sg
encouraging	Pres	Nom	Sg

40B. Participles *cont.*

1. Translate:
   Jesus came into Galilee preaching the gospel of God

   And immediately on the Sabbath(s), entering into synagogue, he was teaching.

   And a leper comes to him urging him and saying to him …

45. Imperative Mood

1. Express in Greek:
   λαλεῖ OR λάλησον

   θεράπευε OR θεράπευσον τὰς οἰκίας μου

   πιστεύετε OR πιστεύσατε τῷ εὐαγγελίῳ

   διακονείτωσαν OR διακονησάτωσαν

2. Parse:

T	V	M	P	N	R	E
Pres	Act	Imp	2nd	Pl	ποιέω	I do
Pres	Act	Imp	2nd	Sg	ὑπάγω	I go away
Pres	Act	Imp	2nd	Sg	ἀκολουθέω	I follow

3. Translate:

Prepare the way of the Lord

Repent and believe the gospel

I say to you, rise, lift up your bed and depart into your house

46. Passive Voice

1. Express the following in Greek:
   πιστεύεται
   ἠκολούθεισθε
   παρακαλοῦμαι
   καλῇ
   ἐκαθαρίζετο

2. Parse and translate:

T	V	M	P	N	G	E
Pres	MP	Ind	1st	Pl	βάλλω	I throw *we are being thrown*
Impf	MP	Ind	2nd	Sg	διδάσκω	I teach *you were being taught*
Pres	MP	Ind	3rd	Pl	θεραπεύω	I heal *they are being healed*
Impf	MP	Ind	3rd	Pl	ὑπάγω	I go away *they were being sent away*
Impf	MP	Ind	1st	Sg	προσφέρω	I bring *I was being brought*

3. Translate:
   And they were being baptized by him in the river Jordan

47. Middle Voice

1. Form 1st Aor Mid Ind 3rd Sg:
   ἐγράψατο
   ἐδοκήσατο
   παρεκαλέσατο
   ἠνοίξατο
   ἐθεραπεύσατο

48. Verbs with Middle Lexical Forms

1. Express in Greek:
   ἀσπάζῃ
   ἠργάσαντο
   ἄρχεται
   προσεύχεσθε
   ἐλογίσαμην

2. Parse:

Aor	Mid	Ind	3rd	Sg	ἅπτομαι	I touch
Aor	Mid	Ind	2nd	Pl	λογίζομαι	I reckon
Aor	Mid	Ind	3rd	Pl	ἀσπάζομαι	I greet
Aor	Mid	Ind	1st	Pl	δέχομαι	I receive

49. The Verb ἔρχομαι

1. Parse forms of ἔρχομαι:

1:7	Pres	Mid	Ind	3rd	Sg	ἔρχομαι	I come
1:45	Impf	Mid	Ind	3rd	Pl	ἔρχομαι	I come
2:3	Pres	Mid	Ind	3rd	Pl	ἔρχομαι	I come
2:13	Impf	Mid	Ind	3rd	Sg	ἔρχομαι	I come

50. Future Tense-Form: Middle and Passive

1. Form Future Middle Ind 1st Pl:
   γραψόμεθα
   ἀκουσόμεθα
   ἄξομεθα
   κρατήσομεθα
   πραξόμεθα
   πεισόμεθα

2. Form Fut Pass Ind 2nd Sg:
   πειρασθήσῃ
   φωνηθήσῃ
   ἀχθήσῃ
   γραφήσῃ
   κηρυχθήσῃ

51. Aorist Passive

1. Identify from principal parts:
   ἤχθην   ἐβλήθην ἐγενήθην
   ἐλήμφθην ἐρρήθην   ὤφθη
   ἠνέχθην

2. List verbs dropping θ: ἠγγέλην

3. Parse:

Aor	Pas	Impv	2nd	Sg	καθαρίζω	I cleanse
Aor	Pas	Ind	3rd	Sg	καθαρίζω	I cleanse
Aor	Pas	Ind	3rd	Sg	ἀκούω	I hear
Aor	Pas	Ind	3rd	Sg	ἐγείρω	I raise

4. Parse:

Aor	Act	Ind	3rd	Pl	ἀναβαίνω	I ascend
Aor	Act	Ind	3rd	Sg	γινώσκω	I know
Aor	Act	Ind	3rd	Pl	γινώσκω	I know
Aor	Act	Ind	3rd	Sg	ἀναβαίνω	I ascend
Impf	Act	Ind	3rd	Sg	γινώσκω	I know

52. Liquid Stem Verbs

1 Consult, identify liquid stems:
   ἀγγέλλω, βάλλω, γίνομαι, ἐγείρω, θέλω,
   κρίνω, λαμβάνω, φέρω

2. Parse:

T	V	M	P	N	Gk	E
Fut	Act	Ind	2nd	Pl	ἐγείρω	I raise
Fut	Act	Ind	3rd	Sg	μένω	I remain
Aor	Act	Ind	2nd	Sg	σπείρω	I sow
Aor	Act	Impv	3rd	Sg	αἴρω	I lift
Pres	Act	Ind	2nd	Sg	κρίνω	I judge
Aor	Act	Ind	1st	Pl	μένω	I remain
Fut	Act	Ind	1st	Pl	φωνέω	I call
Fut	Act	Ind	2nd	Pl	σπείρω	I sow
Fut	Act	Ind	1st	Sg	ἀποκτείνω	I kill

53A. 2nd Aorist Tense-Form

1. List principal parts:

ἄγω	βάλλω	γίνομαι
-θνήσκω	λαμβάνω	ἔρχομαι
ἐσθίω	ἔχω	λέγω
ὁράω	φέρω	

2. Translate:

   he saw   he said   Offer!

53B. 2nd Aorist Tense-Form: Outside the Indicative

1. Conjugate 2nd Aor Impv:
   ἄγαγε   λάβε
   ἀγαγέτω   λαβέτω
   ἀγάγετε   λάβετε
   ἀγαγέτωσαν   λαβέτωσαν

2. Decline Masc 2nd Aor Part:

βάλων	βάλοντες
βάλοντος	βαλόντων
βάλοντι	βάλουσιν
βάλοντα	βάλοντας

3. Parse forms of ἔρχομαι:

9	2Aor	Act	Ind	3rd	Sg	ἔρχομαι	I come
20	2Aor	Act	Ind	3rd	Pl	ἀπέρχομαι	I depart
24	2Aor	Act	Ind	2nd	Sg	ἔρχομαι	I come
25	2Aor	Act	Imp	2nd	Sg	ἐξέρχομαι	I go out
26	2Aor	Act	Ind	3rd	Sg	ἐξέρχομαι	I go out
29	2Aor	Act	Ind	3rd	Pl	ἔρχομαι	I come
35	2Aor	Act	Ind	3rd	Sg	ἀπέρχομαι	I depart
38	2Aor	Act	Ind	1st	Sg	ἐξέρχομαι	I go out

54A. Participles: Feminine and Neuter

1a. Identify:

	Case	Number	Gend	Tense
πυρέσσουσα	Nom	Sg	Fem	Pres
ἔχοντας	Acc	Pl	Masc	Pres
κηρύσσων	Nom	Sg	Masc	Pres

1b. Account for gender:

πυρέσσουσα	Agrees ἡ πενθερά
ἔχοντας ἀνθρωπῶν	implied as object of verb ἔφερον
κηρύσσων	Agrees with implied subject of ἦλθον (Jesus)

2. Form 1st pres fem part:

μαρτυρούσα	κατοικούσα
ἀνοιγούσα	πειραζούσα
γραφούσα	

54B. Participles: Feminine and Neuter *cont.*

1a. Identify:

	Case	No.	Gend	Tense
σπαράξαν	Nom/Acc	Sg	Neut	Aor
φωνῆσαν	Nom/Acc	Sg	Neut	Aor
κρατήσας	Nom	Sg	Masc	Aor

1b. Account for gender:

σπαράξαν	Agrees τὸ πνεῦμα
φωνῆσαν	Agrees τὸ πνεῦμα
κρατήσας	Agrees with implied subject of ἤγειρεν (Jesus)

2. Form 1st Aor Fem Part:

μαρτυρήσασα
ἀνοιξάσα
γράψασα
κατοικήσασα
πειράσασα

55. Demonstrative Pronouns

1. Parse the following:

C	N	G	Gk	E
Dat	Pl	Fem	ἐκεῖνος	that
NA	Sg	Neut	οὗτός	this
Acc	Sg	Fem	ὅλος	whole
Nom	Sg	Fem	ὅλος	whole
NA	Sg	Neut	οὗτός	this

56B. Words That "Take" the Predicative Position

1. Express in Greek:
τοῦτο τὸ σαββάτον
ἐκεῖναι αἱ γλῶσσαι
ἐκείνη ἡ ἡμέρα
ὅλος ὁ ὄχλος
ταῦτα τὰ ἱμάτια
ὅλη ἡ ἔρημος

2. Translate:

And it happened in those days (that) Jesus came from Nazareth of Galilee.

And he came preaching into their synagogues into the whole (of) Galilee and casting out demons.

57. Reflexive Pronoun

1. What sort of pronoun? Parse.

		C	N	G	P
2	Personal	Gen	Sg		1st
2	Personal	Gen	Sg		2nd
8	Personal	Nom	Sg		1st
8	Personal	Acc	Pl		2nd
11	Personal	Nom	Sg		2nd
11	Personal	Dat	Sg		2nd
24	Personal	Dat	Pl		1st
24	Personal	Acc	Pl		1st
24	Personal	Acc	Sg		2nd
27	Reflexive	Acc	Pl	Masc	3rd
40	Personal	Acc	Sg		1st
44	Reflexive	Acc	Sg	Masc	2nd

58. Relative Pronoun

1. Combine; what case?

Peter saw the man whom the Jews knew.	Acc
Paul preached the gospel whose power was clear.	Gen
Jesus healed the girl who was dying.	Nom

2. Identify antecedent, divide; case, no., gender?

Jn 2:22 the word
The believed the Scripture and the word.
Jesus had spoken the word.
Acc, Sg, Masc

Jn 2:23 the signs
Many believed in his name because they saw the signs.
He was doing the signs.
Acc, Pl, Neut

Jn 4:29 the man
Come see a man.
The man told me everything I have ever done.
Nom, Sg, Masc

Jn 4:53 the hour
The father realized that this was the hour.
In the hour Jesus had said to him, 'Your son will live'
Dat, Sg, Fem

Jn 6:42 Jesus
Is not this Jesus, the son of Joseph?
We know Jesus's father and mother.
Gen, Sg, Masc

59. Participles: Middle and Passive Voices

1. Identify:

1:5	Pres	M/P	Pl	Masc	Nom
1:10	Pres	M/P	Pl	Masc	Acc
1:13	Pres	M/P	Sg	Masc	Nom
1:32	2Aor	M/P	Sg	Fem	Gen
1:32	Pres	M/P	Pl	Masc	Acc
1:41	Aor	Pass	Sg	Masc	Nom
1:43	Aor	Mid	Sg	Masc	Nom
2:3	Pres	M/P	Sg	Masc	Acc
2:6	Pres	M/P	Pl	Masc	Nom

2. Express in Greek:
ἀσπαζόμενος
δεχθείς
λογιζόμενος

60A. Perfect Tense-Form: Indicative Mood

1. Consult and list:
a. No Perfect

εἰμί	ἄγω	ἐγείρω	θέλω	ἐσθίω

b. Irregular reduplication

ἀκήκοα	ἀνέῳγα	εἴληφα
ἐλήλυθα	ἔσχηκα	εἴρηκα
ἑώρακα	ἑόρακα	ἐνήνοχα

c. Ending other than κα

κεκήρυχα	ἀκήκοα	ἀνέῳγα
γέγονα	εἴληφα	ἐλήλυθα
ἐνήνοχα		

60B. Perfect Tense-Form: Indicative Mood *cont.*

1. Give Perf Act Ind 1st Sg:

μεμίσηκα	πέπραχα
ἔγνωκα	εἰσελήλυθα
κέκληκα	γέγονα
κέκραγα	

2. Give Perf Mid/Pass Ind 1st Sg:

βέβλημαι	ἀνέῳγμαι
παρήγγελμαι	γέγραμμαι

61. Perfect Non-Indicative

1. Translate:

1:2	it is written/has been written
1:6	being clothed/having been clothed
1:15	it is near/has drawn near
4:15	being sown/having been sown
5:19	he is doing/he has done
5:33	it has happened
5:34	it saves/it has saved
6:14	he has been raised
7:29	it has left
7:30	being thrown/having been thrown
9:42	he is being thrown/has been thrown
10:28	we have followed

62. Verbs Like δύναμαι

1. Translate:

1:40	You are able	2:7	he is able
2:4	being able	2:14	sitting
2:6	sitting	2:19	they are able

63. Pluperfect Tense-Form

1. Form:

ἐτεθεραπεύκειν	ἐδεδήμεν
ἐτεθεραπεύκεις	ἐδέδησο
ἐτεθεραπεύκει	ἐδέδητο
ἐτεθεραπεύκειμεν	ἐδεδήμεθα
ἐτεθεραπεύκειτε	ἐδέδησθε
ἐτεθεραπεύκεισαν	ἐδέδηντο

2. Parse & translate:

1:34	Plu	Act	Ind	3rd	Pl	οἶδα	I know	they were knowing
9:6	Plu	Act	Ind	3rd	Sg	οἶδα	I know	he was knowing
15:7	Plu	Act	Ind	3rd	Pl	ποιέω	I do, make	they were making
4:29	Plu	MP	Ind	3rd	Sg	οἰκοδομέω	I build	it was being built
11:22	Plu	Act	Ind	3rd	Sg	πείθω	I persuade	he was trusting
16:20	Plu	MP	Ind	3rd	Sg	βάλλω	I throw	he was being cast
4:8	Plu	Act	Ind	3rd	Pl	ἀπέρχομαι	I go from	they were going from
7:30	Plu	Act	Ind	3rd	Sg	ἔρχομαι	I come	it was (not) coming
11:13	Per	Act	Ind	3rd	Sg	λέγω	I say	he was speaking

64. οὐ and μή in Negation

1. Classify and translate:
   N.B. see English NT for translation

2:7	ordinary	…;
2:9	ordinary	…;
4:38	expects 'yes'	οὐ …;
6:3	expects 'yes'	οὐ …;
6:3	expects 'yes'	οὐ …;
8:12	ordinary	…;
14:37	expects 'yes'	οὐ …;

65. Subjunctive Mood

1. Form pres act subj:
   ἐγείρω
   μισῇ
   σῴζητε
   ζητῶ
   δέχωνται

2. Form aor pass subj:
   κηρυχθῇ
   βληθῆτε
   ἀκουσθῶμεν
   θεραπευθῇς
   ἀχθῶσιν

3. Parse:

Aor	Pass	Sub	2	Sg	ἀνοίγω	open
Pres	Act	Sub	1	Pl	αἴρω	lift
Pres	Act	Sub	3	Pl	εἰμί	am
2Aor	Mid	Sub	1	Sg	βάλλω	throw
2Aor	Mid	Sub	2	Sg	OR	
2Aor	Act	Sub	3	Sg	ἔρχομαι	come

66A. Uses of the Subjunctive

1. Which construction?

5	Purpose
7a	Indefinite person
3	Prohibition
2	Deliberative
5	Purpose
1	Hortatory
4	Emphatic future negative
6	Noun clause
7b	Indefinite time

66B. Uses of the Subjunctive cont.

1. Find and classify:

1:38	1.	Hortatory
1:38	5.	Purpose
2:10	5.	Purpose
2:20	7b.	Indefinite time
3:12	5.	Purpose
3:14	5.	Purpose
3:29	7a.	Indefinite person
3:35	7a.	Indefinite person
4:12	5.	Purpose
4:15	7b.	Indefinite time
4:22	5.	Purpose
4:32	7b.	Indefinite time
4:35	1.	Hortatory

67A. Conditions

1. Identify:
   Contrary to fact—past & present
   Of fact & Contrary, past & present
   Future
   Of fact—present
   Future

67B. Conditions cont.

1. Classify & translate:

1:40	Future	If you are willing, you are able.
3:26	Of fact—present	If Satan rose up … then he is not able to stand
3:27	Future	unless (if not) he binds the strong one first
3:28	Future	… if they should blaspheme
14:29	Of fact—future (?)	Even if all should be caused to stumble, but not I.
14:35	Of fact—present	if it is possible for the hour to pass from him

68. Adverbs

1. Translate and identify the verb:

5:23	ἐσχάτως	finally	ἔχει; i.e., is at the point of death
7:37	καλῶς	well	πεποίηκεν
10:43	οὕτως	in this way	ἐστίν
14:70	ἀληθῶς	truly	εἶ

69A. 3rd Declension Nouns: Masculine and Feminine

1. Form the dative plural of:

γυνή	γυναιξίν
νύξ	νύξιν
πούς	πόσιν
μήτηρ	μήτρασιν

2. Parse:

πατέρα	Acc	Sg	Masc	πατήρ	father
χεῖρα	Acc	Sg	Fem	χείρ	hand
Σίμωνι	Dat	Sg	Masc	Σίμων	Simon
εἰς τὸν αἰῶνα	Acc	Sg	Masc	αἰών	age
μήτηρ	Nom	Sg	Fem	μήτηρ	mother
νύκτα	Acc	Sg	Fem	νύξ	night

69B. 3rd Declension Nouns: Masculine and Feminine *cont*.

1. Parse:

ἄφεσιν	Acc	Sg	Fem	ἄφεσις	pardon
γραμματεῖς	N/A	Pl	Masc	γραμματεύς	scribe
πόλις	Nom	Sg	Fem	πόλις	city
πόλιν	Acc	Sg	Fem	πόλις	city
γραμματέων	Gen	Pl	Masc	γραμματεύς	scribe
ἀρχιερέως	Gen	Sg	Masc	ἀρχιερεύς	chief priest
ἱερεύς	N/A	Pl	Masc	ἱερεύς	priest
θλίψεως	Gen	Sg	Fem	θλῖψις	oppression

70. 3rd Declension Nouns: Neuter

1. Parse and translate:

ὕδατι	Dat	Sg	Neut	ὕδωρ	water	to water
πνεύματι	Dat	Sg	Neut	πνεῦμα	spirit	to the Spirit
πνεῦμα	N/A	Sg	Neut	πνεῦμα	spirit	Spirit
πνεύμασι	Dat	Pl	Neut	πνεῦμα	spirit	to spirits
πνεύματα	N/A	Pl	Neut	πνεῦμα	spirit	spirits
ὄρος	N/A	Sg	Neut	ὄρος	mountain	mountain
ὄνομα	N/A	Sg	Neut	ὄνομα	name	name
θέλημα	N/A	Sg	Neut	θέλημα	will	will
ὦτα	N/A	Pl	Neut	οὖς	ear	ears

71. 3rd Declension Pronouns

1. Find, parse and classify τις, τίς, ὅστις:

1:24	Nom	Sg	Neut	Inter	what?
2:6	Nom	Pl	Masc	Indef	certain
2:18	Acc	Sg	Neut	Interr	what? why?
3:33	Nom	Sg	Masc	Interr	who?
4:20	Nom	Pl	Masc	Indef Rel	whoever
4:23	Nom	Sg	Masc	Indef	anyone
5:31	Nom	Sg	Masc	Inter	who?
7:5	Acc	Sg	Neut	Inter	what? why?
8:23	Acc	Sg	Neut	Indef	anything
8:29	Acc	Sg	Masc	Inter	who?
11:13	Acc	Sg	Neut	Indef	anything
12:9	Acc	Sg	Neut	Inter	what?
12:13	Acc	Pl	Masc	Indef	some (men)
15:14	Acc	Sg	Neut	Inter	what?
15:35	Nom	Pl	Masc	Indef	certain

72. Adjectives of 3rd and 1st Declensions

1. Parse and translate πᾶς:

Nom	Sg	Fem	the whole Judean…
Nom	Pl	Masc	all the Jerusalemites
Acc	Pl	Masc	all who were sick
Nom	Pl	Masc	everyone is seeking
Nom	Sg	Masc	the whole crowd
Nom	Sg	Masc	the whole crowd
Acc	Pl	Fem	all the parables
Gen	Sg	Neut	during every night
Nom	Pl	Masc	everyone wondered
Acc	Sg	Fem	the whole truth
Gen	Pl	Fem	from all the cities
Nom	Sg	Neut	everything entering

2. Translate into Greek:

μία χείρ
εἷς λόγος
μία γυνή
μία σάρξ
εἷς προφήτης

73. πολύς and μέγας

1. Translate:

he healed many (1:34)
no one casts wine (2:22)
in many parables he was speaking to them (4:33)
they feared a great fear (4:41)
crying out in a great voice he says (5:7)
they were casting many demons (6:13)
no one is good (10:18)
the great among them (10:42)
are you answering nothing? (14:60)
They said nothing to anyone (16:8)

2. Express in Greek:

μεγάλα ἔργα	πᾶς, πᾶς ἄνθρωπος
ἔφαγεν οὐδέν	πολλὴ θλῖψις
πάντες ἁμαρτωλοί	πολλαί ἡμέραι
πᾶν, πάντα	πᾶς ὁ ὄχλος

74. The Infinitive

1. Express the following in Greek:
καλέσαι
φίλεισθαι
βάπτισαι
βάλλεσθαι
κηρύξαι

76. Contract Verbs αω

1. Form:

ἠγάπησα	ἠγαπώμην	
ἠγάπησας	ἠγαπῶ	ἀγάπα
ἠγάπησεν	ἠγαπᾶτο	ἀγαπάτω
ἠγαπήσαμεν	ἠγαπώμεθα	
ἠγαπήσατε	ἠγαπᾶσθε	ἀγαπᾶτε
ἠγάπησαν	ἠγαπῶντο	ἀγαπάτωσαν
ἀγαπηθήσομαι	ἀγαπῶ	ἀγαπῶσα
ἀγαπηθήση	ἀγαπᾷς	ἀγαπώσης
ἀγαπηθήσεται	ἀγαπᾷ	ἀγαπώση
ἀγαπηθησόμεθα	ἀγαπῶμεν	ἀγαπῶσαν
ἀγαπηθήσεσθε	ἀγαπᾶτε	ἀγαπῶσαι
ἀγαπηθήσονται	ἀγαπῶσιν	ἀγαπῶσων
ἀγαπώσαις	ἀγαπῶσας	

76. Contract Verbs αω (cont. from previous page)

2. Form:

ζῶμαι	ἔζων
ζῇ	ἔζης
ζῆται	ἔζη
ζώμεθα	ἔζωμεν
ζῆσθε	ἐζῆτε
ζῶνται	ἔζων

3. Parse:

Aor	Act	Ind	3rd	Sg	ἐπιτιμάω	I warn
Pres	Act	Imp	2nd	Sg	ὁράω	I see
Impf	Act	Ind	3rd	Pl	ἐρωτάω	I ask
Impf	Act	Ind	3rd	Sg	ἐπερωτάω	I question
Fut	Mid	Ind	2nd	Sg	ζάω	I live	OR
Aor	Act	Subj	3rd	Sg	ζάω	I live	OR
Aor	Mid	Subj	2nd	Sg	ζάω	I live
Pres	Act	Ind	3rd	Sg	τιμάω	I honor	OR
Pres	Act	Sub	3rd	Sg	τιμάω	I honor	OR
Pres	M/P	Ind	2nd	Sg	τιμάω	I honor	OR
Pres	M/P	Sub	2nd	Sg	τιμάω	I honor
Pres	M/P	Ind	2nd	Pl	πλανάω	I lead astray	OR
Pres	M/P	Sub	2nd	Pl	πλανάω	I lead astray	OR
Pres	M/P	Imp	2nd	Pl	πλανάω	I lead astray
Fut	Act	Ind	2nd	Sg	ἀγαπάω	I love
Aor	Pass	Ind	3rd	Sg	γεννάω	I beget

77. Contract Verbs οω

1. Form πληρόω:

ἐπλήρωσα	ἐπληρούμην	
ἐπλήρωσας	ἐπλήρου	πλήρου
ἐπλήρωσεν	ἐπληρούτο	πληρούτω
ἐπληρώσαμεν	ἐπληρούμεθα	
ἐπληρώσατε	ἐπλήρουσθε	πληροῦτε
ἐπλήρωσαν	ἐπληρούντο	πληρούτωσαν
πληρωθήσομαι	πληρῶ	πληροῦσα
πληρωθήθήσῃ	πληροῖς	πληρούσης
πληρωθήθήσεται	πληροῖ	πληρούσῃ
πληρωθήθησόμεθα	πληρούσαν	πληρῶμεν
πληρωθήθήσεσθε	πληρῶτε	πληρῶσαι
πληρωθήθήσονται	πληρῶσιν	πληρουσῶν
πληρούσαις	πληρούσας	

2. Parse:

Aor	Pass	Ind	3rd	Sg	δικαιόω	justify
Fut	Pass	Ind	2nd	Sg	δικαιόω	justify
Perf	M/P	Ind	3rd	Sg	πληρόω	fill
Aor	Pass	Sub	3rd	Sg	φανερόω	show
Aor	Pass	Sub	3rd	Pl	πληρόω	fill
Aor	Act	Imp	2nd	Sg	σταυρόω	crucify
Aor	Pass	Sub	3rd	Sg	σταυρόω	crucify
Pres	Act	Ind	3rd	Pl	σταυρόω	crucify

78A. Pragmatics of Participles

1. Find, identify, choose:

4	βαπτίζων	ἐγένετο	Purpose
4	κηρύσσων	ἐγένετο	Purpose
5	ἐξομολογούμενοι	ἐβαπτίζοντο	Temporal
6	ἐνδεδυμένος	ἦν	Periphrastic
6	ἐσθίων	ἦν	Periphrastic
7	λέγων	ἐκήρυσσεν	Instrumental
7	κύψας	λῦσαι	Temporal
10	ἀναβαίνων	εἶδεν	Temporal
10	καταβαίνον	εἶδεν	??
13	πειραζόμενος	ἦν	Periphrastic
14	κηρύσσων	ἦλθεν	Temporal
15	λέγων	ἦλθεν	Temporal

78B. Pragmatics of Participles *cont.*

1. Decide & compare:

1:19	Causal	being a righteous man
21:22	Conditional	with faith
28:19–20	Instrumental	baptizing and teaching
8:11	Purpose	to test him
8:18	Concession	have eyes
9:15	Temporal	When the crowd saw him

79. Periphrastic Participles

1. Choose:
future indicative
pluperfect indicative
imperfect indicative
perfect indicative
present indicative

2. Find, identify, give equivalent: εἰμί + Part

1:6	ἦν … ἐνδεδυμένος	Impf + Perf	he had clothed himself
1:22	ἦν … διδάσκων	Impf + Pres	he was teaching
1:33	ἦν … ἐπισυνηγμένη	Impf + Perf	it had gathered
2:18	ἦσαν … νηστεύοντες	Impf + Pres	they were fasting
5:41	ἐστιν μεθερμηνευόμενον	Pres + Pres	which is interpreted
9:4	ἦσαν συλλαλοῦντες	Impf + Pres	they were talking with
10:32	Ἦσαν … ἀναβαίνοντες	Impf + Pres	they were going up
	ἦν προάγων	Impf + Pres	he was going ahead
13:13	ἔσεσθε μισούμενοι	Fut + Pres	you will be hated
2:17	γεγραμμένον ἐστίν	Pres+ Perf	it is written

80A. Three Key μι Verbs (ε, ο, α): Indicative and Participle

1. Form:

δέδωκεν   ἐθήκατε   στήσομεν

δέδοσαι   ἐστάθησαν   τεθήσῃ

2. Parse:

Fut	Act	Ind	3rd	Pl	δίδωμι	I give
Perf	Act	Ind	1st	Pl	ἵστημι	I stand
Aor	Act	Ind	2nd	Pl	τίθημι	I place
Perf	M/P	Ind	3rd	Pl	δίδωμι	I give
Perf	Act	Ind	3rd	Sg	τίθημι	I place

3. Find, parse, translate:

6:22	δώσω	I will give	Fut	Act	Ind	1st	Sg	δίδωμι	I give
6:29	ἔθηκαν	they laid	Aor	Act	Ind	3rd	Pl	τίθημι	I place
8:12	δοθήσεται	it will be given	Fut	Pass	Ind	3rd	Sg	δίδωμι	I give
8:25	ἐπέθηκεν	he laid	Aor	Act	Ind	3rd	Sg	ἐπιτίθημι	I place upon
14:44	δεδώκει	he had given	Pl	Act	Ind	3rd	Sg	δίδωμι	I give
verse	παραδιδούς	(the) betraying (one)	Pres	Act	Part	Nom	Sg	παραδίδωμι	I betray

80B. Three Key μι Verbs (ε, ο, α): Other Moods, Aorist Forms

1. Find, parse, translate:

1:14	παραδοθῆναι	to be arrested	Aor	Pass	Inf				παραδίδωμι	I hand over
3:19	παρέδωκεν	he betrayed	Aor	Act	Ind	3rd	Sg		παραδίδωμι	I hand over
3:24	σταθῆναι	to be caused to stand	Aor	Pass	Inf				ἵστημι	I stand
3:26	ἀνέστη	it stood	2 Aor	Act	Ind	3rd	Sg		ἀνίστημι	I stand up
verse	στῆναι	to stand	Aor	Act	Inf				ἵστημι	I stand
5:23	ἐπιθῆν	(in order to) place upon	Aor	Act	Sub	2nd	Sg		ἐπιτίθημι	I place upon
6:37	δότε	(you pl) give	Aor	Act	Imp	2nd	Pl		δίδωμι	I give
verse	δώσομεν	we will give	Fut	Act	Ind	1st	Pl		δίδωμι	I give
7:9	στήσητε	that you might cause to stand	Aor	Act	Sub	2nd	Pl		ἵστημι	I stand
7:13	παρεδώκατε	you handed on	Aor	Act	Ind	2nd	Pl		παραδίδωμι	I hand over
8:25	ἐπέθηκεν	he laid upon	Aor	Act	Ind	3rd	Sg		ἐπιτίθημι	I place upon
8:25	ἀπεκατέστη	it was restored	Aor	Act	Ind	3rd	Sg		ἀποκαθίστημι	I am restored
9:1	ἑστηκότω	having stood	Perf	Act	Part	Gen	Pl	Masc	ἵστημ	I stand
10:40	δοῦναι	to give	Aor	Act	Inf				δίδωμι	I give
13:9	παραδώσουσιν	they will hand over	Fut	Act	Ind	3rd	Pl		παραδίδωμι	I hand over
verse	σταθήσεσθε	you will stand	Fut	Pass	Ind	2nd	Pl		ἵστημι	I stand
13:11	παραδιδόντες	handing over	Perf	Act	Part	Nom	Pl	Masc	παραδίδωμι	I hand over
verse	δοθῇ	(whatever) might be given	Aor	Pass	Sub	3rd	Sg		δίδωμι	I give
13:14	ἑστηκότα	having been set up	Perf	Act	Part	Acc	Sg	Masc	ἵστημι	I stand OR
			Perf	Act	Part	N/A	Pl	Neut	ἵστημι	I stand
15:10	παραδεδώκεισαν	they had handed over	Plu	Act	Ind	3rd	Pl		παραδίδωμι	I hand over
15:35	παρεστηκότων	having stood	Perf	Act	Part	Gen	Pl	Masc/Neut	παρίστημι	I stand up

1. Parse and translate:

11:6	Aor	Act	Ind	3rd	Pl		they allowed
11:16	Imp	Act	Ind	3rd	Sg		he was not allowing
11:25	Pres	Act	Imp	2nd	Pl		forgive!
12:12	Aor	Act	Part	Nom	Pl	Masc	leaving
12:19	Aor	Act	Sub	3rd	Sg		he should leave
OR	Aor	Mid	Sub	2nd	Sg		
13:2	Aor	Pass	Sub	3rd	Sg		(no way) left
13:34	Aor	Act	Part	Nom	Sg	Masc	leaving
14:6	Aor	Act	Impv	2nd	Pl		Let (her alone)

82. The μὲν … δέ Construction

1. Find the μὲν … δέ … constructions:
   though John never … all he said was true (10:41)
   in regard to … in regard to (16:9–10)
   Now … but (16:22)
   So soldiers did … the mother stood (19:24–25)
   soldiers came and broke … but when they came to Jesus (19:32–33)
   Jesus did many … but these (20:30–31)

VOCABULARY LISTS

Vocab #1 [L8]
Names – Various Declensions

Ἀβραάμ	12:26	Abraham
Ἀνδρέας	1:16	Andrew
Γαλιλαία	1:9	Galilee
Δαυίδ	2:25	David
Ζεβεδαῖος	1:19	Zebedee
Ἠσαΐας	1:2	Isaiah
θεός	1:1	God, god
Ἰάκωβος	1:19	James
Ἰησοῦς	1:1	Jesus
Ἰορδάνης	1:9	Jordan
Ἰουδαία	1:5	Judea
Ἰουδαῖος	7:3	Jew, Judean
Ἰωάννης	1:4	John
Ναζαρέτ	1:9	Nazareth
Πέτρος	3:16	Peter
Πιλᾶτος	15:1	Pilate
σατανᾶς	1:13	Satan
Σίμων	1:16	Simon
Χριστός	1:1	Christ

Vocab #2 [L15]
Nouns – Masculine – 2nd Declension: λόγος, ου, ὁ

ἄγγελος	1:2	messenger, angel
ἀδελφός	1:16	brother
ἁμαρτωλός	2:15	sinner
ἄνθρωπος	1:23	person, man
Ζεβεδαῖος	1:19	Zebedee
ἥλιος	1:32	sun
θεός	1:1	God, god
Ἰάκωβος	1:19	James
Ἰησοῦς	1:1	Jesus
Ἰουδαῖος	7:3	Jew, Judean
καιρός	1:15	(fixed) time, period
κύριος	1:3	lord, owner, master
λόγος	1:45	word, assertion
οἶκος	2:1	house, family
οὐρανός	1:10	heaven
ὄχλος	2:4	crowd
Πέτρος	3:16	Peter
Πιλᾶτος	15:1	Pilate
ποταμός	1:5	river, stream
τόπος	1:35	place, location
υἱός	1:1	son, descendant

Nouns – Feminine ὁδός, οῦ, ἡ

ἔρημος	1:3	desert, wilderness
ὁδός	1:2	way, road, journey

Vocab #3 [L18]
Nouns – Feminine – 1st Declension: γραφή, ῆς, ἡ

ἀρχή	1:1	beginning, ruler
γραφή	12:10	writing, Scripture
διδαχή	1:22	teaching, instruction
παραβολή	3:23	parable, illustration
συναγωγή	1:23	synagogue, assembly
φωνή	1:3	sound, voice, noise

ὥρα, ας, ἡ

ἁμαρτία	1:4	sin
βασιλεία	1:15	kingdom, royal rule
Γαλιλαία	1:9	Galilee
ἐξουσία	1:22	authority, power
ἡμέρα	1:9	day, time
θύρα	1:33	door, entrance
Ἰουδαία	1:5	Judea
μετάνοια	1:4	repentance
οἰκία	1:29	house, family
ὥρα	6:35	hour, time of day

δόξα, ης, ἡ

γλῶσσα	7:33	tongue, language
δόξα	8:38	brightness, greatness
θάλασσα	1:16	sea, lake

Vocab #4 [L20]
Nouns – Neuter – 2nd declension: ἔργον, ου, τό

δαιμόνιον	1:34	demon, (evil) spirit
ἔργον	13:34	work, deed, action
εὐαγγέλιον	1:1	gospel, good news
θηρίον	1:13	animal, beast
ἱμάτιον	2:21	clothing, apparel
παιδίον	5:39	child
πλοῖον	1:20	boat, ship
πρόσωπον	1:2	face, presence
σάββατον	1:21	sabbath, week
τέκνον	2:5	child, descendant

Vocab #5 [L21]
1st declension masculine nouns: προφήτης, ου, ὁ

Ἰορδάνης	1:9	Jordan
Ἰωάννης	1:4	John
μαθητής	2:15	disciple, adherent
προφήτης	1:2	prophet

1st declension masculine nouns: Ἀνδρέας, ου, ὁ

Ἀνδρέας	1:16	Andrew
Ἠσαΐας	1:2	Isaiah
σατανᾶς	1:13	Satan

Personal Pronoun – 3rd Person [L23]

αὐτός, ή, ό	1:5	he, she, it

Vocab #6 [L25]
Prepositions

εἰς	+ acc	1:9	into, in, toward, to
	+	1:4	for, in order to
πρός	+ acc	1:5	toward, near, at
ἀπό	+ gen	1:42	from, away from
ἐκ	+ gen	1:10	from, out of
ἐν	+ dat	1:2	in, among
ὀπίσω	+ gen	1:7	behind, after (place)
πρό	+ gen	1:2	before, in front of
μετά	+ gen	1:20	with, among
μετά	+ acc	1:14	behind, after
περί	+ gen	1:30	about, concerning
	+ acc	1:6	around, about, near
ὑπό	+ gen	1:5	by
	+ acc	4:21	under
ἐπί	+ gen	2:10	on, upon, near
	+ dat	1:22	on, in, above
	+ acc	2:14	on, over
παρά	+ gen	3:21	from beside, beside
	+ dat	10:27	by, beside, near
	+ acc	1:16	by, at edge of, near

Vocab #7 [L28]
Verbs Ending in ω: λύω

ἄγω	1:38	I lead, bring, go
βάλλω	2:22	I throw, expel, put
γράφω	1:2	I write, record
διδάσκω	1:21	I teach, instruct
ἐγείρω	1:31	I raise up, wake up
ἐσθίω	1:6	I eat, consume
εὑρίσκω	1:37	I find, discover
ἔχω (impf εἶχον)	1:22	I have, own, hold
θέλω	1:40	I wish, desire, will
θεραπεύω	1:34	I heal, restore
λέγω	1:7	I say, tell, report
λύω	1:7	I loose, untie, destroy
πιστεύω	1:15	I believe, trust
φέρω	1:32	I carry, bring

Compound Verbs Ending ω

N.B. These occur as one word without a space

ἀπο στέλλω	1:2	I send away, send out
ἐκ βάλλω	1:12	I drive out, send away
προσ φέρω	1:44	I bring, offer
ὑπ άγω	1:44	I go away

Vocab #8 [L29]
Verbs Ending in εω: ποιέω

ἀκολουθέω	1:18	I follow, am a disciple
ζητέω	1:37	I seek, investigate, strive
καλέω	1:20	I call, invite, summon

N.B. ε does not lengthen in καλέω and compounds

κρατέω	1:31	I seize, hold
λαλέω	1:34	I talk, speak
ποιέω	1:3	I make, do, keep
φωνέω	1:26	I call out, summon

Compound verbs ending εω

N.B. These occur as one word without a space

δι ακονέω	1:13	I serve, help, minister to
παρα καλέω	1:40	I encourage, urge, implore

N.B. ε does not lengthen in καλέω and compounds

Verb To Be εἰμί

εἰμί	1:6	I am

Vocab #9 [L36]
Special Verbal Roots
Verbal Root Ending δ

βαπτίζω	1:5	I baptize, wash
δοξάζω		I praise, glorify
ἐγγίζω	1:15	I draw near
ἑτοιμάζω	1:3	I prepare
καθαρίζω	1:41	I make clean, cleanse
καθίζω		I seat, appoint, sit
πειράζω	1:13	I test, tempt
σώζω		I save, rescue

Verbal Root Ending γ or κ

κηρύσσω	1:4	I announce, proclaim
πράσσω		I do, behave
κράζω	3:11	I cry out, call out

Vocab #10 [L39]

Adjectives

Consonant Stem ἀγαθός, ή, όν

ἀγαθός	3:4	good, useful
ἀγαπητός	1:11	beloved, dear
ἄλλος, η, ο	4:5	other, another
ἐμός	8:38	my, mine (possessive)
ἱκανός	1:7	sufficient, competent
καινός	1:27	new, unused
ὀλίγος	1:19	little, few
ὅλος (pred. pos.)	1:28	whole, entire

Vowel or ρ Stem ἅγιος, α, ον

ἅγιος	1:8	holy, perfect
δίκαιος	2:17	upright, just, right
ἰσχυρός	1:7	strong

Same Form Masculine & Feminine: ἀκάθαρτος, ον

αἰώνιος		eternal, without end
ἀκάθαρτος	1:23	unclean, impure

Vocab #11 [L41]

Personal Pronouns

ἐγώ	1:8	I (1st pers sg)
ἡμεῖς	1:24	we (1st pers plur)
σύ	1:11	you (2nd pers sg)
ὑμεῖς	1:8	you (2nd pers plur)

Vocab #12 [L43]

Coordinating Conjunctions

καί	1:4	and, also
δέ	1:8	and, now, but
διό		therefore
γάρ	1:16	for, then
ἀλλά	1:44	but, yet
οὖν		so, therefore
ἤ	2:9	or, than
τέ		and, even
οὐδέ	4:22	and not, neither, nor
οὔτε		and not
εἴτε		and if

Subordinating Conjunctions

ὅτι	1:34, 15; 2:1	because, " ", that
εἰ	2:7	if
ὡς	1:22	as
καθώς	1:2	as, even as
γάρ	1:16	for, then
ὅτε	1:32	when, while

Vocab #13 [L45]

More Prepositions

διά	+ gen	2:23	through, via
	+ acc	2:4	because of
ὑπέρ	+ gen	9:40	for, on behalf of
	+ acc		above, beyond
κατά	+ gen	3:6	against, toward
	+ acc	1:27	according to, along
ἔμπροσθεν+	gen		in front of, before
ἐνώπιον	+ gen		before, in presence of
ἔξω	+ gen	1:45	outside, out of
ἕως	+ gen		until, as far as
χωρίς	+ gen		apart from, without
σύν	+ dat	2:26	with

Vocab #14 [L48]

Verbs with Middle Lexical Forms

(ἅπτομαι)	I touch, hold, cling to
ἄρχομαι	I begin
ἀσπάζομαι	I greet, welcome
δέχομαι	I receive, take, grasp
ἐργάζομαι	I work, accomplish
ἔρχομαι	I come, go
ἀπέρχομαι	I go away, depart, leave
διέρχομαι	I go through
εἰσέρχομαι	I enter, come into
ἐξέρχομαι	I come out, go away
προσέρχομαι+ dat	I come to, approach
(εὐαγγελίζομαι)	I proclaim the gospel
λογίζομαι	I reckon, calculate, think
προσεύχομαι	I pray

Verbs with Passive Lexical Forms

βούλομαι	I want, intend, will
(φοβέομαι)	I fear, am afraid

Verbs with Mixed (Middle / Passive) Lexical Forms

ἀποκρίνομαι+ dat	I answer, reply
γίνομαι	I am, become, am made, come about, happen, move, etc.
(πορεύομαι)	I go, proceed, live
ἐκπορεύομαι	I go out, proceed

Vocab #15 [L50]
More Endings Ending in ω

αἴρω	I lift up, take up, carry away
ἀκούω	I hear, listen, learn about
ἁμαρτάνω	I sin
ἀνοίγω	I open
ἄρχω	I rule
βλέπω	I see, look at
γινώσκω	I know, understand
διώκω	I pursue, persecute
κλαίω	I weep, cry
κρίνω	I judge, decide
λαμβάνω	I take, acquire, receive
μένω	I remain, stay
πάσχω	I suffer, experience
πείθω	I convince, persuade
πέμπω	I send
πίπτω	I fall, am destroyed
σπείρω	I sow seed, scatter
ὑπάρχω	I exist, am, am present
χαίρω	I rejoice, am glad

Vocab #16 [L52]
More Verbs Ending in εω

αἰτέω	I ask, demand
δέω	I bind, tie
δοκέω	I think, believe, seem
εὐχαριστέω	I am thankful, give thanks
θεωρέω	I look at, observe, notice
μαρτυρέω	I bear witness, testify
μισέω	I hate, detest
οἰκοδομέω	I build, strengthen
τηρέω	I keep, guard

More Compound Verbs Ending ω

ἀνα βαίνω	I go up, ascend
ἀπο θνήσκω	I die, face death
ἀπο κτείνω	I kill, eliminate
ἀπο λύω	I release, free, dismiss
ἐπι γινώσκω	I learn, know, recognize
κατα βαίνω	I go down, descend
παρα λαμβάνω	I take, receive
συν ἄγω	I gather, bring together

More Compound Verbs Ending εω

κατ οἰκέω	I live, dwell, inhabit
περι πατέω	I walk around, behave
προσ κυνέω	I worship, revere

Vocab #17 [L54]
More masculine nouns: λόγος, οῦ, ὁ

ἀπόστολος	apostle, envoy
ἄρτος	bread, loaf, food
διδάσκαλος	teacher
δοῦλος	slave
θάνατος	death
θρόνος	chair, seat, throne
καρπός	fruit, advantage
κόσμος	world, universe, adornment
λαός	people, people-group
λίθος	stone
ναός	temple, sanctuary
νόμος	law, principle
οἶνος	wine
ὀφθαλμός	eye
πειρασμός	test, trial, temptation
πρεσβύτερος	elder
σταυρός	cross
φόβος	fear, reverence, a terror
χρόνος	time, occasion

Vocab #18 [L55]
More Feminine Nouns γραφή, ῆς, ἡ

ἀγάπη	love, affection, esteem
γῆ	earth, ground, land
δικαιοσύνη	righteousness, justice
εἰρήνη	peace, harmony
ἐντολή	command
ζωή	life
κεφαλή	head
ὀργή	anger, wrath
τιμή	honor, price
ὑπομονή	endurance, perseverance
φυλακή	prison
ψυχή	soul, life, person

More Feminine Nouns ὥρα, ας, ἡ

ἀδικία	unrighteousness, wickedness
ἀλήθεια	truth, reality
γενεά	age, generation
ἐκκλησία	assembly, congregation
ἐπαγγελία	promise, pledge
ἐπιθυμία	craving, lust, desire
καρδία	heart, centre
μαρτυρία	testimony
σοφία	wisdom, Wisdom
σωτηρία	salvation, deliverance
χαρά	joy, gladness
χρεία	need, lack

Vocab #19 [L57]
Pronouns: Demonstrative

N.B. Take predicative position

οὗτος, αὕτη, τοῦτο	1:27		this (proximity)
ἐκεῖνος, η, ο	1:9		that (remoteness)

Pronouns: Reflexive & Relative

ἐμαυτοῦ, ῆς	myself
σεαυτοῦ, ῆς	yourself
ἑαυτοῦ, ῆς, οῦ	him-, her-, it-self, self
ὅς, ἥ, ὅ	who, which, what, that

Neuter Nouns ἔργον, ου, τό

ἱερόν	sanctuary, temple
μνημεῖον	tomb, grave, memorial
πρόβατον	sheep
σημεῖον	sign, miracle

Vocab #20 [L58]
Adjectives Consonant Stem

ἕκαστος	each, every
κακός	bad, evil, harm
καλός	good, useful
λοιπός	remaining, rest of

Adjectives: Consonant Stem ἀγαθός, ή, όν

μέσος	middle, among
μόνος	only, alone
ὅσος	as great, as far, as much
πιστός	trusting, faithful
πρῶτος	first, earliest
τοιοῦτος, αύτη, οῦτον	of such a kind
τρίτος	third, third part
τυφλός	blind, uncomprehending

Adjectives: Vowel or ρ Stem ἅγιος, α, ον

ἄξιος	worthy, deserving
δεξιός	right
δεύτερος	second, a second time
ἕτερος	other, different
ἴδιος	one's own, own
μακάριος	blessed, privileged
μικρός	small, short
νεκρός	dead, lifeless, corpse
ὅμοιος	same, like, similar
πονηρός	evil, wicked

Vocab #21 [L60]

Perfect Related

οἶδα (perfect form)	I know, understand (pres)
ᾔδεις (pluperfect form)	I knew (aor)
εἰδέναι (infinitive)	to know
εἰδῶ (subjunctive)	I know
εἰδώς -υῖα -ος	knowing
εἰδότος	

Numbers

N.B. 5 – 100 are indeclinable

δύο (indeclinable)	two
τρεῖς, τρία	three
τέσσαρες, α	four
πέντε	five
ἕξ	six
ἑπτά	seven
δέκα	ten
δώδεκα	twelve
τεσσαράκοντα	forty
ἑκατόν	one hundred

Vocab #22 [L62]

Verbs Like δύναμαι

δύναμαι	I can, am able, am capable
κάθημαι	I sit, stay, sit down
κεῖμαι	I lie, recline, exist

Vocab #23 [L65]

Words Used with Subjunctive

ἵνα (conj.)	in order that, that, so that
ὅπως (conj.)	in order that, that
ἄν (part.)	untrans. of contingency (-ever, would)
ὅταν (part.)	whenever, when, while

Conjunctions Used with Conditions

εἰ	if, whether (indirect qns)
ἐάν (εἰ + ἄν)	if
εἴτε (εἰ + τε)	if, whether (indirect qns)

Interjection

οὐαί	woe, alas

Crasis

κἀγώ (καί + ἐγώ)	and I, but I, I too

Vocab #24 [L68]

Adverbs
Adverbs of Place

ἐκεῖ	there, in that place
ὅπου	where
ὧδε	here, at this point

Adverbs of Time

ἄρτι	at present, just now
ἔτι	yet, still
οὐκέτι	no more, no longer
μηκέτι	no longer, not from now on
εὐθέως	at once, immediately
ἤδη	already, now
νῦν, νυνί	now
τότε	then, thereafter
πάντοτε	always, at all times
σήμερον	today

Adverbs of Manner

ἀμήν	Amen, truly
καλῶς	rightly, correctly
ὁμοίως	likewise, so, similarly
οὕτως	thus, in this way
πάλιν	again, also
πῶς	how?

Adverb of Degree

μᾶλλον	more, rather

Vocab #25 [L69]

3rd Declension Nouns: Masculine and feminine Stems (i.e., Genitive) Ending in ρ

ἀνήρ, ἀνδρός, ὁ	man, husband
ἀστήρ, ἀστέρος, ὁ	star, planet
μάρτυς, μάρτυρος, ὁ	witness, martyr
σωτήρ, σωτῆρος, ὁ	saviour, deliverer
χείρ, χειρός, ἡ	hand

Variations like πατήρ, πατρός, ὁ

μήτηρ, μητρός, ἡ	mother
πατήρ, πατρός, ὁ	father, parent

Stems Ending in ν

αἰών, αἰῶνος, ὁ	age, eternity, past
Σίμων, Σίμωνος, ὁ	Simon

Stems Ending in κ or γ

γυνή, γυναικός, ἡ	woman, wife
σάρξ, σαρκός, ἡ	flesh, body, mortal nature

Stems Ending in δ or τ

ἐλπίς, ἐλπίδος, ἡ	hope, expectation
νύξ, νυκτός, ἡ	night
πούς, ποδός, ὁ	foot
χάρις, χάριτος, ἡ	grace, favour, charm

3rd Declension Nouns
Feminine Ending in -ις

ἀνάστασις, εως, ἡ	resurrection
ἄφεσις, ἀφέσεως, ἡ	pardon, cancellation
δύναμις, δυνάμεως, ἡ	power, ability
θλῖψις, θλίψεως, ἡ	oppression, affliction
κρίσις, κρίσεως, ἡ	judgment, right
πίστις, πίστεως, ἡ	faith, trust, fidelity
πόλις, πόλεως, ἡ	city, town

Masculine Ending in – ευς

βασιλεύς, βασιλέως, ὁ	king
γραμματεύς, έως, ὁ	scribe, expert in law
ἱερεύς, ἱερέως, ὁ	priest
ἀρχιερεύς, έως, ὁ	high priest, chief priest

Vocab #26 [L70]
3rd Declension Nouns
Neuter Like σῶμα, σώματος, τό

αἷμα, αἵματος, τό	blood
θέλημα, θελήματος, τό	will
ὄνομα, ὀνόματος, τό	name, title
πνεῦμα, πνεύματος, τό	spirit, breath, Spirit
ῥῆμα, ῥήματος, τό	word, thing
σπέρμα, σπέρματος, τό	seed, descendants
στόμα, στόματος, τό	mouth
σῶμα, σώματος, τό	body, corpse
οὖς, ὠτός, τό	ear, hearing
πῦρ, πυρός, τό	fire
ὕδωρ, ὕδατος, τό	water
φῶς, φωτός, τό	light, lamp

Like τέλος, τέλους, τό

ἔθνος, ἔθνους, τό	nation, Gentile
ἔτος, ἔτους, τό	year
μέλος, μέλους, τό	member, limb
μέρος, μέρους, τό	part, share
ὄρος, ὄρους, τό	mountain, hill
πλῆθος, πλήθους, τό	large number
τέλος, τέλους, τό	end, goal

Vocab #27 [L71]
Adjectives & Pronouns
3rd Declension

τίς, τί	who, which, what, why?
τις, τι	someone, anyone, a certain
ὅστις, ἥτις, ὅ τι	whoever, who
μείζων, μεῖζον, μειζόνος	greater, larger
πλείων, πλεῖον, πλείονος	more

3rd – 1st – 3rd Declension

πᾶς, πᾶσα, πᾶν, παντός (pred. pos.)	every, all, whole
ἅπας, ἅπασα, ἅπαν (pred.)	whole, all
εἷς, μία, ἕν, ἑνός	one, the first
οὐδείς, μηδείς	no one, nothing

2nd – 1st – 2nd Declension

πολύς, πολλή, πολύ	much, many
μέγας, μεγάλη, μέγα	great, large

Vocab #28 [L74]
Infinitive Related

θέλω	I wish, want, desire
μέλλω	I am about to, destined
δεῖ	it is necessary, fitting
ἔξεστιν+ dat	it is right, permitted
ὥστε	so that, therefore
δύναμαι	I am able, can

Vocab #29 [L77]
Verbs Ending in αω

ἀγαπάω	I love, have affection for, cherish
γεννάω	I bear, beget
ἐρωτάω	I ask, request
ἐπερωτάω	I ask, ask for
ὁράω	I notice, catch sight of
πλανάω	I mislead, deceive
τιμάω	I honor, revere
ἐπιτιμάω	I rebuke, reprove
καυχάομαι	I boast, glory, am proud of
ζάω	I live

Vocab #29 Cont.
Verbs Ending in οω

δικαιόω	I justify, vindicate, make free
πληρόω	I fill, complete, fulfil
σταυρόω	I crucify
φανερόω	I reveal, disclose

Vocab #30 [L80]
μι Verbs

τίθημι	I lay, put
ἐπιτίθημι	I lay upon, put upon
δίδωμι	I give, donate, sacrifice
ἀποδίδωμι	I pay, reward, give back
παραδίδωμι	I hand over, hand down
ἵστημι	transitive: I set, establish, vindicate; intransitive: I stand, stand still, stand firm
ἀνίστημι	trans: I raise, raise up; intrans: I rise up, stand up
παρίστημι	trans: I place beside, present; intrans: I am present
ἀφίημι	I forgive, pardon, cancel, leave
συνίημι	I understand, comprehend
δείκνυμι	I show, point out, explain
φημί	I say, affirm
ἀπόλλυμι	active: I ruin, destroy; middle: I perish, am ruined

RULES OF WORD FORMATION

Verbs Followed by Special Case for Direct Object	Words Easily Confused			
GENITIVE	Neut pl of ἄλλος	ἄλλα	ἀλλά	but
ἀκούω	Fem of αὐτός	αὐτή	αὕτη	Fem of οὗτος
(of person heard, acc. of thing)	Fem pl of αὐτός	αὐταί	αὗται	Fem pl of οὗτος
ἅπτομαι	if	εἰ	εἶ	2nd pers εἰμί
ἄρχω	into, to	εἰς	εἷς	one
	outside	ἔξω	ἕξω	Fut Sg ἔχω
	in, on	ἐν	ἕν	one
DATIVE	Fem sg article	ἡ	ἥ	Fem Rel Pro
ἀκολουθέω	or, than	ἤ		
ἀποκρίνομαι	Subj of εἰμί	ᾖ	ᾗ	Fem Rel Pro
διακονέω	Impf of εἰμί	ἦν	ἥν	Fem Rel Pro
ἐγγίζω	Subj of εἰμί	ᾖς	ἧς	Fem Rel Pro
ἔξεστιν	Masc sg article	ὁ	ὅ	Rel Pro
πιστεύω	Participle of εἰμί	ὄν	ὅν	Rel Pro
προσέρχομαι	not	οὐ	οὗ	Rel Pro
προσκυνέω	a certain, some	τις, τι	τίς, τί	who? What?
ὑπακούω	Subj of εἰμί	ὦ	ᾧ	Rel Pro
ἐπιτιμάω	O! (with vocative)	ὦ		
πέποιθα (perf. πείθω)	Participle of εἰμί	ὤν	ὧν	Rel Pro

RULES FOR CHANGES

Beginning of Stem	End of Stem

Beginning of Stem

VERBS: INITIAL VOWEL CHANGE
Imperfect & Aorist

Augment + stem

ε + ἀ → ἠ	ε + αἰ → ἠ	ε + αὐ → ηὐ
ε + ἐ → ἠ	ε + εἰ → ἠ	ε + εὐ → ηὐ OR εὐ
ε + ὀ → ὠ	ε + οἰ → ὠ	

VERBS: REDUPLICATION
Perfect & Pluperfect

Consonant first letter	**Vowel first letter**
consonant + ε + stem	vowel lengthens
λύω → λέλυκα	ἀκολουθέω → ἠκολούθηκα
except	OR
χ → κεχ σ → ἑσ	
	remains unchanged
φ → πεφ ζ → ἐζ	εὑρίσκω → εὗρον
θ → τεθ ξ → ἐξ	

End of Stem

VERBS ENDING IN MUTES

Addition of σ (Aorist & Future; Active & Middle)			**Addition of θ** (Aorist & Future; Passive)		
κ, γ, χ +	σ	= ξ	κ, γ, χ +	θ	= χθ
π, β, φ +	σ	= ψ	π, β, φ +	θ	= φθ
δ, τ, θ +	σ	= σ	δ, τ, θ +	θ	= σθ

CONTRACT VERBS εω, αω, οω
Adding vowels   Adding consonants

εω							
	ποιε +	ε	= ποιεω	ποιε +	σ	= ποιησ
	ποιε +	ο	= ποιου	ποιε +	κ	= ποιηκ
	ποιε +	ω	= ποιω	ποιε +	μ	= ποιημ
	(long vowel or diphthong)			etc. (except καλέω)		

αω						
	γεννα +	ο, ου, ω	= γεννω	γεννα +	σ	= γεννησ
	γεννα +	ε, η	= γεννα	γεννα +	κ	= γεννηκ
	γεννα +	ει, οι, αι	= γεννα	γεννα +	μ	= γεννημ
	(except pres act inf γενναν)			etc.		

οω						
	φανερο +	η, ω	= φανερω	φανερο +	σ	= φανερωσ
	φανερο +	ε, α, ο	= φανερου	φανερο +	κ	= φανερωκ
	φανερο +	ει, αι, οι	= φανεροι	φανερο +	μ	= φανερωμ
				etc.		

NOUNS: 3RD DECLENSION DATIVE PLURALS

κ, γ, χ +	σιν	= ξιν	αντ +	σιν	= ασιν
π, β, φ +	σιν	= ψιν	δντ +	σιν	= εισιν
τ, δ, θ +	σιν	= σιν	οντ +	σιν	= ουσιν

PATTERNS OF WORD FORMATION

These are generalisations about the significance of endings and prefixes. They do not hold for every New Testament word.

Nouns			Verbs & Adverbs			Adjectives & Prefixes		
SIGNIFICANCE ENDING	EXAMPLE	ENGLISH	SIGNIFICANCE ENDING	EXAMPLE	ENGLISH	SIGNIFICANCE ENDING	EXAMPLE	ENGLISH
PERSON, THING			**STATE OR ACTION**			**GENERAL QUALITY**		
–ος	θεός	god, God	–ω	λύω	I loose	–ος	καλός	good
			–εω	ποιέω	I make, do	–λος	τυφλός	blind
PERSON, AGENT			–αω	τιμάω	I honor	–(α)νος	γυμνός	naked
–της	κριτής	judge	–μι	τίθημι	I place	–ρος	νεκρός	dead
–τηρ	σωτήρ	savior						
–ευς	βασιλεύς	king	**ACTION**			**POSSESSION**		
			–αζω	πειράζω	I test, tempt	–ιος	ἅγιος	holy
ACTIVITY			–ιζω	βαπτίζω	I baptise			
–τις	πίστις	faith	–ευω	πιστεύω	I trust	**BELONGING TO**		
–σις	κρίσις	judging				–ικος	ἐθνικός	Gentile
–ια	μετάνοια	repentance	**CAUSATION**					
			–οω	σταυρόω	I crucify	**MATERIAL TYPE**		
RESULT OF ACTIVITY			–υνω	αἰσχύνω	I shame	–ινος	σάρκινος	fleshly
–μα	κρίμα	judgment	–αινω	λευκαίνω	I whiten	–εος	χρύσεος	gold
ABSTRACTION, QUALITY			**MANNER**			**NOT, UN-, DIS-**		
–ια	σωτηρία	salvation	–ως	σοφῶς	wisely	ἀ–	ἄπιστος	unbelieving
–σια	ἐξουσία	authority				ἀν–	ἄναγνος	unchaste
–συνη	δικαιοσύνη	assembly	**FROM WHERE**					
–εια	βασιλεία	kingdom	–θεν	ἐκεῖθεν	from there	**WELL, GOOD**		
–οτης	νεότης	young age				εὐ–	εὐγενής	of noble birth
			IN WHAT LANGUAGE					
DIMINUTION			–ιστι	Ἑλληνιστί	in Greek	**HARD, UN-, MIS-**		
–ιον	παιδίον	infant				δυσ–	δυσνόητος	difficult to
–ιδιον	κλινίδιον	mat						understand
–ισκος	νεανίσκος	young man						

BASICS OF GREEK ACCENTS

The patterns, or "rules," of Greek accentuation are extraordinarily **complex**, and mastery requires great effort for advanced students of the language. You will not be expected to know these rules. However, for any student who wishes to pursue the study of Greek to **advanced** levels, accents become important, and the best time to learn the basics is at the beginning of your study of the language. For that reason, the basic **essentials** are provided here, which will offer a foundation for future mastery, should that be desired.

(Formal permission has been secured to summarize the work of John A. L. Lee, *Greek Accents in Eight Lessons* [Sydney: Macquarie University, 2005] on this page.)

THE BASIC RULES

Vowels are regarded as **long** or **short**.

Short:	ε, ο
Long:	η, ω, ῃ, ῳ, and ᾳ
Short or long:	α, ι, υ
"Diphthongs" are long:	αι, ει, οι, αυ, ευ, ου, υι, ηυ, ωυ
	(but final αι and οι are short)

Accents

Acute (έ) is found on final, 2nd-last, or 3rd-last syllable (on long or short vowel):

ἀστήρ, βασιλέως, ἄνθρωπος.

Circumflex (ῶ) is found on final or 2nd-last syllable (only on long vowel):

Ἰησοῦς, δῶρον.

Grave (ὰ) is only found on final syllable (on short or long vowel):

τὸν υἱόν, τὸν υἱὸν . . .

Final acute changes to grave if another word follows at once (unless the other word is enclitic).

Length of Last Syllable

The length of the last syllable determines accentuation in these ways:
1. If **short**, the accent may be on last, 2nd-last, or 3rd-last syllable: ἄνθρωπος.
2. If **long**, the accent may be on last or 2nd-last syllable, but not 3rd last: ἀνθρώπου.
3. If **long** and the accent is on 2nd last, it must be *acute* (not circumflex): δούλου.
4. If **short** and accent is on 2nd last which is long, it must be circumflex: σωτῆρα.

VERBS

Verbs have a "**recessive**" accent. The accent pushes away from the end of the word as far as possible, without transgrssing the basic rules above. There are exceptions to this; e.g., the accent does not precede the augment in compound verbs.

e.g., λύω, λύομεν, ἔλυον, λέλυμαι ἐλυόμην, ἐλυσάμην, ἐλύθην

NOUNS & ADJECTIVES

The basic rule for words that decline (such as nouns, adjectives, and participles) is that the accent remains on its **set position** if it can. Every word has its own accent, and this will remain fixed—as allowed by the basic rules. The accent of a word is not always predictable, so accents are best learned as you learn **vocabulary**.

e.g., ἄνθρωπος, καιρός, ἡμέρα

CONTRACTION

There are **two general rules** for contracted words.
1. If the accent was on one of the contracting vowels, it will also be found on the contracted vowel or "diphthong."
   e.g., φιλέω → φιλῶ
   The accent on the contracted vowel is mostly a circumflex.

2. If the original accent was on another vowel, it remains where it was.
   e.g., ἐποίεον → ἐποίουν

ENCLITICS

Enclitics are words that are **unaccented** in most uses. A word that is **followed by** an enclitic has its accent affected. These changes in accentuation are explained if the enclitic is regarded as combined with the preceding word.

The Enclitics

με, μου, μοι, σε, σου, σοι
τις, τι (all forms)
που, ποτε, πως, ποθεν, ποι
εἰμι, ἐστιν, ἐσμεν, ἐστε, εἰσιν (not εἶ)
φημι, φησι, φαμεν, φατε, φασι
γε, τε
There are others, but these are the main enclitics.

Enclitic Patterns of Accentuation
Each pattern shows a monosyllabic then disyllabic enclitic.

ἀδελφός μου	ἀδελφός ἐστιν
ἄνθρωπός μου	ἄνθρωπός ἐστιν
λόγος μου	λόγος ἐστίν
φῶς μου	φῶς ἐστιν
δῶρόν μου	δῶρόν ἐστιν

Nouns and Adjectives

Nouns										

		1st Declension					2nd Declension		3rd Declension			

		Feminine			Masc		Masc	Neut	M/F	Fem	Masc	Neuter	
Sg	Nom	γραφή	ὥρα	δόξα	προφήτης	Ἠσαΐας	λόγος	ἔργον	ἀστήρ	πόλις	βασιλεύς	σῶμα	γένος
	Gen	γραφῆς	ὥρας	δόξης	προφήτου	Ἠσαΐου	λόγου	ἔργου	ἀστέρος	πόλεως	βασιλέως	σώματος	γένους
	Dat	γραφῇ	ὥρᾳ	δόξῃ	προφήτῃ		λόγῳ	ἔργῳ	ἀστέρι	πόλει	βασιλεῖ	σώματι	γένει
	Acc	γραφήν	ὥραν	δόξαν	προφήτην	Ἠσαΐαν	λόγον	ἔργον	ἀστέρα	πόλιν	βασιλέα	σῶμα	γένος
Pl	Nom	γραφαί	ὥραι	δόξαι	προφῆται		λόγοι	ἔργα	ἀστέρες	πόλεις	βασιλεῖς	σώματα	γένη
	Gen	γραφῶν	ὡρῶν	δοξῶν	προφητῶν		λόγων	ἔργων	ἀστέρων	πόλεων	βασιλέων	σωμάτων	γενῶν
	Dat	γραφαῖς	ὥραις	δόξαις	προφήταις		λόγοις	ἔργοις	ἀστράσιν	πόλεσιν	βασιλεῦσιν	σώμασιν	γένεσιν
	Acc	γραφάς	ὥρας	δόξας	προφήτας		λόγους	ἔργα	ἀστέρας	πόλεις	βασιλεῖς	σώματα	γένη

Adjectives													

		1st & 2nd Declension (2–1–2)									3rd Declension		1st & 3rd (3–1–3)		

		M	F	N	M	F	N	M	F	N	M/F	N	M	F	N
Sg	Nom	ἀγαθός	ἀγαθή	ἀγαθόν	ἅγιος	ἁγία	ἅγιον	πολύς	πολλή	πολύ	πλείων	πλεῖον	πᾶς	πᾶσα	πᾶν
	Gen	ἀγαθοῦ	ἀγαθῆς	ἀγαθοῦ	ἁγίου	ἁγίας	ἁγίου	πολλοῦ	πολλῆς	πολλοῦ	πλείονος	πλείονος	παντός	πάσης	παντός
	Dat	ἀγαθῷ	ἀγαθῇ	ἀγαθῷ	ἁγίῳ	ἁγίᾳ	ἁγίῳ	πολλῷ	πολλῇ	πολλῷ	πλείονι	πλείονι	παντί	πάσῃ	παντί
	Acc	ἀγαθόν	ἀγαθήν	ἀγαθόν	ἅγιον	ἁγίαν	ἅγιον	πολύν	πολλήν	πολύ	πλείονα	πλείονι	πάντα	πᾶσαν	πᾶν
Pl	Nom	ἀγαθοί	ἀγαθαί	ἀγαθά	ἅγιοι	ἅγιαι	ἅγια	πολλοί	πολλαί	πολλά	πλείονες	πλείονα	πάντες	πᾶσαι	πάντα
	Gen	ἀγαθῶν	ἀγαθῶν	ἀγαθῶν	ἁγίων	ἁγίων	ἁγίων	πολλῶν	πολλῶν	πολλῶν	πλειόνων	πλείονων	πάντων	πασῶν	πασῶν
	Dat	ἀγαθοῖς	ἀγαθαῖς	ἀγαθοῖς	ἁγίοις	ἁγίαις	ἁγίοις	πολλοῖς	πολλαῖς	πολλοῖς	πλείοσιν	πλείοσιν	πᾶσι	πάσαις	πᾶσι
	Acc	ἀγαθούς	ἀγαθάς	ἀγαθά	ἁγίους	ἁγίας	ἅγια	πολλούς	πολλάς	πολλά	πλείονας	πλείονα	πάντας	πάσας	πάντα

NOUN CASE AND FUNCTION

Case	Function	Example	
NOMINATIVE	1. Subject of a verb	ὁ **κόσμος** αὐτὸν οὐκ ἔγνω	**The world** did not know him
	2. Predicate (with εἰμί)	καὶ **θεὸς** ἦν ὁ λόγος	And the Word was **God**
(VOCATIVE)	(Simple address)	**κύριε**, δός μοι τοῦτο τὸ ὕδωρ	**Lord**, give me this water
GENITIVE	1. Possession ("of …")	τὰ ῥήματα **τοῦ θεοῦ** λαλεῖ	He speaks the words **of God**
	2. After a preposition	ὁ ὢν ἐκ **τῆς γῆς**	The one being from **the earth**
	3. Time "during which"	οὗτος ἦλθεν πρὸς αὐτὸν **νυκτός**	This one came to him **by night**
	4. After some verbs (direct object)	ἀκούων **αὐτοῦ** χαρᾷ χαίρει	Hearing **him** he rejoices with joy
	5. After comparative adjective (…than…)	οὐκ ἔστιν δοῦλος μείζων **τοῦ κυρίου**	A slave is not greater **than the Master**
	6. Genitive absolute	ἔτι **αὐτοῦ λαλοῦντος** παραγίνεται Ἰούδας	While he was speaking, Judas arrived
DATIVE	1. Indirect object of a verb ("to" … "for" …)	λέγει ἡ μήτηρ αὐτοῦ τοῖς **διακόνοις**	His mother says **to the servants**
	2. After a preposition	ὃν ἔγραψεν Μωϋσῆς ἐν **τῷ νόμῳ**	About whom Moses wrote **in the law**
	3. Time "at which"	καὶ **τῇ τρίτῃ ἡμέρᾳ** ἐγερθῆναι	And **on the third day** he will be raised
	4. After some verbs (direct object)	καὶ ἠκολούθησαν **τῷ Ἰησου**	And they followed **Jesus**
	5. Instrumental use	καὶ ἐξέβαλεν τὰ πνεύματα **λόγῳ**	And he cast out the spirits **by a word**
	6. Locative (Dat. of "Sphere")	μακάριοι οἱ καθαροὶ **τῇ καρδίᾳ**	Blessed are the pure **in heart**
ACCUSATIVE	1. Direct object of a verb	ἠγάπησεν ὁ θεὸς **τὸν κόσμον**	God loved **the world**
	2. After a preposition	καὶ ἦλθον πρὸς **τὸν Ἰωάννην**	And they came toward **John**
	3. Time "how long"	ἐκεῖ ἔμειναν οὐ **πολλὰς ἡμέρας**	He remained there **for** not **many days**
	4. "Subject" of infinitive (acc. of respect)	πρὶν ἀποθανεῖν **τὸ παιδίον** μου	Before my **child** dies

PREPOSITIONS AT A GLANCE

Prep.	Case	Freq. NT	Glosses			Forms Before Vowels	
			Spatial	Temporal	Other	Smooth	Rough
Prepositions Used With Three Cases							
ἐπί +	Gen	222	on, upon, near	in the time of	in the time of	ἐπ'	ἐφ'
	Dat	186	on, in, above	at, during	at, during		
	Acc	474	on, over	for, over a period	for, over a period		
παρά +	Gen	82	from beside		by (*agency*)	παρ'	παρ'
	Dat	53	by, beside		in the sight of		
	Acc	59	by, at edge of		more than, against		
Prepositions Used With Two Cases							
διά +	Gen	387	through, via	through, during	by (*agency*)	δι'	
	Acc	280			because of		
κατά +	Gen	74	toward, down from		against (*vs*)	κατ'	καθ'
	Acc	396	along, through	at, during	according to		
μετά +	Gen	365	with, among		with	μετ'	μεθ'
	Acc	104		behind, after			
περί +	Gen	182			about, concerning		
	Acc	451	round, about		with regard to		
ὑπέρ +	Gen	130			for, on behalf of		
	Acc	19	above, beyond		more than, beyond		
ὑπό +	Gen	169			by (*agency*)	ὑπ'	ὑφ'
	Acc	151	under, below		under (*subord.*)		
Prepositions Used With One Case							
Genitive							
ἀντί +	Gen	22			instead of, for		ἀνθ'
ἀπό +	Gen	646	from, away from		from (*source*)	ἀπ'	ἀφ'
ἐκ +	Gen	914	from, out of	from [this point]	out of (*source*)	ἐξ	ἐξ
πρό +	Gen	47	before, in front	before	before (*rank*)		
Dative							
ἐν +	Dat	2752	in, among	in, when, while	with, because of		
σύν +	Dat	128			with, in company of		
Accusative							
ἀνά +	Acc	13	up, upwards		in the midst of		
εἰς +	Acc	2112	into, in, toward	for, throughout	for, in order to		
πρός +	Acc	693	toward, near, at	toward, for	for the purpose of		

VERB TABLES

Table of εἰμί the Verb "I Am"		
INDICATIVE MOOD		
Present	**Imperfect**	**Future**
εἰμί	ἤμην	ἔσομαι
εἶ	ἦς or ἦσθα	ἔσῃ
ἐστίν	ἦν	ἔσται
ἐσμέν	ἦμεν or ἤμεθα	ἐσόμεθα
ἐστέ	ἦτε	ἔσεσθε
εἰσίν	ἦσαν	ἔσονται

NON-INDICATIVE MOODS				
Subjunctive	**Infinitive**	**Participle**		
ὦ	εἶναι	ὤν	οὖσα	ὄν
ᾖς		ὄντος	οὔσης	ὄντος
ᾖ		ὄντι	οὔσῃ	ὄντι
		ὄντα	οὖσαν	ὄν
ὦμεν				
ἦτε		ὄντες	οὖσαι	ὄντα
ὦσιν		ὄντων	οὐσῶν	ὄντων
		οὖσιν	οὔσαις	οὖσιν
		ὄντας	οὔσας	ὄντα

N.B. For the imperative, the New Testament prefers the present imperative of γίνομαι.

μι – Verbs Reference Table

Forms not easily derived from principal parts

Present Active			Present Mid-Pass			2nd Aorist Active			2nd Aorist Mid	
Indicative										
τίθημι	δίδωμι	ἵστημι	τίθεμαι	δίδομαι	ἵσταμαι	ἔθηκα	ἔδωκα	ἔστην	ἐθέμην	ἐδόμην
τίθης	δίδως	ἵστης	τίθεσαι	δίδοσαι	ἵστασαι	ἔθηκας	ἔδωκας	ἔστης	ἔθου	ἔδου
τίθησιν	δίδωσιν	ἵστησιν	τίθεται	δίδοται	ἵσταται	ἔθηκες	ἔδωκες	ἔστη	ἔθετο	ἔδοτο
τίθεμεν	δίδομεν	ἵσταμεν	τιθέμεθα	διδόμεθα	ἱστάμεθα	ἐθήκαμεν	ἐδώκαμεν	ἔστημεν	ἐθέμεθα	ἐδόμεθα
τίθετε	δίδοτε	ἵστατε	τίθεσθε	δίδοσθε	ἵστασθε	ἐθήκατε	ἐδώκατε	ἔστητε	ἔθεσθε	ἔδοσθε
τιθέασιν	διδόασιν	ἱστᾶσιν	τίθενται	δίδονται	ἵστανται	ἔθηκαν	ἔδωκαν	ἔστησαν	ἔθεντο	ἔδοντο
Subjunctive										
τιθῶ	διδῶ	ἱστῶ				θῶ	δῶ	στῶ	θῶμαι	
τιθῇς	διδῷς	ἱστῇς				θῇς	δῷς	στῇς	θῇ	
τιθῇ	διδῷ	ἱστῇ				θῇ	δῷ	στῇ	θῆται	
τιθῶμεν	διδῶμεν	ἱστῶμεν				θῶμεν	δῶμεν	στῶμεν	θώμεθα	
τιθῆτε	διδῶτε	ἱστῆτε				θῆτε	δῶτε	στῆτε	θῆσθε	
τιθῶσιν	διδῶσιν	ἱστῶσιν				θῶσιν	δῶσιν	στῶσιν	θῶνται	
Imperative										
τίθει	δίδου	ἵστη	τίθεσο	ἵστασο		θές	δός	στῆθι	θοῦ	
τιθέτω	διδότω	ἱστάτω	τιθέσθω	ἱστάσθω		θέτω	δότω	στήτω	θέσθω	
τίθετε	δίδοτε	ἵστατε	τιθέσθε	ἵστασθε		θέτε	δότε	στῆτε	θέσθε	
τιθέτωσαν	διδότωσαν	ἱστάτωσαν	τιθέσθωσαν	-άσθωσαν		θέτωσαν	δότωσαν	στήτωσαν	θέσθωσαν	
Infinitive										
τιθέναι	διδόναι	ἱστάναι	τίθεσθαι	δίδοσθαι	ἵστασθαι	θεῖναι	δοῦναι	στῆναι	θέσθαι	
Participle										
τιθείς	διδούς	ἱστάς	τιθέμενος	διδόμενος	ἱστάμενος	θείς	δούς	στάς	θέμενος	
τιθέντος	διδόντος	ἱστάντος				θέντος	δόντος	στάντος		

PARTICIPLES

Present Active			Present Middle & Passive		
λύων	λύουσα	λῦον	λυόμενος	λυομένη	λυόμενον
λύοντος	λυούσης	λύοντος	λυομένου	λυομένης	λυομένου
λύοντι	λυούσῃ	λύοντι	λυομένῳ	λυομένῃ	λυομένῳ
λύοντα	λύουσαν	λῦον	λυόμενον	λυομένην	λυόμενον
λύοντες	λύουσαι	λύοντα	λυόμενοι	λυόμεναι	λυόμενα
λυόντων	λυουσῶν	λυόντων	λυομένων	λυομένων	λυομένων
λύουσιν	λυούσαις	λύουσιν	λυομένοις	λυομέναις	λυομένοις
λύοντας	λυούσας	λύοντα	λυομένους	λυομένας	λυόμενα

1st Aorist Active			1st Aorist Middle			1st Aorist Passive		
λύσας	λύσασα	λῦσαν	λυσάμενος	λυσαμένη	λυσάμενον	λυθείς	λυθεῖσα	λυθέν
λύσαντος	λυσάσης	λύσαντος	λυσαμένου	λυσαμένης	λυσαμένου	λυθέντος	λυθείσης	λυθέντος
λύσαντι	λυσάσῃ	λύσαντι	λυσαμένῳ	λυσαμένῃ	λυσαμένῳ	λυθέντι	λυθείσῃ	λυθέντι
λύσαντα	λύσασαν	λῦσαν	λυσάμενον	λυσαμένην	λυσάμενον	λυθέντα	λυθεῖσαν	λυθέν
λύσαντες	λύσασαι	λύσαντα	λυσάμενοι	λυσάμεναι	λυσάμενα	λυθέντες	λυθεῖσαι	λυθέντα
λυσάντων	λυσασῶν	λυσάντων	λυσαμένων	λυσαμένων	λυσαμένων	λυθέντων	λυθεισῶν	λυθέντων
λύσασιν	λυσάσαις	λύσασιν	λυσαμένοις	λυσαμέναις	λυσαμένοις	λυθεῖσι(ν)	λυθείσαις	λυθεῖσι(ν)
λύσαντας	λυσάσας	λύσαντα	λυσαμένους	λυσαμένας	λυσάμενα	λυθέντας	λυθείσας	λυθέντα

2nd Aorist Active			2nd Aorist Middle			2nd Aorist Passive		
βαλών	βαλοῦσα	βαλόν	βαλόμενος	βαλομένη	βαλόμενον	βληθείς	βληθεῖσα	βληθέν
βαλόντος	βαλούσης	βαλόντος	βαλομένου	βαλομένης	βαλομένου	βληθέντος	βληθείσης	βληθέντος
βαλόντι	βαλούσῃ	βαλόντι	βαλομένῳ	βαλομένῃ	βαλομένῳ	βληθέντι	βληθείσῃ	βληθέντι
βαλόντα	βαλοῦσαν	βαλόν	βαλόμενον	βαλομένην	βαλόμενον	βληθέντα	βληθεῖσαν	βληθέν
βαλοντες	βαλοῦσαι	βαλόντα	βαλόμενοι	βαλόμεναι	βαλόμενα	βληθέντες	βληθεῖσαι	βληθέντα
βαλόντων	βαλουσῶν	βαλόντων	βαλομένων	βαλομένων	βαλομένων	βληθέντων	βληθεισῶν	βληθέντων
βαλοῦσιν	βαλούσαις	βαλοῦσιν	βαλομένοις	βαλομέναις	βαλομένοις	βληθεῖσι(ν)	βληθείσαις	βληθεῖσι(ν)
βαλόντας	βαλούσας	βαλόντα	βαλομένους	βαλομένας	βαλόμενα	βληθέντας	βληθείσας	βληθέντα

Perfect Active			Perfect Middle & Passive		
λελυκώς	λελυκυῖα	λελυκός	λελυμένος	λελυμένη	λελυμένον
λελυκότος	λελυκυίας	λελυκότος	λελυμένου	λελυμένης	λελυμένου
λελυκότι	λελυκυίᾳ	λελυκότι	λελυμένῳ	λελυμένῃ	λελυμένῳ
λελυκότα	λελυκυῖαν	λελυκός	λελυμένον	λελυμένην	λελυμένον
λελυκότες	λελυκυῖαι	λελυκότα	λελυμένοι	λελυμέναι	λελυμένα
λελυκότων	λελυκυιῶν	λελυκότων	λελυμένων	λελυμένων	λελυμένων
λελυκόσι(ν)	λελυκυίαις	λελυκόσι(ν)	λελυμένοις	λελυμέναις	λελυμένοις
λελυκότας	λελυκυίας	λελυκότα	λελυμένους	λελυμένας	λελυμένα

Full Table of the Regular Verb λύω Stem λυ-

Principal Parts													
λύω				λύσω		ἔλυσα		λέλυκα		λέλυμαι		ἐλύθην	
Present Active	Imperfect Active	Present Mid/Pass	Imperfect Mid/Pass	Future Active	Future Middle	Aorist Active	Aorist Middle	Perfect Active	Pluperfect Active	Perfect Mid/Pass	Pluperfect Mid/Pass	Aorist Passive	Future Passive
INDICATIVE													
λύω	ἔλυον	λύομαι	ἐλυόμην	λύσω	λύσομαι	ἔλυσα	ἐλυσάμην	λέλυκα	(ἐ)λελύκειν	λέλυμαι	(ἐ)λελύμην	ἐλύθην	λυθήσομαι
λύεις	ἔλυες	λύῃ	ἐλύου	λύσεις	λύσῃ	ἔλυσας	ἐλύσω	λέλυκας	(ἐ)λελύκεις	λέλυσαι	(ἐ)λέλυσο	ἐλύθης	λυθήσῃ
λύει	ἔλυεν	λύεται	ἐλύετο	λύσει	λύσεται	ἔλυσεν	ἐλύσατο	λέλυκεν	(ἐ)λελύκει	λέλυται	(ἐ)λέλυτο	ἐλύθη	λυθήσεται
λύομεν	ἐλύομεν	λυόμεθα	ἐλυόμεθα	λύσομεν	λυσόμεθα	ἐλύσαμεν	ἐλυσάμεθα	λελύκαμεν	(ἐ)λελύκειμεν	λελύμεθα	(ἐ)λελύμεθα	ἐλύθημεν	λυθησόμεθα
λύετε	ἐλύετε	λύεσθε	ἐλύεσθε	λύσετε	λύσεσθε	ἐλύσατε	ἐλύσασθε	λελύκατε	(ἐ)λελύκειτε	λέλυσθε	(ἐ)λέλυσθε	ἐλύθητε	λυθήσεσθε
λύουσιν	ἔλυον	λύονται	ἐλύοντο	λύσουσιν	λύσονται	ἔλυσαν	ἐλύσαντο	λελύκασιν	(ἐ)λελύκεισαν	λέλυνται	(ἐ)λέλυντο	ἐλύθησαν	λυθήσονται
SUBJUNCTIVE													
λύω		λύωμαι				λύσω	λύσωμαι			Pres Act Ind like		λυθῶ	
λύῃς		λύῃ				λύσῃς	λύσῃ			λέλυμαι:		λυθῇς	
λύῃ		λύηται				λύσῃ	λύσηται			δύναμαι		λυθῇ	
λύωμεν		λυώμεθα				λύσωμεν	λυσώμεθα			κεῖμαι		λυθῶμεν	
λύητε		λύησθε				λύσητε	λύσησθε			κάθημαι		λυθῆτε	
λύωσιν		λύωνται				λύσωσιν	λύσωνται					λυθῶσιν	
IMPERATIVE													
λῦε		λύου				λῦσον	λῦσαι					λύθητι	
λυέτω		λυέσθω				λυσάτω	λυσάσθω					λυθήτω	
λύετε		λύεσθε				λύσατε	λύσασθε					λύθητε	
λυέτωσαν		λυέσθωσαν				λυσάτωσαν	λυσάσθωσαν					λυθήτωσαν	
INFINITIVE													
λύειν		λύεσθαι				λῦσαι	λύσασθαι	λελυκέναι		λελύσθαι		λυθῆναι	
PARTICIPLE													
λύων		λυόμενος				λύσας	λυσάμενος	λελυκώς					
λύοντος		λυομένου				λύσαντος	λυσαμένου	λελυκότος		λελυμένου		λυθέντος	
λύοντι		λυομένῳ				λύσαντι	λυσαμένῳ	λελυκότι		λελυμένῳ		λυθέντι	
λύοντα		λυόμενον				λύσαντα	λυσάμενον	λελυκότα		λελυμένον		λυθέντα	
λύοντες		λυόμενοι				λύσαντες	λυσάμενοι	λελυκότες		λελυμένοι		λυθέντες	
λυόντων		λυομένων				λυσάντων	λυσαμένων	λελυκότων		λελυμένων		λυθέντων	
λύουσιν		λυομένοις				λύσασιν	λυσαμένοις	λελυκόσιν		λελυμένοις		λυθεῖσιν	
λύοντας		λυομένους				λύσαντας	λυσαμένους	λελυκότας		λελυμένους		λυθέντας	

Translating Tense-Forms and Voices

The table provides a guide to translating the various tense-forms and voices of λύω into English. Some verbs will need to be translated in some other way.

Mood	Active (& Middle*)	Passive	Mood	Active (& Middle*)	Passive
Indicative (1st Pers Sg)			**Imperative (2nd Pers Sg)**		
Present	I am loosing; I loose	I am being loosed	**Present**	loose! (general)	be loosed! (general)
Imperfect	I was loosing	I was being loosed	**Aorist**	loose! (specific)	be loosed! (specific)
Future	I will loose	I will be loosed	**Infinitive**		
Aorist	I loosed	I was loosed	**Present**	to loose	to be loosed
Perfect	I loose; I have loosed	I am loosed; I have been loosed	**Aorist**	to loose	to be loosed
Pluperfect	I was loosing; I had loosed	I was being loosed; I had been loosed	**Participle (All Cases)**		
			Present	loosing	being loosed
			Aorist	loosing	being loosed
			Perfect	loosing	being loosed

*The middle voice should be translated as a *kind of active* unless the context demands otherwise. For the present and imperfect tense-forms this means the middle and passive take the same form, but the active and middle have the same translation.

PRINCIPAL PARTS

Present	Future	Aorist Act	Perf Act	Perf Pass	Aor Pass	English
STANDARD REGULAR VERBS						
λύω	λύσω	ἔλυσα	λέλυκα	λέλυμαι	ἐλύθην	I loose
ποιέω	ποιήσω	ἐποίησα	πεποίηκα	πεποίημαι	ἐποιήθην	I make
γεννάω	γεννήσω	ἐγέννησα	γεγέννηκα	γεγέννημαι	ἐγεννήθην	I bear
φανερόω	φανερώσω	ἐφανέρωσα	πεφανέρωκα	πεφανέρωμαι	ἐφανερώθην	I reveal
REGULAR WITH ASPIRATED PERFECT						
κηρύσσω	κηρύξω	ἐκήρυξα	(κεκήρυχα)	-κεκήρυγμαι	ἐκηρύχθην	I proclaim
VARIOUS IRREGULARITIES						
εἰμί	ἔσομαι	(ἤμην) impf.	------	------	------	I am
ἀγγέλλω	-αγγέλω	-ήγγειλα	-ήγγελκα	-ήγγελμαι	-ηγγέλην	I announce
ἄγω	ἄξω	ἤγαγον	------	-ἦγμαι	ἤχθην	I lead
ἀκούω	ἀκούσω	ἤκουσα	ἀκήκοα		ἠκούσθην	I hear
ἀνοίγω	ἀνοίξω	ἤνοιξα	ἀνέῳγα	ἀνέῳγμαι	ἠνοίχθην	I open
		ἀνέῳξεν			ἀνεῴχθην	
βάλλω	βαλῶ	ἔβαλον	βέβληκα	βέβλημαι	ἐβλήθην	I throw
γίνομαι	γενήσομαι	ἐγενόμην	γέγονα	γεγένημαι	ἐγενήθην	I become
γινώσκω	γνώσομαι	ἔγνων	ἔγνωκα	ἔγνωσμαι	ἐγνώσθην	I know
ἐγείρω	ἐγερῶ	ἤγειρα	------	ἐγήγερμαι	ἠγέρθην	I raise up
θέλω	θελήσω	ἠθέλησα	___	------	ἠθελήθην	I wish
-θνήσκω	-θάνουμαι	-ἔθανον	τέθνηκα	------	------	I die
καλέω	καλέσω	ἐκάλεσα	κέκληκα	κέκλημαι	ἐκλήθην	I call
κρίνω	κρινῶ	ἔκρινα	κέκρικα	κέκριμαι	ἐκρίθην	I judge
λαμβάνω	λήμψομαι	ἔλαβον	εἴληφα	-εἴλημμαι	ἐλήμφθην	I take
σῴζω	σώσω	ἔσωσα	σέσωκα	σέσῳσμαι	ἐσώθην	I save
STEMS FROM MORE THAN ONE VERB						
ἔρχομαι	ἐλεύσομαι	ἦλθον	ἐλήλυθα	------	------	I come, go
ἐσθίω	φάγομαι	ἔφαγον	------	------	------	I eat
ἔχω	ἕξω	ἔσχον	ἔσχηκα	------	------	I have
λέγω	ἐρῶ	εἶπον	εἴρηκα	εἴρημαι	ἐρρήθην	I say
					ἐρρέθην	
ὁράω	ὄψομαι	εἶδον	ἑώρακα		ὤφθην	I notice
			ἑόρακα			
φέρω	οἴσω	ἤνεγκα	-ενήνοχα	------	ἠνέχθην	I carry
μι VERBS						
τίθημι	θήσω	ἔθηκα	τέθεικα	τέθειμαι	ἐτέθην	I lay
δίδωμι	δώσω	ἔδωκα	δέδωκα	δέδομαι	ἐδόθην	I give
-ίστημι	στήσω	ἔστησα				I set
		ἔστην	ἔστηκα	------	ἐστάθην	I stand

SUBJECT INDEX

accents, 3, 8, 9
accusative case
  basic meaning, 13
  marking text, 16
  of respect, 85
  time and, 24
acute accent, 8
adjectives
  attributive position, 62
  demonstrative pronouns as, 61
  form of, 40
  function of, 11
  infinitive as, 86
  predicate position, 62, 63, 72
  third declension, 81
adverbs
  formation of, 78
  function of, 11
Aktionsart, 31
Ancient Greek, 2
alphabet, the, 3, 4
antecedent of a relative pronoun, 65
apodosis, 76–77
apostrophe, 7
articles
  definite, 14
  function of, 11
  indefinite, 14
articular infinitive, 85
asyndeton, 46
attributive position, 62
augment, the, 33, 35, 41, 57, 58, 68, 85
autographs, 9

breathing marks, 3, 7, 9
Byzantine Greek, 2
causal
  ὅτι, 47
  participial clause, 90
circumflex accent, 8, 35, 36, 56
Classical Greek, 2
compound verbs, 26, 30, 34–35, 53, 68

computer tools, 22
concessive clauses, 90
concordance, 10
conditions, 75, 76, 90, 96
conjunction
  function of, 11
  verb, 28
consonants, 5
context, role of, 16, 42
coordination of clauses, 46, 48
curse, 96

dative case
  basic meaning, 13
  marking text, 16
  time and, 24
declensions, 19
deliberative subjunctive, 74
Demotic Greek. *See* Modern Greek
dentals, 54
deponent verbs, 51, 52
diaeresis, 6, 8
discourse pyramid, 16
dipthongs, 6
double negation, 83
duplication in the perfect, 68
dynamic equivalence, 45

emphasizing pronoun, 62, 64
emphatic future negation, 74
flash cards, 22
formal equivalence, 45
gamma nasal, 6
gender, grammatical, 13, 20, 59
genitive case
  absolute, 24, 90
  basic meaning, 13
  marking text, 16
  time and, 24
gloss, 13, 42
grave accent, 8
Greek, history of, 2

hortatory subjunctive, 74
identical adjective, 62
imperative
  aorist active, 49, 58
  aorist middle, 51
  aorist passive, 55
  negation of, 72
  μι verbs, 93
  perfect, 69
  present active, 49
  present middle/passive, 51
  relationship to subjunctive, 73
imperfective aspect. *See* verbal aspect, imperfective
indefinite clause, 75
indicative
  aorist active, 37
  aorist middle, 51
  aorist passive, 55
  future active, 39
  future middle, 51
  imperfect active, 33
  imperfect middle/passive, 50, 51
  μι verbs, 92
  negative of, 72
  pluperfect active, 71
  perfect, 67–68
  present active, 28, 29
  present middle/passive, 50, 51
  time and, 31
indirect question, 96
infinitives
  articular, 85
  αω verbs, 87
  marking the text for, 44
  meaning of, 85
  μι verbs, 93
  οω verbs, 88
  perfect, 69
  uses of, 86
inflection, 26
intonation, 8
iōta subscript, 7

Jesus, name of, 15

Koine Greek, 2

Latin, 52
lengthening of -áὺ verbs, 87
lengthening of -ïὺ verbs, 88
lexicon, 10, 19, 20, 30, 35, 40
linear action, 31
liquid stems, 38, 56

manuscripts, 9
marking text
  complete guide, 44
  neuter nominatives and accusatives, 20
  nouns, 16
  prepositions, 25
  verbs, 30
meaning
  choice and, 10
  compound verbs, 35
  formation of, 17
memorization, 22
middle/passive form, 50
Modern Greek, 2
mood, 27
minimalist grammatical approach, xi
mutes, 5, 37, 38, 54

negation, 49, 72, 76–77, 83
New Testament, today's, 9
nominative case
  basic meaning, 13
  marking text, 16
nouns
  agreement with adjectives, 40
  agreement with verbs, 26
  analysis of, 19
  case of, 13
  clause with subjunctive, 75
  endings of, 13

function of, 11, 12
gender of, 13
infinitive as, 86
inflection of, 12, 13
number, 13
stem, 13, 79, 84
"no way", 96

oblique cases, 24

papyri, 9
paradigm, 14, 19, 22
paraphrase, 45
parsing
  nouns, 19
  verbs, 27, 30
participles
  causal, 90
  concessive, 90
  conditional, 90
  function of, 11
  instrumental, 90
  μι verbs, 92
  periphrastic, 89, 91
  pragmatics of, 89–90
  purpose, 90
  temporal, 89
particles
  adjectival, 42
  adverbial, 42
  causal, 90
  concessive, 90
  conditional, 90
  function of, 11
  instrumental, 90
  marking the text for, 30, 44
  negation of, 72
  perfect, 69
  purpose, 90
  temporal, 89
parts of speech, 11
predicative position, 62, 63
perfective aspect. *See* verbal aspect, perfective

Advances in the Study of Greek

New Insights for Reading the New Testament

Constantine R. Campbell

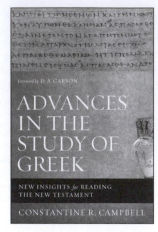

Advances in the Study of Greek offers an introduction to issues of interest in the current world of Greek scholarship. With chapters on a wide range of current issues including linguistic theories, lexical semantics, deponency and the middle voice, discourse analysis, and more Campbell carefully explains these recent advances (and the debates surrounding them) for the study of the Greek New Testament.

Those within Greek scholarship will welcome this book as a tool that puts students, pastors, professors, and commentators firmly in touch with what is going on in Greek studies. Those outside Greek scholarship will warmly receive *Advances in the Study of Greek* as a resource to get themselves up to speed in Greek studies. Free of technical linguistic jargon, the scholarship contained within is highly accessible to outsiders.

Advances in the Study of Greek provides an accessible introduction for students, pastors, professors, and commentators to understand the current issues of interest in this period of paradigm shift.

Keep Your Greek

Strategies for Busy People

Constantine R. Campbell

Seminarians spend countless hours mastering biblical languages and learning how the knowledge of them illuminates the reading, understanding, and application of Scripture. But while excellent language-acquisition resources abound, few really teach students how to maintain their use of Greek for the long term. Consequently, pastors and other former Greek students find that under the pressures of work, ministry, preaching, and life, their hard-earned Greek skills begin to disappear.

Con Campbell has been counseling one-time Greek students for years, teaching them how to keep their language facility for the benefit of those to whom they minister and teach. He shows how following the right principles makes it possible for many to retain—and in some cases regain—their Greek language skills.

Pastors will find *Keep Your Greek* an encouraging and practical guide to strengthening their Greek abilities so that they can make linguistic insights a regular part of their study and teaching. Current students will learn how to build skills that will serve them well once they complete their formal language instruction.